shoestring**reporter**

Books by Joel Thurtell

Up the Rouge! Paddling Detroit's Hidden River,
with photographs by Patricia Beck

Plug Nickel

Seydou's Christmas Tree

shoestring reporter

how I got to be a big city reporter
without going to J school
and how you can do it too!

joel thurtell
hardalee press

Copyright 2010 © by Joel Thurtell

Published by Hardalee Press
11803 Priscilla Lane
Plymouth, MI 48170

All rights reserved. Printed in the United States of America.
No part of this book may be reproduced in any manner whatsoever without written permission except in the case of brief quotations embodied in critical articles and reviews.
For information, address Hardalee Press, 11803 Priscilla Lane, Plymouth, MI 48170.

Cover and interior design by Maya Rhodes

Library of Congress Control Number: 2009906761
Thurtell, Joel Howard

ISBN 978-0-9759969-3-5

For my wife, Karen Fonde, M.D.

contents

Acknowledgments ix
Preface xiii

Introduction *1*
1. Your Newspaper Career *6*
2. I Cudn't Even Spell Jernelist... *9*
3. Pantaloney *14*
4. General Custer's Error *17*
5. Jesse's Undoing *20*
6. Editors NEED you! *25*
7. Double-dippers *27*
8. Surviving as a Writer *31*
9. Ad Hoc J School *34*
10. Checkered Career *37*
11. How to Write Like a Newsie *42*
12. Breaking into the News *45*
13. Breaking into the Times *49*
14. That Times 'Beer Allowance' *59*
15. Reggie's Tip Sheet *65*
16. Beating a Dead Horse *71*
17. Cops & Robbers *73*
18. Sniffin' Stories *79*
19. Get Rattlesnakes! *89*
20. Addicted *94*

21. Getting Hired 96
22. You're Fired! 101
23. Nuts & Bolts 103
24. The Pack-A-Day Gang 108
25. "Never Lead with a Quote" 113
26. Jump-Starting With Papa Joe 116
27. Are Newspapers Dead? 118
28. A New Journalism 125
29. Never Too Old 128
30. Brainwashed 131
31. Bait & Switch 136
32. First Thing We Do… 138
33. Not Well Paid, But… 140
34. Censorship 101 142
35. Page One Envy 145
36. Why Are Editors Dumb? 148
37. It's Not Who You Know 154
38. Got the Picture? 159
39. Byline Fever 162
40. What's the Percentage? 166
41. Think again 168
42. For the Record 172
43. If You Can't Beat 'Em 175
44. A Thimbleful 180
45. A TRUE Ethics Policy 182
46. No Free Lunch 188
47. Second Opinions 192
48. Burial Detail 194
49. Struck Out 196
50. Building the Bullshit Meter 200
51. Prosecuting the Messenger 204
52. Why Not Sell Insurance? 211
Stringer's Oath 214

About the Author 215
Index 217

acknowledgments

Articles, photographs, and illustrations

Page 7, Detroit Free Press business card. Reprinted by permission of the Detroit Free Press

Page 7, Detroit Free Press photo identity card. Reprinted by permission of the Detroit Free Press

Page 11, Author in WJR-AM traffic helicopter. Detroit Free Press, "Job has traffic reporter flying high," August 7, 1986. Reprinted by permission of the Detroit Free Press

Page 22, "Janna Gjesdal: Roots in Detroit, but growing in New York," Detroit Free Press Magazine, August 20, 1978. Reprinted by permission of the Detroit Free Press

Page 24, "Farmers need pickers now," The Detroit News, August 30, 1978. Reprinted courtesy of The Detroit News

Page 29, "Bridge spans colorful past," The Detroit News, March 8, 1978. Reprinted courtesy of The Detroit News

Page 33, Front page, The (Berrien Springs) Journal Era, June 18, 1980. Reprinted courtesy of The (Berrien Springs) Journal Era

Page 40, Cover photograph by Patricia Beck for *Up the Rouge! Paddling Detroit's Hidden River*, published 2009 by Wayne State University Press. Reprinted by permission of the Detroit Free Press

Pages 47–48, "Mexican 'heat' edible," South Bend Tribune, undated 1978 clip. Reprinted courtesy of the South Bend Tribune

Pages 50–52, "Big Abe: Indian, fighter," Detroit Free Press Magazine, January 6, 1980. Reprinted by permission of the Detroit Free Press

Pages 53–55, "Troubled Waters: The Struggle on the Great Lakes for an ancient way of life," The Progressive, September 1980. Reprinted courtesy of The Progressive

Pages 60–63, "The Michiganders Who Want to be Hoosiers," July 6, 1980, The Indianapolis Star Magazine. Reprinted courtesy of The Indianapolis Star

Page 67, "Champion Cherry Pit Spitters Gird for Main Event," The Grand Rapids Press, July 1, 1979. Article reprinted courtesy of The Grand Rapids Press; photograph reprinted courtesy of Michigan Farmer

Page 72, "Town's dinners keep fire engines running," The Detroit News, December 22, 1978. Reprinted courtesy of The Detroit News

Page 80, "Burning resumes despite order," South Bend Tribune, July 13, 1998. Photo by Joel Thurtell. Reprinted courtesy of The South Bend Tribune

Page 82, "Noxious weeds," The (Berrien Springs) Journal Era, June 11, 1980. Photograph by Joel Thurtell. Reprinted courtesy of The (Berrien Springs) Journal Era

Page 84, "Foam on the Rivers" South Bend Tribune, March 11, 1979; Photograph by Joel Thurtell. Reprinted courtesy of the South Bend Tribune

Page 85, "No hole in the dam," The (Berrien Springs) Journal Era, September 10, 1980. Reprinted courtesy of The (Berrien Springs) Journal Era

Page 87, "Council acts on Weakley 'fecal matter' complaint," The (Berrien Springs) Journal Era, September 10, 1980. Reprinted courtesy of The (Berrien Springs) Journal Era with my lost kicker added.

Pages 90–92, "Snakes on Sale," Detroit Free Press, April 22, 1989. Reprinted by permission of the Detroit Free Press

Page 111, "He sat down for a quiet beer and...," South Bend Tribune, February 11, 1981. Reprinted courtesy of the South Bend Tribune

Page 119, "Public meetings should be open to public," The (Berrien Springs) Journal Era, October 17, 1979. Reprinted courtesy of The (Berrien Springs) Journal Era

Page 137, Masthead, The (Berrien Springs) Journal Era, June 11, 1980. Reprinted courtesy of The (Berrien Springs) Journal Era

Pages 150–151, "Indian, 68, hunts roots," The Detroit News, April 19, 1984. Reprinted courtesy of The Detroit News

Page 206, "Journal Era's Editor Rates Medal, Not Probe," The (Benton Harbor) Herald-Palladium, April 22, 1980. Reprinted courtesy of The (Benton Harbor) Herald-Palladium

Page 207, "Staff said no, but judge freed boy," The (Berrien Springs) Journal Era, April 16, 1980. Reprinted courtesy of The (Berrien Springs) Journal Era

preface

I started writing *Shoestring Reporter* soon after I was hired as a full-time staff reporter for the South Bend Tribune. That happened in February 1981. Our first son, Adam, was less than a year old. He, my wife, and I were living in an old rented house on a cattle, pig and horse farm near Berrien Springs, Michigan. As chief of the Tribune's Cass County News Bureau, I took over an empty second-floor bedroom in that rambling house and set up my news office. I joked that as bureau chief, my staff included Jessie, our golden retriever; Sancho Panza, a black-and-white cat; and, of course, our little boy, Adam.

I was very excited, proud and, yes, amazed, that I was on the staff of a moderate-sized daily newspaper. You see, I'd never formally studied Journalism. True, I'd been a politics reporter and music critic on my college newspaper, The (Kalamazoo College) Index. But that didn't last long. I was fired from both those positions. My offense? Being a smart-ass.

Oh, yes, I'd been a carrier for The Grand Rapids Press and I'd worked in the back shop of my hometown newspaper, the Lowell (Michigan) Ledger. I was a printer's helper and did every job connected with making up and breaking down the type of a hot-metal paper — operations that today would mystify most people accustomed to desktop publishing. But during my summer at the Ledger, I didn't write a word.

My closest brush with Journalism in academia was the senior thesis I wrote for my bachelor's degree in history at Kalamazoo College, where the catalog didn't list one single class in Journalism. I wrote my thesis about the opinions of London newspapers on the eve of the War of 1812. I lived for three months in London while reading early 19th-Century papers at the Public Record Office.

For a bit more than a year before the Tribune hired me full-time, I was editor of The Journal Era, a weekly that circulated in Berrien Springs and Eau Claire in southwestern Michigan. That was a part-time job that I combined with my main occupation: I was a stringer for the Tribune and other newspapers and magazines around the country.

As I sat in my bureau, a spare bedroom overlooking cow pastures and wallowing hogs, I reveled in the fact that I, formerly a mere stringer, had made it onto the staff of a real newspaper. How had I managed to do that? I was in love with newspapering, but more than that, I was in love with reporting, because it meant I could give free rein to my curiosity, pursuing hunches and launching them into yarns — I mean articles — that the paper would publish.

I felt I was at the pinnacle of success. Yet I was different from my colleagues on the dailies. I knew of nobody other than myself who was a staff writer without a Journalism school diploma. I was a rarity and, yes, maybe too, an oddity. Yet I had done it. I felt I had arrived. And if I could do it, others could do it, too. I felt like a missionary. I wanted to recruit others into this life of questing after facts, stories, yarns that could be crafted into words on paper that would earn me money and at the same time enlighten people, inform them, give them hope or make them laugh. And yes, did I mention? Make me some money.

That would make YOU money. Yes, others could do what I had done. So I conceived the idea for a book that would coach YOU on how to become a newspaper stringer. I wrote several chapters, including one on Jesse James, made an outline and put it all in a three-ring binder with a hard blue cover. I pondered a title. I'd written a novel, actually a murder mystery, with a newspaper stringer as hero, and titled it, wouldn't you know, *Stringer*. That would have made a good title for my how-to manual, but I didn't want to poach it away from the novel. I've looked through the old manuscript and can't find any sign that I ever resolved the title problem.

A few years ago, I found that hard blue binder, read the outline and unfinished manuscript and realized that I'd been onto something important way back when. But I was still too busy as a workaday reporter. I set it aside again.

Back in 1981, I got busy writing stories for the Tribune. Then, glory of glories, the Detroit Free Press in 1984 hired me — me, a non-J-school guy — as a reporter. In 23 years, I wrote literally thousands of articles for the Free Press.

In the spring of 2007, while I was still cranking out five stories a week, I again found the blue binder. This time, I got excited enough to begin — again — writing the book. I was still not willing to give up on

that murder mystery, so the title *Stringer* was out. How about "String Journalism"? It would do. Gradually, though, it morphed into "String Reporter." Finally, realizing that my career was all about reporting-on-a-budget, doing interesting, fun and sometimes even important Journalism that didn't bankrupt me or the paper, I settled on *Shoestring Reporter*.

By 2007, I was writing loosey-goosey personal columns for the Free Press and before that I'd written seat-of-the-pants columns about my adventures restoring wooden boats for Lightning Flashes, the newsletter of the International Lightning Class Association, a group that promotes the Lightning-class sailboat. Writing in a jaunty, jocular, sometimes self-deprecating way had become normal, even in my newspaper columns. But by now, incredibly, my son Adam — who was a baby when I started this book — was 27 years old. His brother, Abe, was not even conceived when I started writing *Shoestring*, and now he was 24 and prodding me on as, through the summer of 2007, I added chapter after chapter to this book.

The idea of picking up a manuscript that was more than a quarter-century old was exciting. Stringing had worked for me then, and with all the downsizing newspapers are doing, there's ever more reliance on part-timers — stringers — to do the work.

Parts of the old manuscript were fine. I began rewriting the early chapters, and then, new chapters would pop into my brain. Soon, I was melding the old with a new vision for the book. This is the product of a quarter-century wait. In that time, I've learned plenty about the good and bad in newsgathering.

In this new vision, my hope is that readers not only take my advice and start stringing for newspapers, but that they form a corps of independent-thinking Journalists ready for the challenge of thinking for themselves beyond the control of the corporate paradigm-makers who have controlled news by commandeering the brains of the people they hire and pay to write.

This book was nearly finished when I learned that Gannett, the company that owns the Free Press, wanted to reduce operating costs by brooming as many older — and in theory more highly paid — staffers as possible. Though I was not one of those well-heeled staffers, I had the seniority to qualify, so I was offered a "buyout." I took it. I wrote this book largely in the early morning before reporting to work, or on vacations while I was still a Free Press staffer. But I did the fine-tuning while on my "Gannett Grant," the weekly paycheck that kept coming from the Free Press for the better part of the year after I "retired" from the newspaper.

Writing on the Gannett Grant gave me a new perspective. Rather, it brought me back to an old perspective, in that I've actually done some of what could roughly be called stringer work. The economics that stringers contend with more and more again became my economics as I looked down the weeks toward the end of those paychecks, which, I like to think, were earned as I labored to write good stories for poor pay and under deadline pressures that made life stressful and difficult.

As I've prepared the book, new angles have occurred to me that might not have seemed necessary when I was a staff writer. Chapters called "Addicted" and "Get Rattlesnakes!" are among many new chapters, as are "Censorship 101" and "Why Are Editors Dumb?"

You will easily note some chapters were written after my so-called retirement, because I will mention it. I haven't tried to tighten or make uniform those chapters, and I think my situation and mental whereabouts will be pretty clear in some of those later and more recently written chapters.

These chapters are interspersed throughout the text wherever I thought they made most sense. I hope readers won't be confused by this approach, which seemed the most straightforward way to deal with what amounts to a very changed work situation.

I'm suspicious of academic Journalism. Newspaper Journalism is moribund, having been suffocated by the academic training programs that are in thrall to the stifling news media companies who often dole out grants to pay their bills. You could call it the Journalism-Industrial-Complex.

But now as we know, many of these media companies are dying miserable, prolonged and self-dramatized deaths. Let them go. Cry no tears for them. They are as corrupt as the institutions they covered and to which, with great sanctimony, they tried to appear superior.

It is time for the new Journalist. I hope my books will promote the rebirth of independent inquiry along with provocative, courageous Journalism in America.

In trying to thank the many people who helped me find my way in Journalism, I run the risk of neglecting, through forgetfulness, some deserving people. Nevertheless, I owe huge debts to many who had the patience to answer my questions, to guide me and sometimes even to tell me, "No, this is not a story!"

Most of the action in *Shoestring Reporter* takes place in southwestern Michigan, but much of the writing took place between 2007 and 2010. And when I got discouraged or sidetracked on other projects, one person kept pushing me back to the main course with stern lectures about why this project needed to go to print. This intellectually forceful person is Javan Kienzle, who was my copy editor at the Detroit Free Press and who continued in that role, editing the copy of several of my books, including this one. I'm not going to say this book would never have been finished without Javan, but certainly the publication year of 2010 would have been much further out, say by five or even 10 years. Besides prodding me to finish the book, Javan has read it several times, and each time she has caught errors that I missed and that would have embarrassed me had they gone into print. Any errors that make it into book form are strictly my responsibility.

Another person instrumental in bringing this work to publication was Maya Rhodes, who not only designed the cover and interior of the book, but helped me clarify my thinking about what this book would look like and helped me adjust to the realities of publishing on paper rather than in my head.

The man who pointed me toward Journalism, way back in 1974, was Doug Howe, then chief engineer of Western Michigan University's WMUK-FM radio station. It was Doug who advised me not to pursue a career in broadcast engineering, but rather to parlay my training in historical research into a reporting job. Doug introduced me to the late Tony Griffin, news editor at WMUK-FM. It was Tony who handed me my first news reporting assignments and it was Tony who lectured me on what made news and what didn't. During the same time, Professor Arnold Johnston of Western Michigan University's English Department was encouraging me as a writer of fiction. While writing novels and short stories may seem unrelated to newswriting, the help I got from people at Western helped build my confidence as a writer. I was neither a Journalism major nor an English major; I lacked both the academic credentials and the lingo of a trained Journalist, and needed most of all to build credibility with myself.

Scott Aiken of Benton Harbor's The Herald-Palladium newspaper was my prime coach as I felt my way into newsprint. Another Herald-Palladium reporter of that time, Bob Sherefkin, helped me see beyond local markets for my writing. I never worked for the late Bert Lindenfeld, who was then managing editor of the Herald-Palladium, but he gave me advice and backed me at a critical moment.

I often think of the Journalistic adventures I experienced with the late John and Patricia Gillette, co-publishers of The (Berrien Springs) Journal Era, after they hired me as their editor. Weekly Journalism was a new world for all three of us. Until I retired and started blogging, I'd never experienced as much freedom in my writing as I did when I worked for John and Pat. At the time, of course, I chafed and didn't appreciate what I had. Moreover, the Gillettes' side business of publishing out-of-print historical books provided a model for another form of Journalism that continues to fascinate me — creating my own books.

I was a stringer and then a staff writer at the South Bend Tribune for about seven years and worked at the Detroit Free Press more than three times that long. But I never worked for better editors than I had at the Tribune. For intellectual honesty, Journalistic excellence and moral courage, Tom Gruber and Jan Marsh are simply tops.

And then there was Bill Sonneborn, whose South Bend Tribune Michiana magazine motto seemed to be, "If it's interesting, write it!"

No aspiring reporter could have had better role models than the South Bend Tribune reporters whose work I read every day: Sue Morris, Jan Marsh (before she was an editor), Lou Mumford, the late Lyle Sumerix and Gene Walden.

And there was Reginald Stuart. Reggie was chief of The New York Times' Detroit bureau, yet he made time to coach and nurture a neophyte reporter on the opposite side of the state. I'm aware also that I got a boost from Susan Pastor, Times news clerk in the Detroit bureau.

For permitting me to reprint my own and other people's work, I thank The (Berrien Springs) Journal Era, The Benton Harbor Herald-Palladium, South Bend Tribune, The Detroit News, Detroit Free Press, The Grand Rapids Press, Michigan Farmer, The Indianapolis Star, The Progressive, and Wayne State University Press.

Thanks to my sons, Adam and Abe, for listening to me expound, often over dinner, year after year, about my adventures in covering the news. Both of them prodded me to become computer-savvy, and both helped me by creating my Web sites. Not only were they sounding boards, but each inspired me to write stories that would not have occurred to me on my own. As I was finishing the book, it was Abe who double-checked my percentage calculations, detected and corrected my errors and instructed me in the fine points of figuring percentage change.

Most of all, I owe a huge debt to my wife, Karen Fonde, M.D. It was Karen who put up with my penniless pursuit of novel-writing and who saw — better than I did — the opportunity that newspaper stringing held for me. Without her encouragement, advice and judicious criticism, none of this would have happened.

introduction

The New Yorker runs a long story, "Out of Print," explaining how American newspaper Journalism is going down the drain. The New York Times runs its own version of this mordant tale, "Paper Cuts," arguing that the very medium that carries the article is in its death throes.

Who will save Journalism?

Not the people who are practicing it: Their primary challenge is the Internet they so enthusiastically embraced without understanding or planning. Those people don't have a clue how to handle the challenge of the Internet.

But what if things aren't as dire as the papers depict?

Or what if they are facing demise because they believe their own hype?

What if, by believing their own prophecies, they are killing themselves?

Who will save newspapers?

Not the people who own them.

Not the people who run them.

Those people are out to destroy the vessels of their employment.

When we think of newspapers in America, we tend to think of the dailies, the chain-owned papers from the Times on down to small-town dailies. But daily newspapers — chain-owned newspapers — are not the sum of Journalism. It's just that they embody, in our collective mind, at least, much of what we think is good in Journalism: the watchdog role, comforting the afflicted and afflicting the comfortable. That is what Journalism should do, whether its parent is the newspaper or some other medium. And when we think of that kind of Journalism, we often think of papers like the Times or The Washington Post or maybe the Los Angeles Times, Chicago Tribune, or The Philadelphia Inquirer.

Beacons of Journalism.

All in deep trouble.

If newspapers must go, then Journalism at least is worth saving.

Who will save Journalism?

No lone person can do it. But many people, with the right mindset, could save Journalism, though the newspapers that have provided employment and a means of transmitting Journalism may disappear.

Journalism will be saved only if many people are inspired to practice the craft of reporting and writing about events, people and social processes they find important. Many of these people are now excluded from the ranks of newspaper Journalists.

If Journalism can be saved, then maybe newspapers too can be revived.

There is a prejudice among orthodox, Journalism school-trained Journalists to look down on those who have not taken the same courses, pursued the same prestigious internships, and won the same coveted awards that produced the conventional practitioners — themselves.

Such people — orthodox Journalists — will not save Journalism. The saviors of Journalism will come from outside the industry. They will work their way into the craft (NOT a profession!) and, eventually, take over and transform Journalism.

They will accomplish this feat from outside, at first. They will become paid part-time reporters — "stringers" — on the temporary payroll of newspapers.

How will they do this?

By reading this book, *Shoestring Reporter*, a manual outlining how people who are armed only with eyes, ears and intelligence can, with forethought and discipline, become paid contributors to newspapers.

Shoestring Reporter is part autobiography, in that it explains how I became first a stringer, then a part-time newspaper editor, then a full-time staff reporter on a medium-sized paper. And finally, I was hired, with no formal academic Journalism training, as a full-time staff reporter at the Detroit Free Press, then (1984) the ninth-largest newspaper by circulation in the nation.

Shoestring Reporter explains how people who don't have a college degree can be paid for reporting news. Why, I knew a stringer at the South Bend Tribune who had two licenses — as a hairdresser!

I believe people who are not tainted by the orthodox thinking of newsgathering institutions could — if enough of them became involved — save Journalism.

We need many people to write for newspapers from their own personal points of view. We need these people to bring independent, fresh approaches to reporting. We also need to make sure that they don't become corrupted by standard Journalistic thinking.

We may come to see that the current precarious position of many American newspapers is the product of a long process of devaluing newspapers. This process was initiated long ago by the not-so-intelligent bosses who run newspapers. They have unintentionally shown what would happen when they milked newspapers for 20-plus-percent returns; laid off valued writers, editors, printers, ad salespeople, photographers and carriers. They dumbed their papers down, reduced content and provoked people to reject their watered-down product. And this is good. Not good for Journalism in the short term, but good for Journalism as well as the public in the long run, because the very people who have killed off the papers will themselves disappear with their corrupt publications, making room for new publishers, whose content and intellectual direction may well be determined by people who read this book and apply its principles.

This book is not aimed primarily at landing outsiders jobs at the big dailies. Though the chain-owned papers — of which The New York Times is only the best-known of many that are in deep trouble — are cutting jobs, they still hire stringers. But our focus should be on the smaller papers, the ones that are ignored when the big papers narcissistically focus on their own self-inflicted woes, ignoring those outliers in small communities: the papers that still print their news, don't give it away free on the Internet and remain the only source for reports on the high school marching band and the doings of the town's several churches.

To illustrate: I doubt the hotshot covering the demise of newspapers at The New York Times would think of calling Francie VanderMolen, operations manager at The (Berrien Springs) Journal Era in southwestern Michigan. In summer 2009, I called Francie and said, "Does The Journal Era still hire stringers?"

"Yes," Francie replied.

In 1980, I was editor of The Journal Era. I hired Francie, who had no Journalism training, to attend village council and school board meetings and write reports. I — or rather, The Journal Era — paid her ten bucks per meeting, but by sending the same reports to the South Bend Tribune, she was able to make an extra $25 per meeting — not bad, given the more robust purchasing power of the dollar in that time. Francie later became a full-time staff writer on the Tribune, but has returned to The Journal Era where she started.

My big question so many years after I started writing a primer for stringers was simply, Is it still possible, in these terrible times for newspapers, for someone to start a career in Journalism by working as a stringer?

The answer from Francie is concise: Yes, absolutely. First of all — surprise, surprise — small community papers following the ancient business model of printing newspapers on paper with ads and news, then selling them to people who know they can read the ads and news only on paper, well, those newspapers by and large are doing okay. That's not something you'll read in the good old New York Times, but Francie's take on the situation was confirmed by Debra Haight of Niles, Michigan. Debra is a 51-year-old Notre Dame University grad with an economics major who some years ago answered an ad to become a stringer for The (Benton Harbor) Herald-Palladium. She was hired by a Herald-Palladium reporter, Scott Aiken, and now makes a living by selling her reports to five newspapers.

Francie told me that the weekly Journal Era pays one stringer $400-$500 a month to write news about the local school board. Francie also told me The Journal Era is faring well even in a bad economy; nobody on her staff bothers to go out selling advertising, yet the ad customers bring their business to the paper, supporting it nicely. The paper's Web site gives away no news. It simply tells you how to subscribe and how to place an ad. I find this approach typical of small community papers in Michigan and Ontario. You will not read about this in the big dailies as they delve blindly into the causes of their own accelerating suicides.

Shoestring Reporter explains how people can become paid reporters. With chapters on how to think and how to find or conceive unorthodox stories, it promotes a nonstandard approach to reporting. It also explains how outsiders can gain access to information, aka investigative reporting, without spending huge amounts of money on lawyers and photocopies.

Meanwhile, I'm working on another book to help people with Journalism careers. It's not ready yet, but I plan to call it *Shoestring J School*. It will contain a selection of my newspaper stories and **joelontheroad.com** blog essays delving into ways to achieve independence and originality without busting the pocketbook. I'll look at several low- or no-budget investigative articles, too. Taken together or read separately, these books will offer a "how-to" approach to becoming a reporter without spending a fortune on college course-work that may not prepare a person for a working life as a Journalist anyway.

Where *Shoestring Reporter* briefly explains my techniques, tactics and stylistic approaches, *Shoestring J School* will reprint actual published examples of articles that have made things different and, I hope, better. The *Shoestring J School* stories will be blueprints for enterprising would-be reporters to study, imitate and modify — maybe even improve! The articles will appear together with my comments on Journalistic situations that challenged my reporting. For you who want to become unconventional, provocative reporters and writers, *Shoestring J School* will explore in greater depth approaches that worked for me.

And the price of the books is much less than tuition to a conventional J school.

Together, *Shoestring Reporter* and *Shoestring J School* will explain:

- How to become a reporter without going to J school.
- How to do investigative reporting without going bankrupt.
- How to create "different" stories that will excite readers.
- How people from outside the Journalism Establishment of newspapers and J schools can save the noble craft of Journalism from those who are corrupting it.
- The role of "ethics" in Journalism.
- Legal issues and rules for surviving in a nasty world.

Together, these books offer an alternative training course for Journalists, who now have a choice between taking costly conventional academic classes in Journalism or studying a pair of modestly priced books that coach people to become — as individuals — the very Journalistic watchdogs our society so badly needs.

Nor is this the end: I've always believed that there are limits beyond which nonfiction can't reach in conveying reality. Fiction, and in particular, the novel, can portray situations, mindsets, behaviors and causal sequences in ways that can't be touched by nonfiction. My novel *Stringer* is a murder mystery whose central character is, well, a newspaper stringer who stumbles into the plot of a homicide and finds himself searching for motives and culprits while struggling with the mind-inhibiting influences of a small daily paper's newsroom. My novel *Cross Purposes, or, If Newspapers Had Covered the Crucifixion* satirizes the venalities of a fictional big-city newspaper, at the same time illustrating a combination of manic careerism and egocentric self-focusing that cages the brains of many newspeople. Together, these four books form a set called *Shoestring Quartet*.

chapter 1

your newspaper career

Would you like to make a fortune without stirring from your home and without doing any work?

If your answer is "yes," then this book, I'm happy to say, is not for you. But if you're the kind of person who likes independence, who labors to the cadence of your own drum and is not afraid of hard work and harder truths, who knows how to be enterprising and most of all, can think for yourself, then we are kindred spirits and maybe I can help you make at least part of a decent living from your home, after all.

My name is Joel Thurtell, and I am a Journalist. Without realizing it, I was a Journalist since before I could read and write. Does that sound impossible? A Journalist has to know how to put words on paper, right? Actually, the most important thing for a Journalist to know is how to see, how to hear and use the other senses as well. Curiosity is the foundation of Journalism. But okay, in the narrowest of terms, I have been a Journalist — paid for my reporting and writing — for about 30 years.

Until recently, I was a staff writer — a full-time, salaried employee — at the Detroit Free Press, once one of the highest-circulation papers in the country. That is amazing, I think, because I don't have a degree in Journalism. In fact, although I have taught Journalism in college, I have never taken a class in Journalism at any level. Before I was hired by the Free Press, I was a full-time staff writer at the South Bend Tribune. And before that — well, that is my story, and I don't want to spill it too soon.

I didn't get where I am through the ordinary channels, that's for sure. I got there by finding key people, learning how the newspaper employment system works (not one of my jobs was advertised; you might say they were posted through word of mouth), teaching myself how to write the way newspapers like things to be written, by working my buns off and by breaking rules. The purpose of this book is to show how YOU can do what I did.

By "YOU," I mean the outsider, the intelligent, literate, thinking person who likes to read and write and is curious about the world. Some of my observations and tips will no doubt irk people who call themselves newspaper Journalists. If that happens, it's because I mean for you and

Reprinted by permission of the Detroit Free Press

aspiring Journalists like you to use the tricks and tactics in this book to work — yes, to manipulate — the establishment people who consider themselves REAL Journalists.

I'm writing for the people who are not now making an income from newspaper writing, but who think it's something they could do. And if that is what they — YOU — think, you are correct.

I'm very much aware that if you are reading this book with a mind to following my advice, then you are most likely not part of the Journalistic-Industrial Establishment I mentioned. You probably are not employed as a Journalist, and maybe you are not employed at all. It follows that your budget for experimenting with Journalism is pretty limited. Does that mean you are precluded from trying your hand at this work?

Well, there is a reason I titled this book *Shoestring Reporter*. Yes, true, the title evolved from the word "stringer," which means a person who works part-time collecting and writing news. But there is another sense in my title, because when I started out, I was like you — without a job and very much gambling that Journalism would provide me a living. I was on a shoestring. Yet, it turns out, people who are financed on a metaphorical shoestring can do creative, powerful, original work in Journalism.

Once upon a time, I took part in a panel discussion at Detroit's Anchor Bar in which one of the city's top investigative reporters boasted about the tens of thousands of dollars his most recent project had cost, was costing and would continue to cost his newspaper. It sounded intimidating: It made you wonder, How could a lone, poor, isolated Journalist hope to do significant work without a big fat budget?

In the audience, an editor asked panelists to discuss what they might do if they were suddenly given a million dollars to pursue investigative Journalism. My response, when my turn came, was that big budgets promote big waistlines. There is no reason why good Journalism should cost a fortune. If you have a fortune to dispose of, you'll go astray. You'll waste money, waste time, and worst of all, waste mental energy. I plan in this book to show you how fine work can be done by impoverished researcher-writers on, well, a shoestring.

I wish you good luck in plotting your newspaper career. If you have not been lucky enough to land a plum internship after majoring in Journalism at some posh university, *Shoestring Reporter* offers an alternative path into an exciting and fascinating occupation — one you may be able to reshape!

chapter 2

i cudn't even spell jernelist

When I was growing up in a small Midwestern town back in the Stone Age, my Uncle Charlie had this motto taped to his kitchen wall:
6 Munce ago, I cudn't even spell injanear, and now I are won.
Uncle Charlie was a high school grad. And he was very smart. He was a self-taught auto mechanic and electrician before he landed a job designing and installing conveyor systems. He did not have the title "engineer," because he never went to college and couldn't be licensed. But he WAS an engineer by virtue of what he did, and his practical, can-do mind set him apart — and above — the "real" engineers with degrees and licenses who supposedly supervised him. Their creativity and originality were hemmed in by their textbook-ish approaches. Uncle Charlie didn't have much respect for the titled engineers. He called their hallowed but often flawed blueprints "funny papers."

What does that have to do with Journalism? For lack of a college degree and a license, Uncle Charlie could not call himself an engineer. It cost him in salary and prestige. What about Journalism? Sky's the limit, folks. True, there are all kinds of academic programs with well-paid university professors teaching people, so they apparently believe, how Journalists do their jobs. Ask yourself, though, how many of those well-paid profs actually have worked for a newspaper and know the realities of the craft. Better yet, ask the profs. See what they say.

Oh, well, don't waste your effort. Most of the J school profs either never worked for newspapers (you can actually get a PhD in Journalism without ever working on a paper) or did it so long ago that to REAL working Journalists they appear as worn-out has-beens, tired blowhards, weary wannabes.

You can spend lots of time and money getting a bachelor's, master's and even a doctorate in Journalism. But unlike engineers or doctors or lawyers, Journalism is an unlicensed Profession, if it is a Profession at all. For, unlike the other Professions, including doctors, who see licensing as a way to limit competition for scarce jobs, Journalists actually fight the idea of having their competence certified. They argue that it would violate the First Amendment of the U.S. Constitution. Barbers need licenses. Not Journalists. (In a subsequent chapter, "Second Opinions," I'll explain the extent to which workaday Journalists are NOT protected by the First Amendment, at least in the view of some newspaper owners.)

Now look at me: Am I a Journalist? According to my diplomas, I'm far from it. I went to an undergraduate college where not one — yes, NOT ONE SINGLE Journalism class was offered. I graduated with a major in history and one class shy of a major in German. I went to grad school and got a master's, again in history. I passed my oral and written exams for a PhD in history, but scrapped my thesis. That makes me what academics call an ABD — "All But Dissertation." One of the best things I ever did — God, what a bore, hanging out in Academia — was dumping my quest for a doctor's degree.

Think that's sour grapes? Consider this: Would I have flown upside-down in a Blue Angels F/A-18 fighter jet if I'd stayed at the university? Would I have piloted a WJR radio traffic helicopter if I'd gone into teaching? I actually logged two hours of helicopter instruction on that assignment. Yes, I have my pilot's log to prove it! Would I have packed

Crew chief chats with me before takeoff.

With WJR reporter Dennis Neubacher.
Reprinted by permission of the Detroit Free Press

a pair of rattlesnakes in my hatchback and faced an angry, charging western diamondback if I'd gone into teaching? I write about amazing things, and I'll get into this in more detail in my chapter on nonmonetary benefits of this Profession.

Whoops! Did I say "Profession"? I slipped. Truth is, Journalism is a craft. You can have all the fancy Journalism degrees in the world and still not know how to write a logically constructed sentence. But if you have the basic skills of a high school grad, you can do the work — and get paid for it — without spending the time and money to get those pretty diplomas. Why, you might even be hired sight unseen over the telephone, as I was by my Tribune editor.

Don't believe me? Okay, let me tell you about my Auntie Jane. Auntie Jane was my Uncle Charlie's wife. Auntie Jane was a high school grad with a bit of nurse's training. She was your basic housewife, mom to my Cousin Marylyn. But she had a lively wit. She got a clerical job at my hometown newspaper. Never one to hold her tongue, Auntie Jane made it apparent to Scoop Jefferies, her editor, that she had more than the customary dose of moxie and intellect. Scoop asked her to try putting some of her sauce on paper. The result was a weekly column called "Jane's Jabber." Cousin Marylyn recently photocopied her collection of Auntie Jane's Lowell Ledger columns. She gave a copy to me. I've been reading them. They are darned good. Common sense, regular-life topics written about with a unique but polished style unhindered by the dead hand of formal Journalistic training.

In my nearly 30 years as a Journalist, I have written every kind of piece there is to be written at a small, a medium and a large newspaper. Cops stories? Done it. Murders? Done it. Magazine writing, not only done it, I've taught it at a Real School of Journalism! I kid you not, Bowling Green State University in Ohio paid me to suffer the children. Features? Been there.

Investigative? Got the award hardware to prove it. Obits. Why don't they give awards for obituaries? Even sports. Yep, I've won awards. Okay, not for sports. Until recently, I wrote a personal column in the Free Press. Am I a Journalist?

What do I care what you call me!

I may not have those J school degrees, but I wrote copy that my editors liked, and they put it in the paper with my name over it. They PAID me for it! They even gave me merit raises. Now I'm retired and collecting a pension earned from my days as a newspaper writer.

Let me repeat: You do not need a college degree to be a Journalist. In fact, you do not need a degree of any kind.

Still don't believe me? Let me tell you two stories. When I got into this profess — I mean, craft, it was 1978. I became aware of people acting as newspaper and radio reporters who had backgrounds more interesting than anything a college could offer. One of them was a foreman at a fishing lure factory. I kid you not. My favorite fishing lure as a kid was the River Runt made by Heddon, and this guy may well have helped manufacture my lure. Or maybe not, because one day, he heard that a radio station was opening in his town. They needed a news reporter. He got the job. In addition to writing and reading news for WDOW-AM, John Cureton phoned his news to the newspaper and got paid a second time.

There was a woman whose byline was over many stories. When I got to know her, I learned that she had never gone to college, but she had two licenses.

For hairdressing.

I keep telling you: You don't NEED a college degree for this job.

What DOES a Journalist need?

Well, you'd better be able to read. And I mean read intelligently, critically and with comprehension.

You're going to need lots and lots of curiosity.

Definitely you will find it handy to have a reliable bullshit meter. I wish I could sell you one. I could get rich. Instead, in a later chapter, I'll explain how you can build your own manure detector. In other words, you need to know really fast when people are jiving you.

Now here's the biggie: You're going to need — most of all — courage.

Courage, first, because your curiosity is going to make you think of questions. Thinking of questions is not the same as asking questions. Anybody can form a question — smart minds are good at that. It takes guts to ask a question, especially one that might piss someone off. Sometimes questions threaten other people. They might impugn somebody's truthfulness. Or reveal someone as a crook. Why, a good question could threaten a person's ill-gotten livelihood.

Secondly, you will need courage, because your curiosity — once it has forced the question — will reveal facts that people in power don't want to have brought into public view. It is hard to go against the grain. The hint of ostracism is enough to scare off many reporters and editors. They learn that behavior in Journalism schools. It's called Cravenheart 101. (I'm kidding.) But you will need real guts to go ahead and put into print the facts your questions have brought to light.

And, of course, it's not enough for YOU to have a heart for aggressive truth-telling. You'll need editors with spine, too. That's a rare breed, but we need not get into that issue now. Read my soon-to-be-published novel *Cross Purposes* if you'd like further insights into courage and its antithesis.

So, here are the basic traits of character and thinking that you will need to become a Journalist.

Be literate.

Be curious.

Have courage.

None of which is taught in college.

chapter 3

pantaloney

Are you a blogger?

Okay, some of you may not know what a blogger is. Don't feel bad. Not long ago, I didn't know what it meant, either. I probably should be embarrassed. In my case, it's sort of like my Uncle Charlie's motto, "6 Munce ago, I cudn't even spell injanear, and now I are won." Remember that? Well, I actually had a blog and was posting my little essays on what I called my "Web site." I told my son, a computer science major at the University of Michigan, what I was doing.

"So dad," he said, "You're a blogger."

"A what?" I said.

"You're writing a blog — a Web log."

Oh.

Okay.

So I'm a blogger. I write something called **joelontheroad.com**.

Maybe you're a blogger, too.

Does that mean you're a Journalist?

Well, does my blogging mean I'm no longer a Journalist? Did I suddenly lose my license to practice Journalism?

Sound like silly questions? Believe me, in the elitist realm of print Journalism where huge amounts of noise are generated by newspaper practitioners, these questions are quite real. Bloggers get a bad rap in that rarefied world I'll call the Printosphere.

Journalists, it seems, claim some kind of official credential because they call themselves, well, Journalists. And if you're not a blogger, but just someone trying to edge into the Printosphere where staffers are being laid off or bought out and more and more fees are being paid to stringers, you will nonetheless encounter these attitudes of superiority and condescension. Might as well get used to it. But don't worry, you can have the last laugh.

Most of the Journalists I know cash a paycheck cut by some official, accredited news organ. Their employer is recognized as a purveyor of Journalistic stuff, be it news about sports events, recipes, hedge-trimming or city council gossip. They cash those checks issued by recognized news outlets, ipso facto they are Journalists.

The bad rap comes also from people who are not employed by mainline news organizations but, because of their literary output in the nonfiction arena, they are dubbed and certainly consider themselves to be Journalists.

Some of these self-anointed Journalists are real pains in the keister. One of these eminences is a Canadian named George Jonas. In June 2006, Jonas grumbled: " 'Everybody is a critic,' people used to say. Not anymore. Now everybody is a commentator. The Internet has turned my sedentary and unglamorous occupation into a hobby or sport — still sedentary, but no longer as unglamorous as it used to be.

"Gone are the days when a Journalist, as the great H.L. Mencken put it, was just a 'reporter with two pairs of pantaloons.' Now a Journalist is a pundit, no less, with pantaloons galore. And a Web-logger — blogger — is someone who wants to be a pundit without the bother of having to earn a Journalist's pantaloons first, never mind a reporter's."

Now I think I understand what he's saying: Doing the work of Journalists is tough; it takes hard work, experience, and not everyone is up to the task.

I would accept that as fact if I didn't know there are a lot of half-assed Journalists out there.

What makes a Journalist a Journalist?

Having two sets of pants?

What, I'm wondering, does that mean, "a Journalist's pantaloons"?

Does compiling recipes or "pet of the week" listings make someone a Journalist? If so, then why is someone who posts comments on a Web log not automatically considered a Journalist, too?

Doctors need licenses. They can be prosecuted for practicing medicine without one. Ditto lawyers. Same goes for auto mechanics, hairdressers, barbers.

Not so Journalists. The only license they need is a pen and notepad.

The Internet didn't change that.

So what makes Journalists professionals?

Actually, and I'll say this again and again, Journalists are NOT professionals. They are recognized by courts in the U.S. to be practitioners of a craft. In fact, they're lucky in that if they were legally classed as professionals, they couldn't claim pay for overtime.

What, in fact, is Journalism? The short answer is that it's any kind of writing that's about real things, people and places, as opposed to fiction, which is made-up. Beyond that, what can you say? Oh, sure, there are professional organizations that try to warp this amorphous craft to conform to a set of rules, the old "ethical guidelines" so cherished by some newspapers, largely, I think, to exercise social control over and bully their employees.

In the end, though, it's pretty hard to define what a Journalist is.

One thing seems clear to me: Journalism is a craft that anyone with reasonable intelligence can practice.

No license needed. Why, you don't even need a degree in Journalism to do the job. If you did, I'd have been working in some other business.

So why shouldn't bloggers call themselves Journalists?

They can, in fact. I'll bet Mr. Jonas would agree with me on this: Since nobody anoints anyone as a Journalist, nobody can give or take away that title. All it takes is, well, that pen and notepad.

And doing the job. Fairly and intelligently.

To anyone who disagrees, I say "pantaloney!"

chapter 4

general custer's error

"Advise Custer to be prudent," General Sherman wired Gen. Terry before the Battle of the Little Bighorn. "And not to bring along any newspapermen."

Custer wasn't prudent, and neither was Mark Kellogg, the string correspondent for the Western Associated Press who was with Custer when the Sioux attacked. If Custer disobeyed Sherman's order, Kellogg bucked a cardinal rule for writers: Come back alive so you can tell your story.

In the late 19th Century, the Associated Press and its rival, United Press, were fighting over news, trying to scoop each other even in the remotest areas of the country. For that, they needed writers — many writers — and as today, there were never enough full-time reporters to cover every story. Well, actually, there could be enough full-timers — if newspapers were willing to pay their salaries. But there is a cheaper way to hire reporters than paying them full-time and offering fringe benefits like health insurance and retirement pensions.

If you're too cheap to pay all your employees a decent wage, you invent something called a "string correspondent." Now called "stringers," or by the even fancier term, "freelancer," these reporters, and sometimes they are photographers — and they may even be editors — may work full-time or more, but they don't collect a salary. In Mark Kellogg's day, the writers shipped their pages of news copy by pony express, by telegraph or more prosaically, by mail, to the nearest AP or UP office. There, editors read their copy, corrected, deleted, added, and retransmitted it by telegraph to member newspapers around the country.

Stringers were unsalaried, but that doesn't mean they worked for nothing. Somewhere, somebody with a pair of scissors would clip the stringer's stories, creating column-wide strips that were pasted onto narrow lengths of blank newsprint. Usually, the person who did this tedious chore was the stringer him- or herself. At the end of the month, the stringer rolled up that "string" and mailed it to the editor, who pulled a yardstick off a hook on the wall and measured the stringer's monthly contribution. The total number of column inches would be multiplied times the agency or newspaper's column-inch rate of pay. The product of that simple arithmetic would be written onto the writer's paycheck.

When I started stringing, I actually saw one of these paper-and-glue strings. The Herald-Palladium in Benton Harbor, Michigan, was still using stringers and paying them 40 cents a column inch for their work. The polite word for stringers was "correspondent," so once a month, these string correspondents would carry in their rolls of glued-up clippings to be measured for pay.

What kind of abuse do you think this kind of payment scheme might promote? Think about that while I assure you that most newspapers no longer use this archaic system. Yet they all use stringers, from the smallest weekly to the august New York Times. As editor of The Journal Era, I hired stringers. One of them was my wife, who didn't stay long in Journalism. She went on to become an assistant professor and family medicine physician at the University of Michigan Medical School with an M.D. degree from that university. That proves that not everyone needs to stay stuck in the reporting prof— No, NOT "profession" — I mean craft. At the weekly, I hired another stringer. It was her first job in Journalism. She parlayed it into a staff reporting job at the Tribune, just as I had done a few years before.

The trouble with paying by column inch? It encourages writers to "pad" their copy, because the longer the report, the more the pay — unless the editor gets wise and lops off a few inches.

Why do these papers use stringers? The New York Times and the little weekly share a need: They both want on-the-spot reports of events of interest to their readers. That the Times readers are more interested in national and international news while the weekly focuses on schools, cities and towns not too distant from their newsrooms is irrelevant. The staff of every newspaper, from The Wall Street Journal to the Marcellus News, is overworked. It is another cardinal rule that every paper in the country is understaffed.

That is good news for stringers. Editors look upon them with relief. They can lighten the load of reporting that falls on staff writers. Sure, the papers often save the most important stories for staffers, or at least they think they do. But there is enough work left that they farm it out to part-timers, especially in outlying areas. Stringers often (but not always!) sit through small-town school and township board meetings, city and village council meetings and even county commission and court sessions.

There are thousands of stringers working in the United States. When I started stringing in 1978, I counted more than 50 stringers making at least a part-time living by working for one or more of the 10 dailies and

15 or so weeklies in southwestern Michigan. All of those papers are still in business despite all the whining about the forthcoming demise of newspapers. And nearly 30 years later, they still use stringers.

I had been working at the Free Press since 1984, except for a couple of years on "vacation" during what was better known as the Great Newspaper Strike of 1995. Well, call it the strike of '95, '96 and '97, because I was out from July of 1995 till October of 1997. During all my time at the Free Press as a full-time staffer, the paper used stringers. They called them by a fancy name — freelance — as if they were some kind of glorious knights errant, when what they were in fact were part-time reporters paid piece-rate by skinflint papers too cheap to provide them with fringe benefits.

Editors may think stringers work part-time, but many stringers will tell you they often work harder than full-timers. Sometimes they earn more than the staffers. But often, despite long hours, they earn considerably less. Once, the Free Press got so brazen about overworking a stringer that The Newspaper Guild, the union for editorial workers, filed a grievance and an arbitrator later ordered editors to place the stringer on the staff full-time with benefits. That didn't stop the Free Press from using stringers. I wrote five stories a week for the suburban sections. Under the Guild contract, I got five weeks of vacation. Five stories times five weeks absent equals 25 stories a year that editors needed from me, but under the rules I wouldn't be writing them. Who does that work?

Stringers.

chapter 5

jesse's undoing

Rejection is never fun. I've received many, many rejection slips in my time, for novels, short stories, nonfiction books and articles. Early on, my feelings were hurt. Now, I'm numb. I just move on. It's easier now, because I've had some successes, and I know that persistence often overcomes rejection.

At least, I was not having entire articles — produced by dint of lots of time and energy — turned down. All I had invested was the time I took to write a query letter. The query is a way of testing whether editors will buy your story idea.

Let me tell you the story of my very first query letter.

I was living in Manhattan. It was spring 1978. I'd been trying to peddle a novel to agents and having zero luck. Friends encouraged me to try my hand at Journalism. Why not? I had my training in historical research, and I thought I was a pretty cool writer. I decided to start my career as a stringer by sending a query letter to The (Benton Harbor) Herald-Palladium, a daily newspaper about which I knew virtually nothing, nor did I bother trying to find out about it. Instead, I confined myself to learning the name of the managing editor, but not by Googling, because there was no Internet then. I don't recall how I found a copy of a small Michigan daily in New York City, but somehow I did. I read the paper's masthead — the place usually on the editorial page where a paper's top editors are listed — and learned that Bert Lindenfeld was the managing editor. I addressed my letter to him. He quickly sent me a reply, rejecting my proposed story on moral grounds.

I'd suggested that I write a feature that would "describe in more or less a jocular tone Jesse James' contributions to the art of bank robbery. Few people know," I wrote, "that the James brothers, Frank and Jesse, were guerrillas on the Confederate side in the Civil War, and that the terms of peace did not include amnesty for guerrillas. James was an outlaw before he was a bank robber. He proceeded to apply guerrilla techniques to his bank and train operations." The paper, according to my proposal, would publish my story on the anniversary of Jesse James' murder.

Here's what Bert Lindenfeld wrote back: "Thanks, but we're not interested in the anniversary of Jesse James' assassination. As much as we know of him, we'd say that he's well dead and just as well forgotten."

Whew!

Sanctimonious? Wow. What I had not revealed in my query letter was that all of my research into the guerrilla tactics of the James gang so far came from reading an article in Junior Scholastic, where the managing editor apparently thought the topic interesting and suitable for young readers. So I had a laugh and forgot about it. Looking back, I realize that the H-P editor was correct. The story I proposed was something for a magazine. The Palladium concentrates on local governmental doings. They hire stringers to sit through long township or village council meetings and write lengthy reports paid at 40 cents a column inch. They do not pay stringers to research their own ideas, write creative features or think for themselves. The news is what H-P editors deem it to be. Write like that or go somewhere else.

I went somewhere else.

But before I took that hike, I made one more try at the H-P. Through my wife, I'd met Scott Aiken, a Palladium reporter, and he coached me on how to talk to editors. Tom Brundrette was Scott's editor. He was the guy who ordered stringers around, and so I would have to convince him to hire me.

Journalists call the cuttings they make of their own articles from newspaper pages their "clips." I had no clips. What I did have was the typescript of my first freelance piece. It was about Janna Gjesdal, a woman from Detroit who went to Manhattan to try to make it as an actress. I'd seen her in several off-off-Broadway plays, was impressed and decided to write a story about her. At the time I talked to the H-P guy, I had submitted the manuscript to the Detroit Free Press Magazine, but hadn't heard whether they'd buy it. The Herald-Palladium editor looked at the typewritten pages and said, "Our stringers work exclusively for us. I would not want to see your byline in the Freep. They're a competitor."

I could not believe what I was hearing. This small-town paper would never publish my article about a Detroiter in New York, let alone a whimsical story about Jesse James, but they would forbid me to sell it to another paper! Welcome to the wide world of censorship! Restraint of trade? Oh, yes, censorship is a booming business in newspapers. We'll get into that later on.

I wasn't sure I was understanding him. Here's what he was offering me: no benefits such as a pension, overtime pay, health insurance,

notables

Janna Gjesdal: Roots in Detroit, but growing in New York

"Don't ever get a job besides acting that you like."

Janna Gjesdal has followed this advice, and is fond of passing it along. Last September she moved — permanently — from Michigan to New York. So far she has played two major parts in off-off-Broadway plays.

"My decision to come to New York was a decision to make a living as a working actress," Ms. Gjesdal says. But the decision was not easy to make. Leading up to it were eight years of marriage and a 5-year-old daughter. Both the marriage and the child, Ms. Gjesdal asserts, she very much wanted.

She sees her daughter once a month and relations with her ex-husband are fine. At 30, she says, "it was time for the marriage to end and time for me to decide what to do with my life. I managed in those eight years not to prepare myself for anything else."

Neither was she prepared for New York — at least in the sense of having professional connections ready made. Her roots are in the midwest.

The name Gjesdal (pronounced "Jesdal") comes to her from Norwegian grandparents who settled in Iowa. Her father moved to Detroit, and it was there that she grew up. She studied at Oakland University for two years before joining Oakland's Academy of Dramatic Art in 1967. She never graduated and in the meantime the Academy went defunct.

In the late '60s, Ms. Gjesdal says, she found the role of an actress in this society very difficult. Referring to the tense, self-conscious political activism of those days, she says "everything was outward. Acting is very personal. Acting doesn't save the world." If you were political, then acting was difficult to rationalize. And if, on top of that, you were a wife and a mother, a career in acting seemed out of reach — especially from Detroit.

Since her arrival in New York, she has had to work. Following her own maxim, she took a job she didn't like — as a waitress in the Spring Street Bar, where, coincidentally, scenes from "An Unmarried Woman" were filmed.

Through the trade papers she learned that a midtown company called "The Troupe" would hold readings for Ibsen's "Ghosts." Later she found that all major calls are in September. By sheer chance she had picked the right moment to arrive in New York.

She decided to try The Troupe's reading. She arrived to find she was number 160 on the list. She waited for nine hours and read for one minute.

Then she heard nothing. She forgot what The Troupe was. Returning to New York after Christmas, she found a call from The Troupe. They wanted her to read for the part of Maria in Sheridan's "School For Scandal." She got the part, stayed through the first rehearsal, then went home to find her loft had burned.

"I had my first New York part, and no place to live," she smiles.

"What came from working at The Troupe is I'm fine as I am. I'm at the point of seeing agents again." And she does not feel like taking one agent's advice: she is not going to have her hair straightened.

"My hair is naturally straight — I had it curled for the interview."

■ JOEL THURTELL

Reprinted by permission of the Detroit Free Press

use of a company phone, notebook, pen or typewriter. Just sporadic piecework that could be terminated at the pleasure of this editor. Yet a condition of this pretend job was that I not sell my work to anyone else? That's right, he said. Our stringers are pleased to work under those conditions.

I told him I would not be pleased to work like that. There was really nothing more to talk about. Quintessential deal breaker. I walked out.

Incidentally, the Free Press Magazine bought and published my article about the actress. It was my first paid, published work.

After my conversation with the editor, I drove home and tried to call Tom Gruber, Michigan editor of the South Bend Tribune. Once again, Scott Aiken had coached me on how to approach him. I'd left a few messages, but hadn't heard back. After waiting weeks, I got a call from Tom wondering if I'd had experience covering meetings.

I told him about the year I'd spent as an unpaid, or "volunteer," reporter with WMUK-FM, a radio station in Kalamazoo. Once a week, I drove to Portage, a town next door to Kalamazoo. I would sit through the weekly meeting of the City Council. I took notes as I tried to follow what was going on. Mayor Betty Ongley was a teacher, and she had a knack for explaining to the audience the finer points under discussion. I would take my notes back to the studio, write a story, get the engineer/disc jockey on duty to record me reading the report, and go home. Next morning, I'd hear my voice on 102.1 FM.

The Tribune editor said he'd pay me $25 for each meeting article. The morning after the evening meeting, I was to read the story by telephone to the "Code-A-Phone" girls who took dictation from reporters. He assigned me to cover meetings of the school board, village council and two township boards.

That was the basis of my stringing income. Five meetings a month. $125. Peanuts, right? Besides writing up the meetings, I wrote features and sometimes investigative stories about things I learned at the meetings. Eventually, I was earning $400-$600 a month in 1980s dollars. In 2007 dollars, that's $994 to $1,492.

No other news outlet was willing to pay for my meeting reports. But it was at a school board meeting that I learned how the apple farmers couldn't find enough migrant workers to pick their fruit and the school superintendent had recruited high school kids to do the work. I went out to an orchard and snapped photos of kids picking apples in trees. It was a feature story for the Trib. I put the same story, along with a couple of black-and-white film negatives, on a Greyhound bus bound for Detroit. The Detroit News paid me $75 for the story. I'll talk about how I

12-B —THE DETROIT NEWS—Wednesday, August 30, 1978

Fruits, vegetables may rot

Farmers need pickers now

By JOEL THURTELL
News Special Writer

ST. JOSEPH, Mich. — Part of southwestern Michigan's fruit and vegetable crop will go to waste if workers are not found to pick this year's yields, officials say.

While Berrien County agricultural officials could not forecast what proportion of the total harvest is in danger, they stressed that the labor shortage is acute and it is immediate.

Bumper crops combined with declining numbers of seasonal workers in orchards and fields will cause the loss of peach, plum, apple, pear, pepper, tomato, squash and melon crops in Berrien and Van Buren counties. The labor squeeze also is being felt in parts of Kent, Allegan, Kalamazoo and Cass counties.

WITH ONE-THIRD of the peaches yet to be picked, officials foresee the loss of much of that remaining crop.

"A couple of slow years in the past when migrant workers have been turned around and had to go home," explains this year's shortage of migrant arrivals in the area, said James Twomley of the Michigan Employment Security Commission's (MESC) St. Joseph Office.

Some seasonal workers came this year but they have been placed and no new ones are coming in, he said.

"It could get to crops rotting on trees," Twomley said.

Weather is another facet of the problem, according to Harvey Belter, Berrien County Extension Agent for fruit. Cool weather early in the summer slowed ripening of all fruits and vegetables.

"Three hot days in August bunched it all together — Red Havens (peaches), melons, everything. Visualize looking down a barrel with the bottom coming right up to meet you," Belter said.

Belter agreed with Twomley, warning that many crops will rot.

Another consideration for growers is the low prices processors are offering for many crops this year. The headache of finding pickers combined with the prospect of little or no profits will encourage some farmers to let their crops stand on the ground or in the trees, said Berrien County Extension Director Clare Musgrove.

THE MESC's Twomley said that agency is urging farm and church groups to help harvest threatened crops, but with school starting soon, Musgrove disagreed saying, "I don't see this as a source of labor supply at all." Inexperienced pickers often damage crops, Musgrove added.

Harvesting is normally paid on a piece-rate basis set by the state Department of Labor, but new workers, if they are slow, are guaranteed a minimum of $2.65 per hour. Children as young as 12 may work if they have their parent's permission.

Prospective pickers are urged to contact the MESC office nearest them for placement, Twomley said.

Musgrove said that rather than labor, he hoped that the MESC would recruit workers from area towns and cities who could commute to the fields or orchards using their own transportation.

Reprinted courtesy of The Detroit News

found Bob Kirk, the News state editor, in the chapter about serendipity, hustling and networking.

Seventy-five bucks. Let's see, That's $245 in 2008 currency, using an inflation calculator: **www.westegg.com/inflation/**

I'll take it!

chapter 6

editors NEED you!

"I'm gonna pay the stringers by the inch, and stop paying for photos," my soon-to-be-former publisher told me as I was leaving my job as editor of the Berrien Springs weekly. "They should consider themselves lucky to have their stuff in print."

Nothing personal, mind you. Although I'd spent lots of time recruiting smart people to cover local meetings and write features, my old boss wanted to cut expenses. He figured a good way to do it would be to chisel the piecework writers and photographers. It made me angry. I had learned that alone I could not write all the copy the paper needed to print. I felt the stringers improved the breadth and depth of reporting and the overall quality of the paper. The publisher's pay scale was so ludicrously low he might as well have fired them, and in the case of the photogs, that's just what he proposed. I hated to see them lose their jobs, and I hated to see the work I'd done to improve the paper go for naught.

Not to worry. Soon after I left, the publisher brought the stringers back. What changed his mind? Suddenly, he alone was responsible for filling the paper. And, doggone it, he realized that he couldn't do it by himself.

Fear of the news hole suddenly clamped its icy hand on him. Remember this: Editors live in terror of not being able to provide enough copy by deadline. Every day at dailies, panic-stricken e-mails surge through computers as editors — suddenly freed from the mindless and endless meetings they've attended most of the day — get down to the basics of putting out the next day's paper and discover that GOSH! There's no copy. Please, please, somebody, fill the paper.

Staff writers are not always a help, either. They know their editors are spendthrifts with copy. Say I'm a staff writer and I'm heading out on vacation next week, and say I have actually written an extra story or two. If I let my editor know about it, she'll use those stories when I'm gone. When I get back, instead of being ahead, I'll be behind. What is the point of busting my butt to write extra copy if it's going to be squandered while I'm gone? My solution: I would write those stories before I left town, but keep my mouth shut. I have my own little story bank.

This is good for you, the stringer. I've made sure that news-hole fear will prevail in my absence. My editor will be calling stringers to replace the copy she thinks I haven't written. Then, when I return, I feed her stuff I'd socked away, while getting my feet on the ground and ready to pursue more stories.

Find it hard to believe editors would so lack foresight as to be caught flat-footed every day, locked in a vicious cycle of repetitive behavior? It is rare to find an editor who has actually banked stories for use on a day when staff writers, say, are on vacation or someone gets sick or a story just plain falls through. Of course, as I say, sometimes reporters hoard stories. Regardless, editors need stringers. They need you more than you need them.

chapter 7

double-dippers

Wouldn't you like to be paid two, three, four or more times for a single piece of work? That is what book authors do, of course. Stringers can do it, too. As a full-time staff writer, I couldn't do it.

That's right. If you work full-time for one newspaper, as I did, you are paid for writing stories that appear in that paper. If the paper is part of a chain, or belongs to the Associated Press, it may offer your stories to a wire service, which in turn offers them to newspapers, radio and TV stations around the country. I've heard from old friends in faraway places who have seen my Free Press stories — with my byline — in their hometown papers. The exposure was nice, but I wasn't paid an extra dime for my work.

The independent contractor, aka stringer, is in a far better position. He or she can sell a story over and over again. The cardinal rule is simple: Don't offer it to competing papers in the same area. For instance, in my stringing days, I never sent a story to the Free Press if the News was going to print it. But more than once, I sent a feature story to the News after a Free Press editor rejected it. The News would print the stories and I got to laugh at the Freep, and one particular editor, for letting themselves be scooped.

I remember feeling a bit nervous about sending the same story to different papers. But I gradually realized that the editors didn't care. They had a need to fill their news hole with the most interesting copy they could find. If their readers were in Detroit, say, and readers of The Indianapolis Star read the same story, so what? There was no overlapping readership, meaning that people in Indianapolis who read my story were not likely to see it in Detroit.

If they did, big deal. You can call it double-dipping, but the correct word is "syndication." You've heard of syndicated columnists, right? Well, syndication is what I did when I took a story that ran in the South Bend paper and ran it in the weekly paper where I got to choose stories because I was the editor.

In those days before digital imaging and jpegs, I had a little stainless steel canister that I used to develop black-and-white film. I would develop my negatives in a dark closet of my house, then send a negative or two down to South Bend. I would also put my typewritten story and a negative into an envelope and put the envelope on a Greyhound bus bound for Detroit. The News editor would send a copy aide to the bus station and sometime after that my story and the photo would run in that paper.

When I started sending stories to the News in 1978, they paid $75. By 1984, I was receiving $200 for a story with a photo or two. Okay, but that was a long time ago. In 2007, an editor at the Free Press was paying stringers (we euphemistically call them "freelancers") $125 per story without photos. Now, if you can double or triple market that story, it might be worth lots more. But notice how the fee has adjusted for inflation in a curious way — by going down!

Todd Bush, the hero of my first newspaper novel, is a stringer. In fact, the book's title is *Stringer*. Todd knows his relationship with editors at the fictitious Flaggsdowne Argus-Palladium is based on mutual contempt. Sometimes, relationships actually thrive on equally misconceived disrespect. So it often is with stringers and the editors who hire them and who have the power to fire them, too.

Even if editors don't abuse stringers or treat them with outright contempt, it's important to understand that editors have one aim only: filling that news hole. If you are lucky enough to receive calls from editors assigning you to write certain stories, great. But remember, the editor only wants to fill an often local, onetime need. The challenge for the double-dipping stringer is to parlay that story idea into something that can be sold in more than your own local venue.

It helps to know what editors at other papers are publishing. For instance, when I started stringing, I had an idea for a story about my hometown, Lowell, Michigan, which has a unique feature. It is split in two by the Flat River. Main Street crosses the Flat on a bridge. When I was growing up, there were quite a few stores built on pilings in the river so they could face Main Street. My grandfather's meat market in the 1930s was one of these buildings, and the building is still there. Most are gone — wiped out in fires. The town didn't have a fireboat, and when one of those buildings on stilts caught fire, there was no way to get hoses into the back, because their rears sat extended out over the river. (See? I'm starting out on this story again!)

I visited Florence, Italy, and saw the Ponte Vecchio — a bridge with stores, sort of like what Lowell had. Okay, a very rough parallel, but good enough for Journalism. Early in my stringing career, I called Bill Sonneborn, then editor of the South Bend Tribune Sunday Michiana magazine. Bill, it turned out, was in the Army in World War II and knew

Main Street Bridge: A touch of Italy's famed Ponte Vecchio in Lowell, Mich.

PHOTO BY TIM BIEBER

Scenic attraction in Lowell
Bridge spans colorful past

By JOEL THURTELL
News Special Writer

LOWELL, Mich. — It doesn't attract as many tourists as Italy's Ponte Vecchio, but Lowell's Main Street Bridge bears a certain similarity to that 14th-century pedestrian span over the Arno River in Florence.

Lowell's bridge, barely 100 years old, not only links separate halves of the Kent County town but serves as a retail district for its 3,000 residents.

The Ponte Vecchio is lined with small stalls specializing in jewelry and souvenirs, while the Lowell structure supports two barbershops, a boutique, a television store and an auto-parts outlet.

A visitor intent on window-shopping here might not even notice that M-21, Lowell's main artery, crosses the Flat River 15 miles east of Grand Rapids.

Facing the bridge, the stores extend north and south from Main Street and are supported by concrete and wood pilings planted in the river bottom.

ALTHOUGH A CENTRAL location is important to merchants anywhere, it is difficult to understand why Lowell's pioneers erected shops over water, unless perhaps they anticipated a fire and wanted a ready source of water.

That hasn't always been helpful, however. An early wooden span was swept by fire in 1904.

Shops were rebuilt in the same locations, but a year later the Grand River backed up over a wide region of western Michigan and forced tributaries such as the Flat to rise so forcibly that sections of the bridge were torn away.

Historians cannot determine why Lowell's elders constructed stores along the bridge in the first place, then rebuilt there after two disasters.

One explanation is that in the 1880's real estate prices were relatively high, so some merchants chose sites where they would not need land titles.

ANOTHER GUESS goes like this: In the mid-19th century the Flat River was a narrow, shallow, fast-running stream, but just before the Civil War grain millers began damming it for a source of power. One dam went in where the bridge now stands (and a successor remains there).

As the water level rose, shopkeepers who had built close to the embankment faced gradual flooding and either moved their stores or put pilings under the buildings.

Despite all the water below, a big mill was gutted by fire in 1943. In 1958, six stores and a tavern burned out.

Nor is fire the only hazard. In 1955, old pilings under the Kroger store collapsed from rot and caused its entire sugar stock to float away in the Flat.

Some shops could become a nuisance to the millers, too. At the turn of the century the owner of a produce store sold bananas picked from tough, many-branched stems. When these were empty, he tossed them out a back window into the river, forcing a nearby mill to open its dam, lower the river and remove the debris from turbine machinery every few weeks.

NORTON AVERY, who operated a photographic studio on the bridge before World War I, recalls sending an assistant to the front door to make sure no horse-drawn carriages were approaching when he was about to print portraits.

The vibration of buggies on the plank roadway of that era caused his equipment to tremble and could ruin his pictures, he said.

Now 85, Avery saw his former shop razed recently, after its roof began sagging away from an adjacent building toward the river.

But enough others survive to make a trip to Lowell an interesting diversion for tourists.

Reprinted courtesy of The Detroit News

Florence. I pitched the story, with the lead making the Ponte Vecchio comparison. He went for it. I visited Lowell, took some pictures, interviewed some old-timers and wrote an article that ran in the magazine. I also pitched the story to Bob Kirk, state editor of the News. Bingo: Double-dip. He bought the story and used one of my photos.

As I sit here reflecting on that story, written almost 30 years ago, I'm realizing I could, with a few changes, sell that same story today. My first thought is to try the News again. As a Free Press staffer, I was banned from writing for the News. But hey, I keep reminding myself, I don't work for the Freep any more.

With a little retouching, I could send it out as a travel story, especially with that Ponte Vecchio angle. Too poor to fly to Italy? Hop over to Lowell and enjoy their fake Ponte Vecchio. And oh, by the way, have lunch at the Flat River Grill!

See what I mean? There are countless ways to dress up a story and pitch it to different markets.

Again and again and again.

chapter 8

surviving as a writer

By May of 1978, I'd been writing my first novel for about six years. I'd lived in Ann Arbor; Mexico; Ann Arbor again; Togo, West Africa, and on a farm in western Michigan. I'd lived in Manhattan for six months on the theory that I'd be closer to the movers and shakers in book publishing and would more easily find an editor or agent who would be excited about my book.

Half a year of shrieking subways and concrete everywhere, with still no book contract, persuaded me that I could pursue my goal from some distance. I headed back to Michigan, by way of Mexico, with the idea of landing some kind of job. My wife was already working in Berrien Springs as a teacher in the county juvenile home. We'd rented a small house with an unfinished attic. I bought a big wooden desk and we muscled it up the stairs into my garret study. Next, I needed to earn some money.

In the years we'd known each other, my wife had watched me writing my novel. I'd never earned a nickel from my writing. She had an idea how to change that. In high school, she was editor of the high school page in The Ann Arbor News. As a student at the University of Michigan, she took a couple of Journalism classes and was an intern reporter at The Ann Arbor News. She could see some things about my personality that she thought might make me a Journalist. I was trained as a historian and I was inclined to hoard and study documents. My doctoral dissertation was about Mexican Indians in Colonial times. Other than the fact that my sources were long dead, I was looking into everyday questions about life and death among 17th-Century people. Maybe my skills could be translated to the here and now. Karen had a friend, another teacher in Berrien Springs named Rose. Rose was married to Scott Aiken. Remember Scott Aiken? Scott was — and still is — a reporter with the Benton Harbor paper. Karen engineered a meeting. Not only did I make a great friend that day, but Scott began coaching me on how to become a stringer.

He explained that stringing is a part-time job that would allow me time to work on other projects. The pay was not huge, maybe $50 a month from a small weekly. But he knew stringers who were making

$1,000 a month, and one who worked for several papers was making twenty-five grand a year in 1978 — more than most full-time staff newspaper writers of the time. Some of these stringers were running what amounted to local news bureaus, and they were more than busy.

Scott has a degree in Journalism, but he explained that no degree is needed for stringing. College degrees won't help if you can't produce. When I first started writing this book circa 1981, I counted 50 stringers working for 10 daily newspapers and roughly 15 weeklies in southwestern Michigan and northern Indiana. I met a woman who quit her job as a staffer on The Kalamazoo Gazette to have a baby. Rather than go back full-time to the Gazette, she started stringing for them, along with the South Bend Tribune, the Three Rivers Commercial-News and the Sturgis Journal. She covered regular beats as if she were a staff reporter: city and village council meetings, township board meetings, school board meetings. She wrote features based on ideas she picked up in meetings or in conversations with officials. She would send the same story to all those newspapers and at the end of the month each paper would cut a check in her name.

When I was editor of The (Berrien Springs) Journal Era, I would cover the same meetings I'd been writing about for the Tribune. I would write my story and phone it in, dictating to the Tribune "Code-A-Phone" girls. Then I'd hand my copy to Jan Shafer, who ran The Journal Era's Compugraphic typesetting machine. My story would run in the daily paper and again in the weekly. I would send my best stories by Greyhound bus to Detroit, where the News would run them.

Somebody accused me of "double-dipping."

Hey, there's no law against plagiarizing yourself.

But here's the important thing: I had an agent for my first novel who thought it was great, but a bit idiosyncratic. Why not write something more conventional, then work my way back to the first book after finding some loyal readers for my later novels?

No problem. With paychecks coming in from various newspapers, I started working on a new novel. It was a murder mystery. The hero is an escapee from a mental hospital. He's been diagnosed as a paranoid schizophrenic because he believes he is Don Quixote. The narrator is the kind of part-time newspaper reporter we have come to know as a "stringer."

The title of the novel is *Stringer*.

The murder is solved by the madman.

That's right, the hero of the book is a lunatic.

Thanks to stringing, I was able to write that crazy book.

Surviving as a Writer | 33

Reprinted courtesy of The (Berrien Springs) Journal Era

chapter 9

ad hoc j school

You can found your own J school without spending a dime, and without anybody knowing what you're up to.

That's what I did.

I was so stealthy, in fact, that even I didn't know what was happening.

The dean of my little undercover J school was my friend Scott Aiken. He coached me on how to land a job as a stringer, and hardly a week went by when the two of us didn't meet for lunch or at least trade war stories over the phone. His then-wife, Rose, was a teacher in Berrien Springs, and so was my wife, Karen Fonde. Until our first son was born in April 1980, Karen and I would meet Scott, Rose, and other teachers at a restaurant in Berrien Springs. There, over a pitcher of beer, I'd hear from Scott about his latest reporting adventures. I'd tell Scott about my freelance projects and get free advice on how to work sources, what were my rights under Open Meetings and Freedom of Information laws, how to talk to cops, and so on. The bar visits ended after the birth of our son, but the phone chats and lunches kept on happening.

I was working for a rival paper, and it was occupationally hazardous for Scott to be talking to me. His newspaper, The (Benton Harbor) Herald-Palladium, had a nonfraternization policy, meaning he wasn't supposed to have anything to do with the likes of scoundrelly South Bend Tribune writers, even lowly stringers like me.

But Scott met with me anyway, and through Scott I got to know other Tribune writers he wasn't supposed to "fraternize" with: Jan Marsh, Lyle Sumerix and Lou Mumford, the three reporters in the Niles, Michigan, bureau of the South Bend Tribune. Nor was he supposed to acknowledge the existence of Sue Morris, the sage reporter who ran a one-person bureau smack in enemy territory, downtown St. Joseph. Eventually, Jan would become Michigan editor and boss over Sue, Lyle, Lou and me.

If Scott was the dean of my J school, Jan was head of the investigations department, Lyle was head of the police and fire division and Lou headed up the features operation.

What I was doing might be called "networking." If anybody had accused me of intentionally striking up friendships to enhance my professional career, I'd have retorted first that Journalism is not a profession and secondly, I was meeting these people because, well, they were great people, great friends, and their lives fascinated me.

I'd spent a lot of time in libraries reading about history. Suddenly I was with people whose work was an integral part of history. These were people, Journalists, who were taking raw information and transforming it into the rough record of the community's history. They were distilling many, many facts into cogent story lines that would become the town's and the region's tale and would eventually help define the community. As a student, I'd stood outside that process. Now, as a stringer, I was actively engaged in collecting facts, organizing them and putting them into words that contributed, subtly, another point of view — my own — and I was becoming part of the historical record.

Journalists are gossips. They love to talk. When they talk to each other, they invariably talk shop. I was just drinking it in. It reminded me of another time in my life when I got to look through a window into an alien culture. I was playing bit parts in Kalamazoo's New Vic Theater, and while it was not exactly Broadway, theater people are a distinct bunch and by working with the actors, director and crew, going to their parties, I was actually one of them, albeit my role was small. But I thought about those theater days as I assumed this new role, the reporter. In order to act like a reporter, I had to learn my part.

How does a reporter talk to sources? Does the role fit differently when talking to cops than when, say, talking to a school superintendent? A lawyer? A shopkeeper? Bob Sherefkin was the Bob Woodward of our group, seemingly born to inquire suspiciously into the subsurface operations of businesses and government. Bob was constrained by the same Herald-Palladium rule that forbade reporters meeting their counterparts on other papers, but, like Scott Aiken, he didn't let the paper's law stop him from being my friend. Over beers or riding together to stories, I heard Bob telling about how he got the big tip, the big smoking gun, and I'd recall his yarns when I ran into stonewalling and lying officials.

The secret is to throw yourself into the role, don't hold back, play the part to the hilt. You won't have to learn the lines, because you're living the part of a Journalist, talking to real people, not actors, who are giving or holding back what you need to write stories.

Sue Morris taught me how to glean what I needed from Berrien County Circuit Court criminal files to write weekly reports on judges' sentencing of felons. By the way, this is a little-thought-of form of reportorial work that could mean bucks to an enterprising stringer. I simply drove to the county seat every Friday, pulled the files on everyone who'd been sentenced, noted who got what sentence and what the crimes were and once home, wrote a "roundup" story that I'd telephone to South Bend.

I noticed something about Sue's writing: Sue rarely quoted people directly. Why's that, I wondered. Because, Sue replied, it's rare that a reporter has a totally intact quotation, and rather than quote someone incorrectly, she preferred to paraphrase. It was a position that took guts, as many editors demand quotes because quotations spice up a story, regardless of their accuracy. Sometimes reporters find it's easier when dealing with dumb-ass editors to simply say yes and fudge the quotes. The longer I worked as a reporter, the more I respected and imitated Sue's approach.

On her desk, Jan Marsh always had a stack of clippings from other newspapers — the Detroit Free Press, The Detroit News, The New York Times, Newsweek — with articles that she was sure could be "localized." She was a synthesizer, able to see the potential of a New Jersey story, how it might be refocused in southwestern Michigan.

When you know the individual writers, you start reading their work more closely. Lou Mumford, a joker in person, has a fine wit in print. Lyle Sumerix was the consummate cops reporter; we used to wonder if he'd have a police scanner playing in his bedroom even after he retired. (As it turned out, when Lyle retired, he left the world of news and turned to community work. He died late in 2009.)

One day when I was a staffer for the Tribune, I got a call from Lyle. He'd been listening to the scanner (it is actually illegal to monitor police scanners for commercial pursuits, which news reporting very much is; but most people in the news business don't know this, and if they do, they don't care) and heard police back-and-forth about a high-ranking Berrien County sheriff's officer who was firing off his service revolver in a drunken and unofficial chase in my area, Cass County. With Lyle's tip and after a few calls, I had the story.

And a good story it was. I stopped making jokes about Lyle retiring to eavesdrop on police scanners.

Once you start working as a stringer, if you're a savvy person, you can create your own classroom, your own seminars, over lunch with the "professors" who don't know they're your unpaid tutors in this fascinating endeavor of finding and reporting the news.

chapter 10

checkered career

"You've had a checkered career," the associate managing editor of the Chicago Tribune told me.

Man, did he hit the nail on the head. But he couldn't have known it from reading that sheet of paper, which was a personal creation I called my résumé. It was a piece of fiction worthy of a novelist, which I was. Not that it contained outright lies, I want you to know.

Although he was near the pinnacle of his career, this editor was making a classic error in judgment that is common to newspaper managers in this country. He was confusing my paper track record with what I had actually done. I had also provided him — days in advance — a pile of clippings: stories I'd written for The New York Times, The Progressive, the Detroit Free Press Magazine, The Detroit News and of course, my alma mater, the South Bend Tribune.

What editors are really looking for, even though sometimes they don't realize it, is writers who write. People who produce. Sound weird? Of course a writer can write, by definition. Not necessarily. Sometimes it's not easy to tell — even from published articles — whether a full-timer is really producing, because editors often "help" staffers appear better than they are. There are internal incentives for doing this, which I have portrayed in my novel, *Cross Purposes*.

Stringers rarely enjoy the luxury of being given the star treatment. There's not much incentive for editors to gussy up the work of part-timers whose faces they might not even recognize. Sink or swim is the motto for stringers. Most of what I showed the Chicago Tribune editor was stringer work, and the variety of publications should have been a sign that I was a producer. Any polishing was done by yours truly.

Okay, okay. I can imagine editors shaking their heads as they recollect nightmare sessions rewriting some stringer's poorly written copy. There certainly are stringers who turn in shoddy work, just as there are staff writers who could pass for semiliterate. That's why we need people like YOU, people who will work hard to improve the standard not just for stringers, but for ALL Journalists.

My résumé threw the Trib editor off. It was maybe a tad offbeat.

What he should have been looking for was this: a person who senses what a newspaper story is, has the ability to find that kind of story, and can collect enough information to write the tale in a way that a reasonably intelligent person can understand. Since I was going for a full-time staff writer job, he didn't need to know if I could shoot a publishable photo to illustrate my story, but the proof was there before him. These are the only things a stringer needs to do. But if you're trying to make the leap to salaried staff writer, there is one thing more that you need.

Yes, that doggone résumé.

Another word is "bullshit," because nobody pretends that these fabricated documents are real. Oh, yes, the facts must be correct. Put down outright fabrications, aka lies, and chances are you will be burned in future by your own ill-considered prevarications. The facts on my résumé were correct. Think that's not important? I'll say it again: Woe unto the applicant who lies on a résumé. That is, makes up from whole cloth supposed "facts" about his or her past. A fake diploma, once discovered by managers, is a fireable offense. But leaving things out?

That's what I mean by the Chicago Trib editor hitting the nail on the head with that term "checkered career." Not that I brought up that part of my past, of course. The gearshift on this guy's brain was frozen in the standard career forward position. I learned the hard way that no matter how interesting a true yarn I told about my past, it would not land me a job, but instead brand me as an interesting character who could not possibly be happy in the job this employer was thinking of offering me. The untold story, one of many invisible spots on my résumé, was this: Once upon a time, with a brother, I owned a taxicab and I drove it for the Ann Arbor Yellow and Checkered Cab Co.

Get it?

Checkered career.

Ha-ha. But you wouldn't find that on any résumé I submitted to a newspaper. Bad enough that I put down grad school in history, and the Peace Corps. That's what the editor meant by "checkered." Now, had I lied and put down some baloney about taking Journalism classes and working on my college paper, I might have landed the job. But if anybody found out my lies, I'd be fired. The truth is, I've never had a J School class and I got fired twice from my college paper. Not good résumé material: Takes too much explaining, and when you have to explain or otherwise excuse a résumé, you might as well head out the door.

There was nothing on there about farm work, grinding castings in a foundry or running a belt sander in a furniture factory. Nothing in there about shoveling burned beans in a grain elevator or delivering mail for the Paw Paw Post Office.

I learned the hard way that even a semi-honest résumé can cause trouble for editors in the hiring mode if the record shows a history that deviates much from the standard past editors want to see in new hires. They are hiring reflections of themselves over and over and over again. They want to see applicants with college degrees in Journalism and if you can point to one or more internships at newspapers, great. Any entry that might indicate some knowledge of how the real world turns is a downer.

Another source of trouble for nonconforming writers is age. I ran into that barrier at the Chicago Trib. The final words of that editor were, "I see that you're 37 years old. Normally, we start new reporters on the police beat. I'd hate to put a 37-year-old guy in a police cruiser."

Yes, ladies and gentlemen, age discrimination is alive and well in the newspaper industry, right along with race, sex and every other kind of prejudice. The age thing has worked against me every step of my career. When you break into Journalism at the ripe long-play age of 33 1/3, you'd better expect trouble. Fact is, my birth date makes me so old, I can't even be classed as a baby boomer.

Around the same time I found out about my checkered career, I applied for a slot in a European Union Journalism study abroad program. The U.S. side of this program was run by the J School at Columbia University, no less. Home of the Columbia Journalism Review, where I got the idea from a little back-of-the book ad offering a fully paid year studying and writing in Paris. Actually, when this happened I had just become a full-time staffer at the South Bend paper. Master's in history, Peace Corps volunteer in Africa, able to speak and write French — hey, by that time I was even an award-winning reporter. The prof at Columbia told me later that Columbia "put their chips" on me. But the French said, "Non!"

Too old. I was 37.

Hmmm. Too old? Too old for what? I was 60 years old in 2005. I wasn't too old, along with a photographer who was in her 50s, to paddle a canoe 27 miles up the Rouge River in Metro Detroit, a dangerous odyssey where we traversed 72 logjams and four dams and risked our lives any number of times. The October 2005 Free Press series, written by me with photos by my co-author, photojournalist Patricia Beck, won the Water Environment Federation's 2006 Harry E. Schlenz Medal for Achievement in Public Education. Wayne State University Press has

Chapter 10

Reprinted by permission of Detroit Free Press

published our book about this adventure. It's called *Up the Rouge! Paddling Detroit's Hidden River*. The Library of Michigan named *Up the Rouge!* a Michigan Notable Book for 2010. You can order a copy of the print book as well as the audio book at **www.uptherouge.com**.

While I was organizing that canoe trip, I also applied for a mid-career Journalism fellowship at the University of Michigan. I figured that since I had started my Journalism career at age 33 1/3, the fact that I was about to turn 60 meant I was indeed in the middle of my career. Given that I've had three print books and an audio book published in 2009 and my blog, **joelontheroad.com**, was named by Detroit's Metro Times newspaper "best independent blog raising hell" when I was 63, I think my claim was legitimate. This book, *Shoestring Reporter*, will be published in the fall of 2010, to be followed by others, including *Cross Purposes, Stringer* and *Shoestring J School*, the other elements in *Shoestring Quartet*. *Mouse Code* is in production, along with *Exchange Student* (*Schützenfest* in the German edition) and a sequel to *Up the Rouge!* Fairly decent production for a guy in mid-career, if you ask me.

Did I get called to an interview at the University of Michigan? Negatory, good buddies. I got a polite rejection note. But at a party more than a year later, a Journalist who actually got one of these fellowships the same year I wanted one told me, "You would have made a great Fellow. Too bad you're too old!"

Believe me, the age thing is very real. I was hired at the Free Press when I was 37. A few years later, a mid-thirtyish city editor was mystified because I seemed to be doing things more appropriate for a younger reporter: "For a guy who's 45, Joel, you sure do have a lot of energy."

Isn't that cute? Let me see here, where did I leave my cane?

For the stringer who can produce what editors need on time, age is irrelevant. A cagey stringer with telltale white hair could make sure his or her face never was seen by an editor. Telephones and e-mail make this possible.

Better yet, if you can manage to remain independent, if you don't need to be a full-time staffer, you won't need a résumé.

Enjoy your checkered career and live it, too!

Let your work be your résumé.

chapter 11

how to write like a newsie

Never written for a newspaper, right?

Don't write at all?

Somebody who doesn't write would be a poor candidate to write for newspapers. But you never know till you try. Let me give you a little test of your newswriting ability. Call up the last half dozen e-mail messages you sent. Doesn't matter to whom — friends, family, business letters. Read them carefully. Do you get right to the point? Waste no words?

Not half bad, right? You were relaxed when you wrote those letters. You weren't tense, worrying, Oh, my God! I've got to think of an entertaining way to write this! You were thinking about the point to be made. You were focused.

Hey, you're hired!

When I taught writing classes, I noticed that my students often felt they were not writers. Some would complain of suffering from something called "writer's block." I don't believe in writer's block. The problem is not some psychological stoppage, some mental dam that won't let ideas cross. Instead, the problem is motivation. Wanting to write. I'll give you an example. Right now, I'm about two months past deadline on an assignment I didn't want and didn't ask for. I was asked by friends to write an article about a charitable foundation. Ask them what they want, how long it should be, they don't know. "Make it interesting!" Try to interview them to get their ideas and some nice quotes and they act like I'm wasting their time. Just write it! Get it to us timely. Lots of dumb-ass roadblocks. So, of course, I don't write. I feel an obligation to write, but when somebody pressures me, urges me to write and on top of that, "Make it interesting!" I freeze up. I put it off.

This is not writer's block. In the period that I neglected to write that little article, I banged out many of the chapters of this book and I wrote dozens of stories for the Free Press.

Writer's block? I call it writer's rebellion. If you are having trouble writing, ask yourself why. Is it because you maybe aren't very interested in the subject? Is it because you feel pressured and are resisting some dumb obligation? In my own case, I know part of my problem is that I fear what I write won't meet my own standards simply because my sources also are my editors and will screw up what I write. Makes me cringe.

I think I've found a partial solution. At the top of my story, I'll write: "No byline, please."

My problem boils down to this: I don't believe in the story. I should not have agreed to do it. I could have refused, but thought it would be a matter of a few minutes to crank out a little story.

If you WANT to write, if you BELIEVE in your subject, you will suffer no blocks. But there is one hurdle we all have to get over.

Getting started.

Sometimes, having delved into a subject, I find myself overwhelmed with information. I'm not sure where to begin. Working for newspapers has forced me to start stories, even when I didn't think I was ready.

Here are a few things to keep in mind when starting to write:

First, there is NO ONE RIGHT WAY to start a story. Rather, there are myriad starting points, because each of us has an imagination capable of conjuring all kinds of beginnings.

Some starts are better because they lead naturally into the regions you want to explore in a story. I'll often reject a clever top after realizing it doesn't lead to the points I want to make. False starts like that can be avoided, I find, if I fill out a photo request before starting to write.

This is a little mental game I play with myself. When I sit down to write the story, and if I'm facing deadline in, say, half an hour or less, stress can tend to lock up the old brain. Nowadays, the photo request is the first writing I do on a story. The photo department has an electronic form with a blank section topped with this question: WHAT IS STORY ABOUT?

Wow. That says it all. I mean, you just can't get more basic.

WHAT IS STORY ABOUT?

If you can answer that question in a few words, you will have started your story without realizing it. This is actually what happened to me. There were times when I had already started writing my story and was told the photo people wanted to illustrate it. Okay, sit down, fill out the form. Hmmm. What's this about? Somehow, filling out that form was less stressful, less fraught with deadline pressure, and suddenly I'd be writing a whole new top to the story. I'd dump what I had started and replace it with my answer to WHAT IS STORY ABOUT?

Now, whenever I start a story, even if it doesn't require photos, I pretend to fill out a photo request.

Okay, here's another mental trick. Often, especially when my kids were young, I'd come home and over dinner I'd regale my family with my adventures of the day. Some of my assignments were quite exhilarating. For instance, there was the time I flew in a Navy Blue Angels F/A-18 fighter jet straight up, upside-down; it was the most intense and exciting thing I've ever done. My wife and my boys heard all about it. Or there was the time I rode on a U.S. Coast Guard icebreaker punching a course through ice into Lake St. Clair. Listen to yourself as you tell others your story. How do you start? What elements do you withhold for use as a kicker at the end? Let your own oral storytelling build your writing.

Once you've figured out what your story is about, start writing as if you were dashing off an e-mail to a friend, or to your mom or dad. Don't worry about being formal. Informal is fine. If you really want to sound like a newswriter, remember that the better part of Journalism is imitation. There are certain forms that newswriters follow, and it helps to understand what is going on in an article.

Look at your local newspaper. Compare the writing with premier models, like The New York Times and The Wall Street Journal. Notice how stories begin and how they flow, how points are made and how the writer brings the enterprise to an end.

Above all, keep in mind that you are writing a story, and it should entertain your readers. There is one reader above all others that you should try to amuse. You. If your writing pleases YOU, it will most likely entertain others.

Be Audience Number One.

I ride in a Navy jet.

chapter 12

breaking into the news

I'm not sure if the catchphrase "networking" had been coined when I first started stringing in 1978. I recall hearing from supposedly sage people that it's smart to join professional organizations if for no other reason than that they connect you to people who can help you get work. So I joined the Society of Professional Journalists.

No club helped me get any of my reporting jobs. It was my friend Scott, the Herald-Palladium reporter, who guided me to my first paid reporting job as a stringer for the South Bend Tribune. That summer, I met another H-P staffer who gave me a wonderful tip and coached me to become a stringer for other newspapers. This was Bob Sherefkin, then a farm writer and today a reporter with Automotive News in Detroit. I suppose this would pass as networking.

By late summer, I'd been reporting stories long enough and reliably enough that Tom Gruber decided to let me try covering the Berrien County Youth Fair. In truth, he had nobody else to do it.

It meant 16-hour days taking notes as the various grand champions and reserve grand champions in beef, dairy, hog, sheep, goats, chickens, not to mention apple, peach, rhubarb pies and so on were judged. It meant taking photos of the winners. It meant sitting in that hot garret office above our house and writing stories about all these winners. It meant driving to the State Police post late at night and dropping off my film so somebody could pick it up next morning and deliver it to the paper. It meant reading my stories over the phone the next morning before I headed to yet another round of contests and reporting.

As I went from the dog show to the sheep pens, I had some company. This was Bob Sherefkin. When he learned about my stringing, and no doubt figured out how green I was at this Journalism thing, Bob began instructing me in the fine art of Journalism salesmanship. He looked at some story I'd written for the Tribune.

"How'd you like to make $75 for that story?" he said. "Call Bob Kirk at the News. He's looking for out-state stories, and he'll pay you $75."

Not bad. That would be like $245 in 2008 dollars. So I did as Bob suggested and sure enough, Bob Kirk asked me to send him the story and some negatives. What a deal!

Next time I saw Sherefkin, I told him about my luck. Not luck, he said; your stuff is good. "How'd you like to make $75 every week?"

Just keep sending those stories to Kirk, he said.

So I started sending my stories out, and became a regular Double-Dipper.

Not everyone will have such mentors. But you don't need them. You've got me. Knowing what I know, I could move to any town in the country, or for that matter, Canada, and start plying my stringing trade. Just follow in my steps.

The key breaks for me were names of editors. I struck out when I first tried to string stories, but I got lucky with Tom Gruber. Once I was writing for pay, I was able to sell stories to other editors. Tom pointed me to Bill Sonneborn at the Tribune's Sunday Michiana Magazine, where I sold many stories. I tried to sell Bill a story about Mexican cooking, but he steered me to the features editor. That's where it ran. Once the door is open, possibilities appear that you never imagined. While I couldn't interest Free Press city desk and features editors in my ideas, I sold several stories to the Free Press' Sunday Detroit Magazine. In fact, the very first freelance piece I sold was to the Free Press mag.

It's easy to find editors' names. But they change, often quickly. For instance, at the time I wrote this, I could have given you the name of my editor who was buying lots of stringer-written stories for the weekly Community Free Press. But that wouldn't do you any good now — she's in a different job and the CFP editions are history. Do your own research. The fact that papers change editors and editions doesn't relieve them of the need to publish more copy than their staff writers can produce.

What's this? You say you're living in Los Angeles and not writing stories about the burbs of Detroit? You think there aren't any editors in LA or Seattle or Boston or Pittsburgh or Kalamazoo or Peru, Indiana? Buy the paper and comb the masthead for names.

Good luck!

Article on next two pages: reprinted courtesy of the South Bend Tribune.

Mexican 'heat' edible

By JOEL THURTELL
Berrien Springs Correspondent

"Too greasy for me!"

"Well, I can stand the grease, but not the spice!"

Grease and spice are the twin myths of Mexican cookery. Some Mexican food is sure to be greasy, I won't dispute that. But without mentioning the good man's name nor southern colonelcy I will simply add that certain old fashioned North American cuisine suffers from the same greasy constitution, although most of our food does not. And if I eat in a good Mexican restaurant or with a Mexican family, I do not expect my meal to be greasy.

The complaint against "spiciness" is harder to disprove. The first, a qualification: I am not discussing Mexican food as it is prepared in the United States, where because of their perceptions of Americans' taste chefs tend to err towards either extreme — blandness or heat.

And by "heat" I don't mean the simple, familiar heat of plain old temperature, but the fearful, raw fire that erupts from an innocent mouthful, scorching tongue and throat. This heat is only whipped hotter by drinking water.

Ironically, Mexicans themselves often spread the myth of their own spicy food.

"Muy piquante," a Mexican grins as he ladles heaps of pickled chili peppers onto his tostada. When I assure him that I have eaten food "mucho mas piquante" in other countries (my palate shrivels at thought of Africa) his disbelief turns to offense.

But his national pride notwithstanding, I risk losing an offer of seconds (well, maybe it was thirds or fourths, my memory is not clear on the point) and continue my argument. Except in poorer families and market food, where the chili pepper is added as a meat substitute, the hot spices are set not in the food, but on the table.

I have lived in several middle class Mexican homes and not once have I seen a meal come to the table with homicidal intent. But the chili sauces lie in dishes on the table waiting for my use — or abuse. Of course there have been tricksters who point to a dish, slyly assuring me it is "menos caliente" — not quite so hot. But normally if I left the table feeling like a dragon, the fault was mine.

In these homes, and in good restaurants too, the use of chilis is left to the guest's discretion. The reason for this, believe it or not, is that there really exist Mexicans who do not eat any peppers. Others use them moderately. And others, not always Mexicans either, seem intent on proving themselves above the laws of chemistry.

When I left Mexico this year I took with me several recipes, specialties of my hostess, Senora Teresa Davalos de Luft. Senora Davalos directs the Regional Museum of Patzcuaro, Michoacan. Patzcuaro is an old Spanish town located in the mountains between Mexico City and the Pacific. Senora Davalos is nearly as famous for her cooking as she is for her zeal in preserving and displaying the crafts of Mexico's dying folklore.

In the middle of a hectic day at the museum, Teresa Davalos climbs the steep cobbled road leading to the tall adobe house she and her artist-archaeologist husband, Enrique Luft, have built. Now, during the siesta hour, she will command the kitchen. While in the past couple years this family has acquired a refrigerator, most shopping is still done on a day-by-day basis. A large market is run daily in Patzcuaro, and fruit, vegetables, meat and spices can be bought as they are needed.

The kitchen work area consists of a large counter made of clay tile. On the left is a sink with running cold water. To the left and built into the stone and tile counter is the charcoal stove.

As cooking began, I sat talking to Enrique Luft about my chances of getting recipes from his wife.

"I don't think Teresa can give you any recipes," Enrique Luft said. He was interested, but doubtful because, as he said, "she is an artist. She could make a feast out of a bare turkey bone, but I don't think she can tell you how she does it."

But my old friend don Enrique proved wrong. It is true that Teresa Davalos cooks spontaneously — "thunderously" and "uproariously" are similar words that come to mind. I don't believe she owns a cookbook, for like all great chefs de cuisine she is guided by higher principles.

"To know the condiments," she lectured me, "that is the secret. Oregano, marjoram, silantro, the various spices — this is the secret for making a meal to please everyone."

"Yes, yes," I say, but I want more than generalities. "But how?"

In the recipes that follow, Teresa Davalos de Luft tells how, and even if we are not so spontaneous, thunderous and uproarious in our culinary operations, nor conversant with higher principles of kitchen wizardry, well, it won't matter. All of that has already gone into these recipes. No more intuition needed.

FISH SAUCE

This sauce goes well with shrimp, whitefish, abalone, but it is not recommended for oysters.

Eight ounces yogurt
Eight ounces mayonnaise
Five to six garlic cloves, mashed

Place above in a bowl, add a pinch of black pepper. "Don't overdo — just a little — we will taste it!" says Teresa. "I use many spices, but it is possible to use more or less than I say."

Very finely cut five or six sprigs of silantro and add to sauce. If silantro is not available, use parsley.

Mix well. Place in serving dish. That's it.

TACITOS (LITTLE TACOS) WITH GREEN SAUCE AND CREAM

30 tortillas (figure four to five tacos per person)
One-half pound sliced ham

Dice ham finely (chicken may be used in place of ham). Place a small line of meat along diameter of tortilla, then roll like a cigarette; not too much meat — these are tacitos! Put tacos in a greased casserole; preferably use pork fat. Fry, place aside in pan with lid.

SALSA VERDE OR GREEN SAUCE FOR TACITOS

One pound green tomatoes — these must be true green tomatoes, not simply unripe tomatoes

Cut each tomato into four pieces. Place in blender with seven garlic cloves and four green (mild) chili peppers, all diced. (Chili peppers may be omitted) Also add a handful of silantro — again, parsley may be substituted; salt, black pepper. Grind in blender.

Now back to the tacos. First layer sauce over them. Above sauce spread:

One-half pint cream
Salt (easy does it)
Cheese

Place in oven for five minutes for au gratin.

Es todo! That's all; put tacos on a serving platter garnished with leaves of lettuce.

"The secret," Teresa says, "is garlic and condiments."

And for a true Mexican effect, the chef may offer a selection of chili sauces, available where Mexican food is sold. These should appear quite plainly on the table — a challenge!

COSTILLAS DEL PUERCO CON SOYA
(PORK CHOPS A LA TERESA)

These are to be served with fried potatoes.

Two pounds small potatoes
Two pounds pork chops
Eight cloves garlic (unless otherwise specified, garlic cloves should be large, and note that we never specify otherwise)
Soy sauce

Boil potatoes in their skin. When ready, pour off water. In a pan with a little pork grease fry the potatoes in their skin. Add salt and set aside, covered.

For the pork sauce grind eight garlic cloves together with salt, pepper, soy sauce. In a Mexican kitchen this operation will be performed with metate and mano, which are a pair of porous stones roughly equivalent to a mortar and pestle, the metate being a rough, bowl-shaped stone.

The rules are quite specific here: Garlic, soy sauce, salt and pepper are to be milled and left in the metate, into which the pork chops are laid for half an hour to marinate. Lacking the requisite utensils, I simply mash the garlics one by one with the flat of our Chinese cleaver — a good stable cutting board comes in handy here — and marinate the chops in a glass bowl.

After the marinade, fry the pork chops. I suggest heating a little pork grease in the pan first.

Serve the meat and potatoes with

Recipe contest extra sections are available

Extra copies of The Tribune's recipe contest supplement delivered with the Sunday, June 18, edition are available at 10 cents each from the Circulation Department.

Final contestants who brought samples of their entries for the judging and have not picked up their pans or dishes may do so in the third floor Personnel Department office of The Tribune.

WORKING IN the kitchen of her Patzcuaro, Mexico, home is Teresa Davalos de Luft. Her Mexican cookery, admittedly greasy and spicy as is the cuisine of the country, is described as "fantastic." The museum director cooks from a charcoal stove.

several slices of tomato. On each tomato slice put a tiny bit of Tabasco sauce. Avocado slices may be added.

PUERCO CON FRIJOLES (PORK WITH BEANS)

Two pounds black beans
30 tortillas
Two pounds small pork chops
One cup white rice

Soak beans a day ahead. Slice pork chops into thin pieces. Boil with a little pork fat. When boiled, put meat with beans. Take time to get beans cooked and meat soft. Salt to taste; add parsley plus a medium-sized onion unsliced. Separately make rice.

This recipe includes, gratis, a set of aesthetic instructions for proper display of the chef's work.

On each plate put rice on one side, pork and beans on the other. "Then," Teresa says, "adorn a separate plate with diced onion and diced hot radishes along with diced silantro (or parsley). This meal should be served with lemon slices and if possible, chilis habaneros de Yucatan, which may be available where Mexican food is sold. These are big orange chili peppers and one may omit them or make a substitution. But if chilis habaneros are used, Teresa warns, they must first be put in the fire, heated, and while hot, peeled. Otherwise they will be too hard, and worse — less piquante!

Dice three of these big orange chilis without seeds; dice two onions; add warm water, salt, oregano, oil, and vinegar. Place in a glass dish on the table. Those with courage may try this sauce on the pork and beans.

The above meal may be served as described, but some may want to add hot tortillas. Some may want to make tacos by spreading pork and beans, rice, along with onion, silantro, lemon, on a tortilla and rolling it up.

MUTTON WITH SAUCE

Those who are offended by the sound of "mutton" may substitute the word "lamb". Remember that whenever one prepares mutton, or even the young mutton known as lamb, one must be careful to remove the fell, or thin membrane that separates the meat from the wool.

Five pounds mutton, or lamb;
try to get a leg
10 garlic cloves
Black pepper
Two bay leaves, cumin, marjoram

Grind 10 garlic cloves, a pinch of black pepper, cumin, and marjoram together with salt. Place in a large pot with two bay leaves and leg of mutton or lamb. Pot should be filled with water at start. Cook for three hours, allowing water to boil off. Do not add water!

When ready this may be served together with its caldo, or broth. One may add carrots, potatoes, cauliflower, or even cabbage — one or a combination. But Teresa Davalos recommends it without vegetables. "Vegetables alter the meat flavor," she says. Add a pinch of pepper and at your discretion some teaspoons of Tabasco sauce.

At end, add three big cloves of garlic to the broth, mixing well. Add slices of avocado. Serve.

One may serve the meat alone, perhaps with tortillas and a chili sauce. Or you may serve it in its broth.

These recipes are guaranteed not to scorch your mouth — unless you let them!

chapter 13

breaking into the times

"Journalists are copycats," Scott Aiken warned me. "Don't trust them with your ideas. They'll steal them and think nothing of it."

Really? People who went to J school would STEAL your ideas?

"Really," Scott said. "Don't give them too much."

I didn't believe Scott. Besides, as a stringer, I had to sell my work to editors, sometimes before I wrote it. That meant revealing my ideas. In some cases, I tried to line up customers before I started work just to be sure it would be worth my while.

The summer of 1979 was a hot one for the Indian fishing rights issue in Michigan. The state was trying to regulate all fishing so it could promote sport fishing, which brought in revenue from the sale of fishing licenses and was very important to the state's multimillion-dollar tourism industry. But Michigan Indians claimed the state couldn't regulate them because they had retained the right to fish under treaties their forebears signed with the federal government. Noel Fox, a federal judge in Grand Rapids, agreed with the Indians. Lots of nastiness and outright racism were being promoted by the state's Department of Natural Resources. And the DNR had a pipeline to the Associated Press. Also, outdoor writers who accepted free fishing jaunts from professional guides, and so had a big conflict of interest, were nonetheless writing not exactly fairly about the issue. It seemed to me that some balance was needed. I wasn't paid by the Indians, nor was I getting freebie fishing trips, although one was offered to me by a guide who claimed to have taken outdoor writers on free fishing trips.

I pitched my story first to Tom Gruber at the Tribune, and he said go ahead. That meant — as long as I wrote a story — he would pay me something for the research I did. But a trip was mandatory. I needed to interview the linchpin of the whole Indian case, a bigger-than-life Ojibwa fisherman named Big Abe LeBlanc. And I had to keep the bills down. So, Karen and I pitched a tent at a national forest campground near Big Abe's place at Bay Mills in the Upper Peninsula, and I interviewed him. Oh, I did accept a gratuity. In parting, Big Abe gave me a big chunk of smoked lake trout. We ate it. Later, I got sick. Was it the trout?

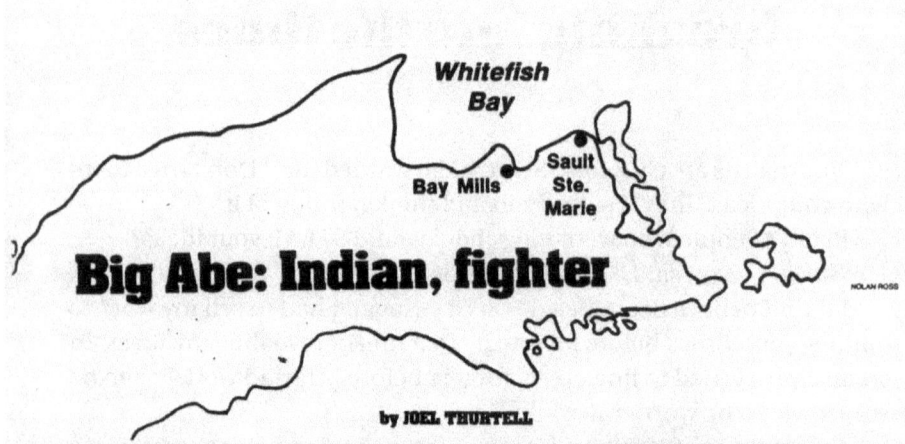

Big Abe: Indian, fighter

by JOEL THURTELL

Abe LeBlanc told a lot of people he was going fishing on September 28, 1971, people like the Michigan Department of Natural Resources and the press and broadcast media. He jammed a copy of an 1836 treaty into his pocket, launched his small aluminum fishing boat in Whitefish Bay and set off on what turned out to be the biggest legal crusade ever taken on by Michigan Indians.

Big Abe was not alone on the water that day. He had let the DNR know where and when he would be on the bay, and patrol boat number four carrying state game officers was watching every move he made, waiting to see the telltale track of his gill nets—white-bottomed plastic milk jugs bobbing in the boat's wake. Like a perpendicular grid, the gill net is a curtain through which fish swim, and if they are large enough, their gills tangle in the rectangles.

Several reporters were watching, too, and the DNR boat at first was hesitant. But when LeBlanc had about 300 feet of net in the water, the patrol boat edged closer, and state game warden Bruce Andrews yelled, "You're under arrest!"

"The hell I am!" LeBlanc retorted, and waved the copy of the treaty in the officer's face.

"I told him I had a treaty right to fish," LeBlanc now recalls. "We dickered back and forth, and eventually he wrote me out a ticket."

Joel Thurtell is editor of the Berrien Springs Journal Era and a freelance writer.

Framed, that ticket now hangs on a wall in the Upper Peninsula Legal Services office in Sault Ste. Marie. But Abe LeBlanc's fish story really began long before that DNR citation, in 1958 in fact, when he first spoke out for Michigan's Indians against the old Conservation Commission, which was beginning to discuss regulation of commercial fishing.

Now he went fishing to test the state limitation on a Michigan Supreme Court ruling in a case involving William Jondreau, a Chippewa fisherman. Earlier that year Jondreau had been arrested for fishing illegally off the Keweenaw Peninsula. But the Michigan Supreme Court held that Jondreau was fishing legally under federal treaties. Immediately, however, the state attorney general's office said that the Jondreau decision applied only to the waters where Jondreau was fishing.

Big Abe LeBlanc was mad. Though he had been running an illegal trap net operation on the St. Mary's River all along, and the DNR knew it, to force the DNR's hand he would have to set gill nets. He maintained that the Jondreau ruling extended as far as Whitefish Bay. He may well have been misreading the decision—his brother Arthur, head of the Bay Mills Chippewa Reservation, thinks he was. But however incorrect his legal judgment was, Abe LeBlanc set the stage for a major fishing rights controversy, and the argument still rages today.

The Jondreau decision tends to be forgotten in the wake of Big Abe's watery confrontation with the DNR, which resulted in People vs. LeBlanc. LeBlanc lost the case and lost it again on appeal, then appealed again and won. Now it was the DNR's turn to appeal, to the Michigan Supreme Court.

In December 1976, when word came that the state's high court ruled in the Indians' favor in the final appeal of People vs. LeBlanc, Big Abe was returning from a delivery trip to Chicago, where much of the Indians' catch is sold. Those fish he had just sold were not contraband after all.

"I was so shook up I actually pulled off the side of the road and busted out crying," he says. "I called my wife and she was elated too. Our family is close-knit. We take care of each other, cry with each other, laugh with each other. I got home about 10 p.m. and the next day we celebrated." Celebration took place in a classic LeBlanc arena—Big Abe's Bar, down the road from Big Abe & Son Fisheries.

Big Abe has become a symbol of Indian fishing rights over the years, but how did he come to be cast in this dramatic role?

Maybe it's in his blood. His great-great-grandfather on his mother's side was Chief Waishkey, one of the signers of the treaty now in question. His grandfather, Andrew Waishkey, was the last hereditary chief of the Bay Mills Chippewas. When Big Abe was 10, was not yet six-feet, six inches tall and 300 pounds, and had not yet given himself the name "Big Abe," his father, Arthur W. LeBlanc, was elected tribal chairman.

A tribal chairman is a full-time counselor, welfare agent and advocate for his people, in this case the 625 Chippewas of Bay Mills. A.B. recalls many all-night sessions at his home. "As I grew older, and having a big mouth, I was involved in our rights question."

Maybe it's because Big Abe makes good news copy. He tells state officials to go to hell, for example. In mid-September, radio stations in northern Michigan carried reports of dockside shouting matches between Big Abe and white sport fishermen. Perhaps that is why, when I mentioned to Sault Ste. Marie tribal lawyer Daniel Green that I might be interviewing A.B., Green gently tried to steer me toward other fishermen.

"A.B. is not characteristic," the soft-spoken Green remarked. "He's the single-largest entrepreneur, a fish buyer who sets small guys up in business so they can fish for a share. He's very outspoken and because his case went to the Supreme Court in '76," Green says, Big Abe has had his fair share of press coverage. The insinuation, quite clearly, was that this big character is warping the public conception of the Indian fisherman, who, unlike Big Abe, is poor, and poorly equipped.

Big Abe disagrees with one of Green's statements: he is not the biggest Indian fish dealer, he says. King Fisheries is bigger. It is his

BIG ABE ▶

Reprinted by permission of the Detroit Free Press

BIG ABE
CONTINUED

egotism more than anything else that sets A.B. LeBlanc apart from other Indians. Most Indians would go out of their way to keep away from the limelight. And mostly, Indians are communal rather than self-oriented.

And then, Bay Mills *is* poor. A drive along the community's main road is enough to prove that. Tiny houses, trailers, junk cars all testify to a society that is barely subsisting. And against this background, Big Abe LeBlanc stands out, along with this historical fact: if he had not set his net and waited for the DNR to arrest him, many of those little guys Green talks about would not be fishing today.

No doubt about it, Green smiles. LeBlanc is "flamboyant...very impressive." Green describes one of his own experiences with the huge Chippewa. During a tribal party, LeBlanc collared Green, laying a huge arm over the lawyer's shoulder. Big Abe "was well in his cups," Green recalled, and proceeded to give him an earful about tribal business.

And like it or not, Big Abe's large crewcut head and bulbous nose are taken as symbols of tribal Indians, even though quite clearly he is not a typical Indian.

A white commercial fisherman had some other words to describe Big Abe. When I mentioned the subject of my call to Leland fisherman Bill Carlson's secretary, she took a deep breath, followed by a foreboding "Oh, boy!"

Although Carlson's deeper impressions of LeBlanc remain his own, he willingly described his Indian counterpart superficially. "Big Abe probably does them (Indians) more good than harm," Carlson said. "He's colorful, idealistic. He's a demagogue. He is a struggling business individual trying to put something together that is profitable. Don't expect more from him. He's not an intellectual hero."

Carlson is not surprised that many people identify the Indian fishing rights issue with Abe LeBlanc. "Abe has been around the situation longer," Carlson says, and many Indians now fishing "have no long history as commercial operators."

But distortion creeps in all too easily here. It is wrong to imagine the now 55-year-old LeBlanc as if he were a successful fish buyer back in 1971, when all the fuss really began for him. Back then, says Green, "nobody was making money," and LeBlanc was a part-time fisherman, like everyone else who fished from Bay Mills. Nor did fishing put him in his present eminent entrepreneurial position.

In 1968 Big Abe had a business brainstorm. Bingo was then illegal in the state of Michigan, but Abe reasoned that his game, Car Bingo, would be exempt if he set it up in the Bay Mills reservation, which is a federal jurisdiction. Car Bingo is just like regular bingo except you play it through a drive-in hot dog standstyle speaker-microphone placed in your car window. "Rain or shine, we play any time" is the motto, although games are only scheduled on Sundays. Big Abe claims it is "a social thing for the people who come there to play, but a moneymaker for those of us who run it."

Three years later, about the same time the DNR was ticketing him for illegal gill netting and fishing without a license, A.B. was applying to the federal Small Business Administration—and getting—a $50,000 loan to buy and remodel a tavern a few miles west of his house in Bay Mills.

"Big Abe's Bar," he called the place. He opened it in 1972.

It set him on his feet. "I made me a little money and started buying some fishing equipment." Now that equipment includes two 16-foot Mirrorcraft aluminum boats, one with a 25-horsepower and the other with a 40-horsepower motor. And he also owns a 45-foot steel tug which he captains himself.

As *People vs. LeBlanc* and in 1973 *U.S. vs. Michigan* were wending their separate meandering courses through the courts, Big Abe found himself up to his neck in fish business. He was on the lake part-time himself, he was recruiting other Indians to fish on a share system using his equipment, he was buying fish wholesale anywhere he could find them, including Canada, and he was processing, packing and transporting fish as far away as Chicago.

Ask Big Abe why he went out and had himself arrested, and he'll say it was a civil rights thing. That is easy enough to believe. Celebrities like Dick Gregory and Marlon Brando were arrested for fishing illegally alongside Indians in Washington state. But big names have not made it back to Michigan. Instead, the region has brewed its own bigger-than-life figure, one with huge biceps, whose belly soars out in front of his belt, a chain-smoking wisecracker who, perhaps in imitation of the movie stars who never come to Bay Mills, feels a need to pop dark glasses onto his nose whenever a camera approaches.

In the face of these antics, it is not surprising that some Indians see more than pure civil rights activism in Big Abe's motives for getting himself arrested. Soo tribal chair Joe Lumsden says that after the 1976 ruling, Big Abe "felt he had won the case and he could do any goddamn thing he wanted to."

"I set the regulations," was the LeBlanc doctrine then, Lumsden says, and "people talked about Abe letting them fish. Since his name was on the suit, he assumed it was *his* right, and there was a time when you would have thought it was his right alone."

Big Abe denies this charge, and his brother Arthur is not quite as harsh as Lumsden. "It was a combination," says Arthur—a combination of egotism and idealism. No doubt about it, though, says the elder brother, "Abe's got one of the biggest egos around here, or he wouldn't have the name 'Big Abe'. He put that handle on himself."

A.B. LeBlanc is the youngest of three children. There is something in that. First there was Bertha, now Bertha Parrault, 59. Then came Arthur, now 57, and finally A.B., the youngest. It is often the burden of the child at the end of the line that people—often many people, all ranked by age above him—continually tell the child what and what not to do. A.B. LeBlanc likes to prove his elders—or anybody in authority—wrong. Parallel with this complex runs the name.

The man has succeeded in propelling that image of sizable defiance before himself and before the public. He had been daring the state to come get him ever since 1958, when he announced that henceforth he would fish without the grace of a state license. In 1968, when there was some doubt about the legality of what has to be his zaniest business—Car Bingo—Big Abe went ahead with the operation. And here again is part of the Big Abe image—he is making money, hustling, making it in the white man's world and hauling in the bucks.

Car Bingo and Big Abe's Bar are sidelines, however. First of all, Abe LeBlanc is a fisherman.

"Abe and I started to fish with our dad when we were big enough to choke herring," Arthur recalls. "Choking" fish is slang for squeezing the fish through the openings in the gill net. Abe was about 12 when he started doing this. In those days, in the 30s and 40s, the herring industry was the only winter employment for many Indians. The LeBlanc boys worked with their father when they were not in the Bay Mills Indian School.

BIG ABE ▶

BIG ABE
CONTINUED

Albert LeBlanc finished the eighth grade at the Bay Mills Indian school and spent two years at Brimley High School. He quit school at 16 and went to work in a Brimley lumber yard, fishing part-time in the fall. World War II broke out, and in 1943 he joined the Navy, serving in the Panama Canal Zone and later in Hawaii in the Seabees. He was a stevedore in the Navy, but in 1945 he received a medical discharge.

Returning to Bay Mills after the war, he went into fishing, working summers for Brown Fisheries at Whitefish Point and heading out in his own rowboat in the fall. In 1945 he was married, and he and Amelia LeBlanc have raised ten children, seven girls and three boys. Three other boys have died.

In the 50s both LeBlanc brothers were fishing, but Arthur was getting caught up in tribal politics, and in 1957 he was elected tribal chairman at Bay Mills. About the same time Abe was finding his own stage in the politics of the fishery.

In 1958 the Michigan Fish Producers Association held a convention and invited Dr. Ralph McMullen, then the Conservation Commission director, to address them. As McMullen began outlining state plans to limit commercial fishing, Big Abe stood up and interrupted him.

"In all your plans," A.B. charged McMullen, "have you ever taken into consideration the Michigan Indian fisherman who does not need your goddamn state license?" From then on, Big Abe fished without a license, and he continued his policy of mouthing off to state conservation officials, a policy that some Indian leaders say gave his brother Arthur as tribal chairman as many

? headaches as the DNR.

As I drove into the parking lot of the big new building with the name Rainbow Country Fisheries, I heard a foghorn voice blaring at the rear of a big refrigerator truck with "Big Abe Fisheries" emblazoned on its side. On the loading dock I glimpse a great-bellied hulk of a man, and his yelling voice, I note, is not raised in anger or excitement. It is a conversational bellow.

I am kept waiting in the outer office. Then he makes a show of seeing me from behind his desk. Rising to greet me, the big fisherman's globular prow, sheathed in a faded black T-shirt, cruises toward me. A little fluffy white dog paddles along in his wake—"Fluffer," a purebred American husky.

We walk through the plant's outer office area, past the pinball machines on our left and the retail fish sales counter on our right, into the inner sanctum, a large, brightly lit room with Big Abe's desk in the center, a work table at one end and a couch at the other. Fluffer chooses the couch. Big Abe sits at his desk. I find a chair and face him across the desk. This is a busy man, I'm told, who got to work at six this morning and was sorry he'd forgotten I was coming

BIG ABE ▶

BIG ABE
CONTINUED

or he'd have some coffee ready. The door stays open. People float in with messages—one of his seven daughters who tends the sales counter up front, or his secretary, a recent graduate of the Bay Mills Indian School.

A few papers lie scattered on the desk top and a single ball point pen peeks over the rim of a tiny goldfish bowl. On the walls, gamefish swim peacefully, emitting stray bubbles, on color prints. Here and there a feathered Indian dances on a painting. An office helper sets a cup of steaming coffee before me while Big Abe rummages around looking for his stated position on *People vs. LeBlanc*.

"Where's that tape? You know, the one about Indian rights. Where's that tape player?"

Neither the player nor the tape, made by the Massachusetts-based Educational Development Company and including the several sides of the fishing rights question for presentation in community college classes, is immediately at hand. Fencing with interruptions, I proceed, grateful that the tape, probably another of Big Abe's subterfuges, is out of reach.

The telephone rings. As he picks up the receiver, Abe flips a switch, and a desk speaker bathes the room in the ongoing dialogue.

"Long distance for Big Abe LeBlanc."

"Speaking."

"Good morning, Big Abe LeBlanc."

"Good morning, Ding Dong."

Ding Dong is another fish dealer. Vociferous ragchewing now between the two cronies as they trade market news. Right, Big Abe agrees, he's taking in a lot of lake trout, too—four or five tons today alone. Paying 65 cents a pound now, but that's got to come down.

He's not ignoring me,

Gillnetting for whitefish

though. In fact, he uses me to launch a trial balloon. A certain white commercial fishery in Leland is in cahoots with the DNR and the Michigan Fish Producers' Association, Abe reveals to Ding Dong and just by the way to me. Just heard about that one last night and not about to mention who told him, but "they're going to sue to stop us from fishing," Abe's outraged larynx fires the words like gunshots, and righteously he concludes, "if it weren't for the goddamn Indians, there wouldn't be a net in the lake."

Now the tape is brought forth, just as I am trying to pry into Abe's life history. We must hear the tape, and Big Abe's voice, now set at a high level of volume, runs over the ground we have already, laboriously, covered. The story of *People vs. LeBlanc* spews forth automatically from the desk top as the big Chippewa beams at the machine. I interrupt often, each time hoping he will forget to switch the machine back on. Eventually it works, but later as I look through my notes, I find two sections that duplicate each other.

Finally, he gets up. He's going home to get some breakfast. Pointedly, I'm not invited. When he gets back, he'll show me a boat. While he's gone, I snoop around. Where is this boat? An office girl takes me to it. There, at the corner of Big Abe Fisheries, is a dented old aluminum fishing boat, a 14-footer. I go back to his office and hang around.

Suddenly an awesome belch. Not exactly ruffles and flourishes, but the man definitely believes in entrances. And now he's wearing a clean gray T-shirt, no holes. Must be I made a good impression.

Two days after my interview with Big Abe LeBlanc I felt the aftermath, and it was not intellectual. It was indigestion, sharp gas pains, to be frank, at about 3 a.m. I had eaten too much of the smoked whitefish Big Abe gave me.

But my talk with Big Abe left me with a mental uneasiness too. Unlike other people whose profiles I have written, Big Abe hardly cooperated in helping me understand who he really is. This is not too surprising, considering that traditionally whites approach Indians usually to take something from them, whether it's land in 1836, fishing rights today, or a story about the life and times of an Indian fisherman.

Yet when the subject's guard is rigidly up, it can also be unwittingly way, way down. A big man, used to throwing his bull and his loud buzzsaw voice around, A.B.'s weaknesses at times are also more evident than he realizes. Could I talk to Amelia—Mrs. LeBlanc?

"Let's keep her out of it," he growls. So there is one hole in his armor.

As far as the rights issue is concerned, from Big Abe I got rhetoric, but no explanation. He is the leader in a holy war, St. James before the troops.

But why, if Indians are catching only 5 percent of the lake trout and sportsmen are taking a good four-fifths, is the DNR so deathly afraid of them?

Soo chairman Joe Lumsden says the root is not racism. Racism, he says, is a tool. The DNR and sporting groups use it to rile up anglers. Lumsden thinks the key word is "control." The DNR is jealous of Indians' recently substantiated right to regulate themselves. Sure, the Indians need regulation, Big Abe contends to me. Indians know that without regulation there will be no fishery, and they want to preserve it as a way of life for their grandchildren.

Could it be that this big-bellied, loud-mouthed man, whose little yellow frame house in Bay Mills has held 10 kids, two dogs, who is now raising seven pigs, whose $200,000-per-year fish-packing business seems modest compared to the sporting lobbyists' annual budget, is even more of a threat to the state then he himself realizes?

Abstractions are foreign to A.B. LeBlanc. He says the final issue boils down to this: "I have to catch enough fish to buy my kids a pair of shoes, to build a decent home. Why should I be different from Jones down the road who has a nice house?"

And at the bottom of the whole dispute, there is his big point:

"Why should we have to change our ways to satisfy the government?" ■

I did lots of research, read congressional hearing transcripts and other records and wound up writing different versions of the story for the Detroit Free Press Magazine, The Progressive, National Fisherman, and the Tribune. But I wanted more. I wanted to write it for The New York Times.

I wrote what is called a Query Letter. In the letter, I covered the issues

Troubled waters

The struggle on the Great Lakes for an ancient way of life

Joel Thurtell

Fishing is a way of life for the Chippewa and Ottawa Indians of the Upper Great Lakes. Explorers entering the region two centuries ago found Indian families settling in fishing villages on the lakeshores each spring, then splitting up to move inland in the fall. Their equipment—spears, basket-traps, dip-nets, and coarse fiber seines—had changed little in more than two thousand years.

Descendants of those tribes still inhabit the region, now sharing its waters with the sport and commercial fisheries of Sault Ste. Marie and tiny Bay Mills. Fishing still shapes their lives, although their early gear has largely been replaced by tough nylon gillnets, and today many have turned to established fisheries for income.

The Michigan Indians are now free to make their own rules for fishing—a right written into treaty law long before Michigan became a state and recently reaffirmed by a Federal district court. Maintaining that right has not been easy for the Michigan Chippewa and Ottawa. While fighting in court to keep their fishing heritage, the tribes have faced a hostile press, an angry white community, and a determined effort by the state of Michigan to strip them of their treaty rights.

Foes of the Indians' ancient fishing ways have focused on the tribes' self-regulated use of the modern gillnet. These nylon webs, almost invisible in the water, are designed to trap fish of marketable size when they swim into

---

Joel Thurtell is the editor of The Berrien Springs, Michigan, Journal Era.

48 / SEPTEMBER 1980

the openings and snag their fins and gills in the mesh. The openings range in size from one-and-a-half to six inches, depending on the kind of fish sought.

It may sound like an efficient way to catch a single kind of fish, but the gillnet distinguishes fish only by size, not by species. Along with the whitefish reaped by Indian and commercial gillnetters come the feisty lake trout, rainbow trout, coho salmon, and other game fish prized by sport anglers and stocked in the region's waters by the Michigan Department of Natural Resources (DNR).

Sport fishing enthusiasts like to think of these game fish as their own, paid for by their fishing-license fees. Not all of them could wait for the Federal court ruling they hoped would keep Indian gillnetters out of the water: In the months that preceded it, tension mounted and erupted in violence against Indians and their fishing equipment. Nets were slashed or stolen, boats were swamped or sunk, and Indians were sometimes fired on.

When Judge Noel Fox upheld the Indians' fishing rights in 1978, the assaults continued. The judge's ruling had been an attempt to settle the dispute over fishing which had raged since 1971, when the DNR began enforcing fish and game laws for Indians and non-Indians alike. In angry response to the policy switch, one Chippewa, Albert "Big Abe" LeBlanc, had jammed a copy of the treaty into his pocket and set out to fish in Lake Superior. He was ticketed by the agency, and the lawsuits following his arrest led to a state supreme court ruling five years later.

Although the state high court ruled that LeBlanc could indeed fish under treaty law, getting the same right for his people was another story. Other Indians turned to the Federal Government for support against the state, and it was in Fox's court that fishing rights were extended to the rest of those originally included in the treaty. An appeals court upheld the decision in July, and Michigan Attorney General Frank Kelley is taking the case to the U.S. Supreme Court to prevent "irreparable harm."

In his ruling, Fox called the local Indians "political successors in interest" to the Indians who first signed the treaties. "The mere passage of time has not, and cannot, erode the rights guaranteed by solemn treaties that both sides pledged on their honor to uphold," he wrote. Under his ruling, the state was forbidden to regulate Indian fishing on more than 23,000 square miles of Lakes Michigan, Superior, and Huron—an area almost the size of West Virginia that the tribes had ceded in the 1836 treaty.

Many refused to accept the decision. One group of Michiganders began circulating "wanted" posters, offering a cash bounty for the arrest of "illegal" gillnetters. The posters showed a photograph of Indians fishing, which somehow made its way from the DNR, through the 100,000-member Michigan United Conservation Clubs, and into the hands of a group calling itself Stop Gillnetting Now.

In self-defense, Indians increased their rowboat crews from two people to three—the third person staying on shore to guard cars and gear, prime targets for vigilante vandalism.

"We don't want any more Wounded Knees on our hands," said

Reprinted courtesy of The Progressive.

the executive director of the Michigan United Conservation Clubs, Tom Washington, insisting that his group meant no harm to the Indians. But at the same time, Washington and various officials, including state fisheries biologists, have continued to fuel the fires of anti-Indian bigotry.

"We've got a real problem in Michigan now," Washington said when he first heard that the court had upheld Indian treaty rights. Indian fishing not regulated by the state, like poaching on a closed reserve, was "raping the environment."

With a well-circulated magazine and a vocal lobby in Lansing, Washington has had ample forum for his views. Smaller sporting groups, such as the Michigan Council of Trout Unlimited and Michigan Steelheaders, as well as sport industry groups such as the Great Lakes Charter Boat Association, have joined his "environmental" cause. And the DNR has also joined the pro-sporting club, raising the banner of "conservation" over the anti-treaty coalition.

The DNR asked Michigan Governor William Milliken to meet with the Indians and discuss placing limits on Indian fishing—ostensibly, to reduce the "growing tension" between the races. At the same time, the agency appealed Fox's ruling. The agency claims that the Indians are pushing lake trout into extinction, but its own figures tell another story.

In a 1978 hearing before the House Subcommittee on Fisheries and Wildlife Conservation, DNR figures put the Indian share of the lake trout catch for all of the Great Lakes at 7.3 per cent. Sport anglers, on the other hand, took 80.4 per cent.

After hearing one DNR official plead his case, Representative James Oberstar, Minnesota Democrat, expressed his disbelief: "Using horseback calculation, I came up with 3.3 million pounds of sport lake trout taken, plus 500,000 pounds, by your estimate, of illegal lake trout taken by nontreaty [white] commercial fishermen," he said. "That brings the figure up to 3.8 million pounds, as compared to 300,000 pounds, by your estimate, of lake trout taken by treaty. And yet you and virtually every other witness on the opposing viewpoint has put the total blame for the decline in the fishery on treaty fishermen."

When asked to explain all the fuss over so few fish caught by self-regulated Indians, DNR Director Howard A. Tanner gave a revealing response:

"You have to talk about depletion biologically, and then you have to talk about depletion economically," he said. "In order to provide an attractive sport fishery, we have to have a very high-level abundance to make the fish available. Given that high-level abundance, for a charter boat captain, or for a sport fisherman, it provides a very attractive fishery where a lot of money is spent and a viable economic base is laid."

As Tanner continued with his explanation, pointing out that lake trout are twenty-five to thirty times more valuable when taken by sport anglers than in commercial use, the real DNR position became clear. It wasn't a concern for the environment that underlay Tanner's analysis—it was economics.

How did the state environmental protection group come to play a chamber-of-commerce role? At first hearing, the agency's linking of ecology and business may have sounded plausible. Even though fishing-related tourism nets Michigan business $250 million annually, stocking the waters with lake trout is a losing game, DNR officials say. They estimate the total cost at $200 per fish; the return via boat captains, motel owners, tackle dealers, and others in tourism is $80. This feeble return requires protection from all dangers, they say—and commercial fishing, bringing in just $4 wholesale per fish, is one very real danger.

Besides a cash return, sport fishing provides more than thirty million pounds of fish each year to sport anglers' families and friends, officials add. The anglers "buy" this food source when they buy their licenses to fish. "One hundred per cent of the fishery program in our state is funded by license buyers," claims Washington.

But the economic argument holds little more water. Licensing fees do not pay the full bill for DNR stocking in Lake Michigan, the subcommittee learned; Federal funds pay almost half the cost of hatchery rebuilding and expansion. One expert called to testify carried the point even farther: Carlos Fetterolf, executive secretary of the joint U.S.-Canadian Great Lakes Fishery Commission, estimated that the "vast majority" of lake trout stocking is done with Federal public funds, not individual licensing fees. He added that without control of the parasitic sea lamprey, there would be no sport fishing to argue about, and lamprey control costs are split between the United States and Canadian governments.

While other states stock game fish in the Great Lakes, none faces the controversy seen in Michigan, since none stocks and regulates as many fish as Michigan does. Of more than forty million lake trout stocked in Lake Superior from 1958 to 1976, almost half were placed by Michigan agencies, with the rest coming in smaller numbers from Ontario, Wisconsin, and Minnesota. The story is much the same for Lakes Michigan and Huron: There, again, Michigan leads the way in game fish stocking.

As it turns out, the DNR's own statistics may make the case for self-regulated Indian fishing—a fortunate irony, since the Indians have had few outlets for their own side of the story. With fewer than 7,000 constituents dotted over seven northern counties, far from the newspapers and wire service bureaus of the state capital, Indians compete with a

'Fishing is our way of life....'

medley of private and state voices, including the state Department of Commerce. Each year, that agency spends $35,000 to hype sport fishing. In the midst of these campaigns, Indians say, their views often come out distorted or garbled in the press.

What is the Indians' side of the story? Hardly a dire tale of tribespeople crowding sports enthusiasts off the waters. Between the Michigan Chippewa and Ottawa tribes, fewer than 200 people are licensed to fish by tribal conservation committees. These committees supervise teams of game officers equipped with boats and four-wheel-drive vehicles. Since last summer, tribal regulations have also permitted DNR game wardens to cite Indians who break conservation rules. Those charged with violating tribal regulations are prosecuted by the tribal lawyer before a tribe-appointed judge. The whole picture is one of careful, reasoned fishing—not one of wanton environmental destruction and anarchy on the waters.

Indians say they are as concerned about conservation as the DNR, since they want to preserve fishing as a way of life for their children. For the present, fishing provides much-needed jobs in a depressed local economy; Overall unemployment is 25 per cent in Michigan's Upper Peninsula, and for Indians, it has hit 60 per cent. Many Indians who do find work earn less than $5,000 annually, and most supplement their incomes with gardening and other jobs in the seven-month non-fishing season. Setting up operations is not cheap: A fifteen-foot aluminum boat, an outboard motor, a trailer, four-wheel-drive car, and gillnets add up to about $15,000. Nor is fishing an easy job, and piloting the small boats on the often-treacherous Great Lakes makes fishing as risky as it is low-profit.

But fishing is more than a matter of economics for the Indians—it's a heritage. As Bay Mills tribal leader Arthur LeBlanc says, "The Bay Mills Indian community has not spent years in court merely because it wishes to have the state recognize our legal right to fish. Fishing is our way of life, and we have been fighting to preserve it."

So far, the Indians' fight has won little support from civil rights advocates, who in the past have shown more sympathy for Indians fighting similar legal battles in the distant state of Washington. Nevertheless, the Michigan Indians, bolstered by the favorable court decision, are once again investing in the fishing equipment they were formerly afraid to buy. Tribal leaders say that the recognition of Indian fishing rights may focus attention on fishing practices of the entire Great Lakes in the future, practices now dominated by the Michigan DNR's pro-sporting bias. While pointing out that there will always be room for sport fishing, Sault Ste. Marie tribal leader Joseph Lumsden says he believes most Michiganders, if they had the choice, would prefer the new source of cheap protein that such a policy change would bring.

With sport fishing already feeling the pinch of rising fuel costs, that choice may present itself sooner than Lumsden expects. The number of families able to pay $160 a day for a charter boat, plus food, lodging, and transportation costs, has already dropped, and as sport fishing becomes inaccessible to all but the wealthiest, popular support may swing to those who fish as a means of sustenance, not as a luxury. The Michigan Indians' right to maintain their heritage of self-regulated fishing will then exist not just in the courts, but in the minds of their non-Indian neighbors. ■

and mentioned the people I'd talked to. Big Abe LeBlanc, for one. I was not then a subscriber to the Times. But I had a resource. Andrews University. It has an excellent library. There, I could read the Times. I saw articles with Reginald Stuart's byline datelined Detroit. Using a phone directory, I found the telephone number for the Times' Detroit bureau, which happened to be on the eighth floor of the Free Press building. I called. The phone was answered by Susan Pastor, a Times stringer. I told her who I was and that I wanted to write for the Times. She did not tell me to go to hell. She suggested I send some clips. I mailed my favorite stories to the Times. I gave the Times a subscription to the little Journal Era weekly I was editing. That way, I figured, when I raked muck or wrote some clever feature, they would see it if they didn't use our paper to line a birdcage.

For the Indian fishing rights story, I went to Andrews University, just a short bike ride from my house, and pulled a copy of The New York Times Index. No stories on Indian fishing in Michigan. Good. I wrote a query that was much like the story I wanted to write for the Times. Very soon, I got the Times' reply: "You wrote a beautiful query, but we're going to staff it," Bureau chief Reggie Stuart told me.

The story was written by Iver Peterson, a Times staff writer who went to Bay Mills, interviewed Big Abe LeBlanc and the other people I mentioned in my query and wrote the story I wanted to write.

I was upset when I saw the story, though my file suggests that I must already have known that I'd lost the assignment. I called the Times office in Detroit. I spoke to Susan Pastor. (Susan once gave me an excellent piece of advice. I was in awe of the Times, which I still think is the best newspaper in the world. I mentioned my reverence for the Times to Susan. "Sure, it's a great newspaper," she said. "But remember, it's still a newspaper.")

Never before had she let me talk to Reggie Stuart, the bureau chief. Now she put me through to him. I let him know I was pissed. I felt betrayed. I recalled Scott Aiken's warning not to trust other Journalists because they'll steal your ideas.

I calmed down as I listened to Reggie Stuart. That, at least, was how I remembered it. Thirty years after Reggie and I talked, I dug out my "New York Times" file and found my handwritten notes from our conversation. It always helps to go back to the sources. Turns out, I have my own record of the incident, and it differs from the way I remembered it.

"What happened with your fishing rights story?" Reggie said. "Two points. Yes, I am interested in pursuing the prospects of your stringing for the Times. About Judge Fox's ruling," he said, Times people had been tracking the fishing rights controversy and when the judge's ruling came down, there was interest in the implications of the ruling nationally. "Nobody was freed up to do it. I wanted to do it. It bounced around. New York wanted to staff it, do a situation piece. There's one dumb problem — we're way over budget."

"Over budget" meant then and now that there's little or no money to pay stringers their fees and expenses. Since a staffer is, well, on staff and receiving a set salary, it appears cheaper to send that person rather than pay an outsider to do the same work.

But Reggie held out hope. There are two ways I could write for the Times: He or someone from the Times might call me and ask me to do a story, or I might write a spot news story, in which case I would call him or an editor in New York.

"Two or three more months only will we be on this emergency basis," he said. "So call me when something's cooking.

"No promises. But do me this favor. Send me a bill for Xeroxing the court ruling and send me a copy of your (South Bend Tribune) series, and we'll work out something. Keep me posted."

I got the message: Keep pitching stories.

I decided to take Reggie Stuart at his word. I had other stories up my sleeve. Taxes were a hot button in those days. Michigan was seen as having higher taxes than neighboring states. A former Catholic priest-turned-lawyer living near the Indiana border decided to go for a little attention. He proposed that Cass County, in Michigan on the Indiana border, should secede from Michigan and join the Hoosier State.

This was not even my story for the Tribune, but I didn't care. I'd learned something about the so-called sanctity of beats and subject territory from my experience with the Times. Which is where I pitched my idea for a Cass County secession story. Bingo. Reggie Stuart liked it, talked to his editors and suddenly I had an assignment for the Times. No byline, but seventy-five bucks was fine with me. I pocketed the money and sold the longer versions of my story to the Free Press Magazine and to The Indianapolis Star Sunday Magazine.

Soon, I was writing another story for the Times, this one an assignment from the national desk. Another seventy-five bucks!

Having my work published in The New York Times — me, a poor stringer in an obscure corner of Michigan — was a very heady experience. One day, as I was laying out pages for the weekly, I got a call from Reggie. He was in the area working a story and wondered if he could stop at our office and meet me. The bureau chief of The New

York Times, headquartered in a tall Manhattan building that made the ground shake when its presses ran, got a tour of our Journal Era newsroom on the ground floor of a little brick building on Ferry Street leading to the St. Joseph River.

Wahoo! I had an in at the Times!

Until Reggie Stuart left Detroit.

Which happened very soon.

Then I was out at the Time*s*.

chapter 14

that times 'beer allowance'

Odd situation I have with The New York Times, which wants to charge me a $520 fee for reprinting in this book a story I wrote for them 30 years ago. It's a situation that YOU as a wannabe stringer can learn from. Back in the day, the Times paid me only seventy-five bucks for the story. Can you believe the cheek? Now they want to charge me seven times what they paid me, just so I can reprint my own story. And they still owe me beer money!

It began back in my freelancing days. When I sold my work, I was careful to make it clear that I was selling "one time rights only" to my stories. The story in dispute, about the proposal of some wacky Michiganders that their county of Cass in southwestern Michigan ought to secede and become part of Indiana, made for some fun writing. It was a preposterous notion; everybody knew it was simply a headline-grabber for a handful of would-be political opportunists. I sold versions of my yarn not only to The New York Times, but to the Detroit Free Press Magazine and The Indianapolis Star Sunday Magazine. I own the copyright to the text I sold to all of those publications, including the august Times. That means I'm free to quote the entire story at length.

I learned about this from Michael Gross, attorney for the Authors Guild. Because I have a book contract with a bona fide publisher, Wayne State University Press, I am able to belong to a union for writers of books. *Up the Rouge! Paddling Detroit's Hidden River*, the book I wrote with photojournalist Patricia Beck, makes this membership possible. I pay ninety bucks a year in dues, which allows me to ask the Authors Guild attorney for legal advice. I'm passing this information on to YOU, because aspiring stringers should know that they have this advantage over staff writers: Whatever they write, as long as they don't sign a contract with the publisher — belongs to them.

Fine enough. But for *Shoestring Reporter*, my Journalism textbook, I wanted more: I wanted to reprint my Times article as it appeared in the Times. Why? Because it would be COOL, that's why. It's a Times article. I want it to appear in my book exactly as it appeared when printed in the Times. Ego? Damned straight. But it's a neat story in its own right, and I wanted to show you how it appeared in that pinnacle of

The Michiganders Who Want To Be Hoosiers

By JOEL THURTELL

WHEN John Steiding studied regional planning at Maryland's Frostburg State College, the department's catalog didn't list a course called "Secession Administration 405." Maybe it would have been better for him if it had.

As director of the Cass County (Michigan) Planning Commission, Steiding at 34 finds himself working for a county that is talking about seceding from Michigan and joining Indiana.

Talking, of course, is not the same as action, and there is talk against secession as well as for it. But the handful of businessmen from Edwardsburg, Mich., who started this movement in October, 1979, insist they are serious and they have already fought (and lost) one court battle in their effort to place the secession question on next November's election ballot.

As a court appeal drags on and secession hopefuls seek support, county bureaucrats like Steiding can't help wondering what would happen to their government and their own jobs if Cass did secede. For instance, fumes Steiding, a round-faced, heavily sideburned man, what would happen to local land records and court cases pending, or what would be the status, suddenly, of convicts in the Cassopolis jail if this 21½ by 24-mile box of a county poised on the Indiana line were abruptly to topple into Hoosier jurisdiction?

But secessionists are not trifling with such technicalites because they have their own list of problems which they say the Michigan legislature has caused for every Michigander who lives outside the Detroit metropolitan area.

Citizens for Secession (CFS) is the brainchild of William L. LaBre, a 35-year-old lawyer, chamber of commerce president and former Roman Catholic priest, who says the group formed as a last resort because its members are frustrated after years of vain efforts to reform Michigan's workmen's compensation laws.

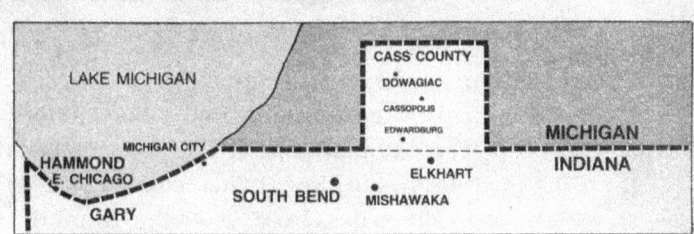

If Cass County secessionists get their way Indiana's northern border will have this new look.

THE SOUTHERN Michigan rebels point out that the location of Edwardsburg 2½ miles above the Indiana border poses problems. One charter CFS member, Richard Christiansen, complains that his factory, which caters to the recreational vehicle industry centered around nearby Elkhart in Indiana, has a tough time competing with Indiana firms because the cost of workmen's compensation is six or seven times higher in Michigan.

After a long session of bellyaching in LaBre's office, a dozen businessmen from Edwardsburg met in a country restaurant called the Dock, where the owner, Ron Linton, was sympathetic to their cause and a member of the secessionist group. There the secessionists swore allegiance to a cause that would anger government stalwarts and which was to provoke picketing by anti-secessionists carrying signs advising LaBre, Christiansen and their ilk, "If you want to live in Indiana, move there."

LaBre published a short manifesto in which he complained that "the lack of understanding or desire to correct the economic problems which cripple Cass County and Southwestern Michigan so badly has led to the loss of at least 350 jobs in Cass County to Indiana in the past year alone, due to higher employment costs."

The proclamation added that "Michigan has a rate of property taxation at least double that of Indiana. Michigan has higher insurance rates due to the Legislature's desire to have low risk areas of the State share the high-risk costs of the metropolitan area," and "today it costs the average homeowner over $1,000 a year more to be called a Michigander. Can you afford it?"

One secessionist who thinks it's too much is Bob Bretschneider. As proprietor of an Edwardsburg sand and gravel company, Bretschneider now has to cope with Michigan's new Wetlands Act which is intended to protect the state's marshes. Bretschneider believes the law means more red tape—and expense—for his business. Indiana has no comparable regulation on digging, dredging or mining in marshes, and if he had to choose between Bretschneider's business and the future of Michigan wildlife, he'd go for his friend, says LaBre.

"I'M MORE concerned about

The intersection of Cassopolis and State Line roads marks the border that some Cass County citizens would like changed.

people than I am about ducks," he says.

Leaving, says planner Steiding, is just like a child who gets mad, picks up his toys and threatens to go home if he doesn't get his way. Sure, Steiding admits, Michigan's workmen's compensation system is bad—everyone from the governor on down would agree. The cost is exorbitant to businesses, while the pay-out to workers is no better than in Indiana.

But LaBre figures the idea of secession was a gleam in LaBre's eye long before the lawyer concocted arguments to support it. Robert Craig, also an attorney and vice-chairman of the county planning commission, guesses that LaBre and his bunch are pulling "a grandstand stunt," the product of a few ingenious brains, a publicity gimmick, "pat, but not profound."

Craig says the secessionists merely want to draw attention to

Reprinted courtesy of the Indianapolis Star

That Times 'Beer Allowance'

the plight of business. Kenneth Myers, a secession supporter, is chairman of the Cass County Board of Commissioners. Craig guesses that Myers wants to use secession as a trade-off. For some tax relief, the idea of secession will be allowed to sink deeper than the lakes and bogs that dot the rural county.

Secessionist Ron Linton scoffs at that theory. "I don't think we're going to get any special treatment from Lansing (Michigan's capital)," says Linton.

If Craig labels secession "cute but cheap," Steiding, who works under Pat of the secession drive, a little uneasy. But he calls LaBre, who was laicized four years ago by a special papal dispensation, "a priest who went bad."

Steiding accuses LaBre of being a chronic quitter. First he drops out of the priesthood, then he wants to drop out of Michigan.

Not too surprisingly, LaBre denies the charge. A small, portly, round-faced man with dark, penetrating eyes, LaBre won't speak of his departure from the Roman Catholic clergy. But simple arithmetic shows it came not too long before his marriage to his wife Pat.

"My husband is not joking," says Pat of the secession drive. And LaBre denies it is a publicity gimmick.

"Even the morning dew has the purpose of getting some moisture into the ground, even if it is going to evaporate when the sun comes out," he says. "But I don't like those kinds of things (gimmicks). It would have no real function, no influence. What you would probably get is some very placating statements from Lansing. But what changes substantially? If that (a publicity gimmick) was the case, I wouldn't want any part of it. I would oppose it."

Indeed, a placating statement did come from Lansing, over the signature of Governor William Milliken and addressed to the Cass County Board of Commissioners. It said:

"Although I think seceding from Michigan in no way would benefit Cass County or the balance of the state, I do believe the course taken by the county board to open these questions to public debate is extremely beneficial to the public."

But the county board told secession leaders that the question would be placed on the board's agenda only if the secession group produced petitions signed by 10,000 who voted for governor in the last election.

While the opposition from Lansing sounded gentle, there was genuine alarm in Cassopolis, the Cass County seat, a pretty resort town dominated by an old stone courthouse surrounded by pretty 19th Century wood frame houses and located on a hill overlooking placid Stone Lake. In Cassopolis there was hostility to the idea of secession.

Steiding, when asked for an interview, said, "Given the area of your subject, you will not find this office very co-operative." He softened later, but still said, "If three people in Cass County talked about a plan for genocide, you guys (reporters) would have the whole county for it."

Steiding says only half the

The Cass County Courthouse (upper left) was the scene of the secessionists' fight to have the issue placed on the 1980 general election ballot. An old pioneer log cabin (above) overlooks scenic Stone Lake. Former priest Bill LaBre (left) heads secession drive.

people originally involved in organization of the secession group will now admit it. LaBre says that appears to be true because two people were forced to go underground. Operators of small retail businesses, they were threatened with boycotts when their names were linked to secession, LaBre says. He claims that 50 persons showed up at a pro-secession rally a week after the group was formed.

Last October and November secession was a media event. All three television stations in South Bend covered it, as did Indianapolis stations. The wire services picked up the story. Articles appeared in the New York Times and Wall Street Journal. The Detroit newspapers prepared their own stories on the secession while the Kalamazoo Gazette, which serves northern Cass County, simply reprinted the New York Times story.

In Cass the exposure was a bit embarrassing. A counter-movement formed and organized a demonstration within sight of LaBre's law office in Edwardsburg (population 1,107). Picket signs advised the rebels to love Michigan or leave it.

LaBre, a native of Escanaba in Michigan's upper peninsula, says he grew up with the idea of separatism. For years, dissidents in Michigan's often forgotten north have talked about seceding the upper peninsula from Michigan and forming a 51st state to be called Superior. LaBre's mother Mrs. Luke LaBre (the name in French-speaking Canada, from which the family comes, means "the lip" or "the lippy one") says she doesn't recall any such talk in her house while Bill was growing up. But maybe it's in the blood.

At any rate, secession rubbed many the wrong way. Reporter Gene Walden, who covers Cass County for the South Bend Tribune, said, "It's just that no self-respecting Michigander—born beneath the crystal blue northern sky, calloused tough as wolverines by the brisk winds off Lake Superior—could ever swallow the idea of becoming a 'Hoosier.'"

No RHETORIC can explain just where secession stands under the law.

Although the Constitution provides for states or parts of states to secede and form new states or join other states (Article IV, Section 3.1) the Federal charter also requires the Michigan legislature to approve the move and most observers sees this as the biggest stumbling block.

Indiana's lieutenant governor Robert Orr, however, called industrialists fleeing Michigan's alleged bad business climate "economic boat people," and pledged his support for Cass' admission to Indiana if the movement ever gets that far.

How far the movement gets will depend upon whether the Cass County Board passes an ordinance allowing its citizens the right to initiative, that is, to directly move for secession. In mid-February, a Cass circuit judge ruled Cass Countians had no such right.

A signature-gathering campaign is part of the secession strategy to induce the county board to put the question on a

Continued on Page 14

Michiganders

Continued from Page 9

ballot, providing a favorable court ruling can be obtained on an appeal. LaBre concedes it will be sometime in August before an appeal can be heard—too late for a favorable ruling to put the secession question on November's ballot, and as far as the county board is concerned "don't hold your breath," LaBre advises. Despite all these roadblocks, the secessionists insist they will persist in trying to get the question on a ballot in 1982.

THE AREA known as Cass County is part of a larger area of Michigan and Indiana which for decades has been nicknamed Michiana. (The Cass secessionists will name the county Michiana if they enter Indiana because Indiana already has a Cass County.)

Cass County in Michigan adjoins the Indiana line. Wayne Hothem, the county's co-operative agricultural extension agent describes Cass as "a geologist's nightmare." Lacking its own identity, Cass seems to reflect the areas that border it.

In the townships closest to Indiana, like Ontwa, home of LaBre, 80 percent of the employed population commutes to Elkhart County, Ind., to work. Overall, 34 percent of Cass workers head toward Indiana each morning and another 22 percent drive to neighboring Berrien County, Michigan.

It is not all one-way. Says Cass County Commissioner Steve Toth, "I was raised in South Bend and moved out of there (to Cass) in 1937. I wouldn't go back on a bet."

Cass County is agricultural mainly and its chief attraction for tourists is its many lakes. But over the years the county has changed from a resort to a kind of country suburban atmosphere. Driving through Cass on a bright afternoon is nothing but pleasant and it is easy to see why many Hoosiers have forsaken their own flatlands for the wooded rolling countryside of Cass.

Much of the land is prairie, but it can very quickly become rough, and much of its northeastern sector would at first sight seem useless. But the rather turbulent countryside there is peppered with the backs of countless hogs. Cass markets more hogs than any other county in Michigan.

To illustrate the kind of fragmented

2 for 1 DRAPERY CLEANING

Two Pairs Cleaned for the Price of One. Pay Only for the larger Pair.

Our **Adjust-a-Drape** process restores that "just-bought" look to your draperies. Exact length and even hemlines are guaranteed.

25% OFF HOUSEHOLD ITEMS

Blankets, Pillows, Chair & Sofa Slipcovers, Sleeping Bags, Bedspreads, Quilts.

Tuchman CLEANERS

Bring Your Draperies to Any One of our 30 Convenient Locations. Take-down and Rehang Service Available.

Call 545-4321

YOUR NEIGHBORHOOD DRY CLEANER

30 CONVENIENT STORES

Plain 2 Piece
SUITS, DRESSES & CLOTH COATS
$3.19
Reg. $3.99
Present Coupon With Order
Expires 7/12/80

Plain
SLACKS, BLOUSES SKIRTS, SWEATERS
$1.67
Reg. $2.09
Present Coupon With Order
Expires 7/12/80

ANY LAUNDRY BUNDLE OR SHIRT ORDER
10% OFF
Present Coupon With Order
Expires 7/12/80

SUEDE, LEATHER FUR, FAKE FUR
20% OFF
Present Coupon With Order
Expires 7/12/80

Citizens For Secession Chairman Ron Linton runs the Dock, a restaurant where the separatist group was formed.

area he plans for, Steiding complains about the multitude of newspapers he says he has to read just to keep on top of county events. The South Bend Tribune has the biggest circulation overall, he says.

But in the southeast part of the county, the Elkhart Truth reigns. Dowagiac has its own 4,000-circulation daily newspaper, but in the northwest, around Silver Creek, people read the Benton Harbor Herald-Palladium. That area's strawberries and orchards tie it strongly to the Benton Harbor produce market. Yet down in the southwest corner of Cass, where students are actually bused to school across the county line into Berrien, people read the Niles Daily Star, while at the top of the county, in Marcellus, the Kalamazoo Gazette is boss.

In Berrien County, next door, old-time politicians recall mumblings about secession 15 or 20 years ago. Politicans in Niles never have been happy with Berrien's county government, claiming that all the county's construction and patronage centers in St. Joseph-Benton Harbor. So once they talked of seceding the southern half of Berrien and creating a new county.

There was no talk of joining Indiana then as Cass County secessionists urge now. But Niles, in a situation somewhat parallel to that of Cass County, is practically a satellite of Indiana, South Bend in particular. For example, when the Niles Chamber of Commerce holds its annual meeting it is in South Bend's Century Center. Last year's meeting saw Michigan Congressman Dave Stockman, whose district includes Niles, speaking to a Michigan Chamber of Commerce on Indiana turf.

LaBre, the tenacious lawyer, is doing the legal legwork for the secessionist group in his spare time and, while there isn't much time left to place the question on November's ballot, even if all roadblocks could be hurdled, he thinks there's plenty of time to set it before voters two years from November.

Does Bill LaBre, the former Catholic priest, see himself as leading some kind of holy war against Lansing? After all, he does credit Pope Leo XIII's famous encyclical "Rerum Novarum" as the basis of his secession philosophy. The encyclical urges that decisions be kept at the smallest social level. But a holy war?

Smiling, LaBre says, "That sounds extraordinarily like Don Quixote, doesn't it?"

Whether the Citizens for Secession was just a crackpot scheme, a huge propaganda stunt or a serious movement remains to be seen. But if it were to come about, by and by, it would be a nightmare for planners like John Steiding. And maybe for others.

As Cass Commissioner Johnnie Rodebush says, "It's just too far out. Every doctor, lawyer, mechanic and other professional would suddenly find themselves without a license."

★ ★ ★ ★ ★

newspapers, the Times. For an obscure writer, a nobody literally working from a garret in Berrien Springs, Michigan, it was a real coup. The seventy-five bucks was nice, but the story under a Times head — that's where the glory lay. Times cachet. Big-city cred. I mean, that's part of my book's title, right? How I Got To Be A Big City Reporter… Well it gives me whatever laurels a no-byline New York Times story can lend. The Times seemed to be claiming that I should pay them for the appearance they created as well as for the words I wrote. I was hoping they'd relent and waive the fee. But if they insisted on charging me a fee, I decided, I'd omit that clip. Incidentally, The Progressive quite enthusiastically gave me permission to reprint my Indian fishing rights story from their September 1980 issue. The Indy Star approved my request to reprint — as they ran it — my Cass County secession story from its pages. The Detroit Free Press gave me permission to reprint from their pages the whole darn Big Abe LeBlanc fishing rights story, too. And then there's the Times.

When the Times assigned its "curtain-raiser" on Indian fishing rights to a staffer, I was angry, and shared my beef with the Times Detroit bureau chief. He persuaded me to photocopy the crucial judicial ruling in the fishing rights case and mail it to him. On June 4, 1979, the Times bureau chief sent me a note with a check to cover my cost of photocopying the judge's ruling. He noted that a Times staff writer was then on his way to interview people for an Indian fishing rights story with my articles and the court ruling "in hand." Besides payment for the photocopies, the Times bureau chief wrote, "I'll try to squeeze out a beer allowance to cover your other troubles." "Other troubles"? It never occurred to me there might be problems with the Times — 30 years down the road.

That "beer allowance"?

I never got it.

Now they want to take it away.

Regardless, the words I wrote belong to me. You'll see that I've reproduced that story *using my own format.* Remember that what you write, even if you sell it to a newspaper for one-time use, belongs to you. Just be careful not to sign a contract forgoing your long-term right to use your work. (I'm sorry to say that I actually did such a dumb thing with articles I wrote for the amateur radio magazine QST, although I kept my right to publish them on my Web site.)

As a stringer, even though you don't have the fringe benefits a staff writer would enjoy, you at least have this advantage: You can rerun, resell your work when and where you like. A staffer doesn't have that right.

chapter 15

reggie's tip sheet

Okay, so I didn't get my "beer allowance" from The New York Times. What I received, gratis, from Reginald Stuart, former Detroit bureau chief of the Times, was worth more than a decade's worth of 12-packs. Reggie gave me, in the space of maybe a five-minute phone conversation, what amounts to a primer on how to report and write a story for the Times. And if it's good for the Times, it'll work anywhere.

I lost the assignment to write about Indian fishing for the Times, but I heard what Reggie said about keeping him posted about interesting local phenomena with national interest. The idea that a county might secede from one state and join itself to another seemed like a throwback to the Civil War, and it occurred to me that it might just have that "national interest" Reggie was looking for. I can't find the query letter I sent to Reggie about Indian fishing rights. But in my carbon copy of a June 3, 1979, letter to Reggie, I warmed up the secession subject by telling him how the Niles (Michigan) Daily Star staff lived in Indiana and kept their watches on Hoosier time. In the same letter, I pitched a story about the annual cherry-pit-spitting contest in Eau Claire, Michigan. I wrote a long paragraph with a high pun-per-sentence count that apparently didn't intrigue Reggie.

By the way, while the Times passed on cherry-pit-spitting, The Grand Rapids Press bought it. But Reggie Stuart jumped on the Cass County secession story. I considered the assignment from The New York Times the biggest event — professionally — in my life and took copious notes on what Reggie told me. Here they are:

"We're going to give you a run for your money. I pulled a lot of teeth, got money loose for you to write this. Write this thing, amplify your letter. I told them about your caliber, I told them I could have put your query on the wire. Write a tight story, 800 words maximum. Write a situation story, not with a hard news lead. Use names with middle initials, ages, jobs, occupations, specific titles, what role they play. If he's a local attorney, for how long? Is he a local boy, or does he come from South Bend? Did he migrate from South Bend? Is he an invader?

"Tell the history of the county, of the region. You hit a pertinent point about tax advantages. Get specifics. What advantages are there?

404 S. Kimmel
Berrien Springs, MI 49103

3 June 1979

Dear Reginald Stuart,

Here is the latest from Judge Fox' office--this opinion belongs with the other two documents I sent you, but his secretary sent it to me later.

I am pursuing the Indian fishing rights issue for the South Bend Tribune, and if you should change your mind and decide to have me do a piece for the Times on this subject, I will be keeping abreast of things.

Another tidbit about Indiana colonialism in Niles, Michigan and recalling your surprise upon hearing that the Niles Chamber of Commerce staged its annual meeting in South Bend. The following item comes from a Benton Harbor Herald-Palladium reporter who used to work for the Niles Daily Star: the majority of reporters and editors at the Daily Star, including the managing editor, lives in South Bend and run their watches an hour behind the rest of us in Michigan.

Did you happen to see a little photo-feature in the Sunday Times recently about an armadillo race? I'm no sports reporter, but I'm sharpening up for an athletic contest which takes place every fourth of July in Eau Claire, a few miles from here. It's the great cherry pit spitting contest, the winner of which gets listed in the Guinness Book of Records, no tongue in cheek. I know of one person who has been training for some time, and I'm trying to work up a story that would be based on inter-views ~~sputums~~ with players--how do they condition?, is it good to keep a stiff upper lip?, and so on,...and then, of course, some wide angle shots--spittin images, naturally, photographed from someplace upwind.

If you would like, I will send you some negatives and a story after the event and purely on spec (short for 'spectoration), of course.

Sincerely,

Joel Thurtell

Champion Cherry Pit Spitters Gird for Main Event

By Joel Thurtell

EAU CLAIRE — All sports are divided into two leagues, the first called "big," and the second "bush." The division, as sane as it is ancient, is no more readily apparent than in the venerable sport of spitting cherry pits.

But there the similarity between conventional, organized sports and pit spitting ends.

Champion spitters come from the bushes, true, but due to the nature of this sport the best and the worst will always remain in the bushes. Nor will a spitter, no matter how proficient he becomes, ever get rich or do a TV commercial.

And where other sports spawn magazines in their special area as well as dozens of honors for winners, cherry pit spitters recognize only one publication and only one high honor — mention in "The Guinness Book of Records."

Since 1976 winners of the annual Cherry Pit Spitting Contest, held on a farm near Eau Claire, have dominated the slight paragraph in Guinness devoted to "cherry stone spitting."

When long-distance spitters gather at the Tree-Mendus Fruit Farm on Saturday, they will be pitting their skills against top contenders from across the Midwest.

But the path to the championship rounds is not an easy one. It is strewn with the pits of countless cherries and seeds from tons of watermelons — all consumed in the quest for mention in Guinness. And in this bizarre contest where participants must eat a good part of their ammunition, even the taste of victory can be sour — for the main prize is a tart cherry tree.

So, while the bush leagues feed us with both the winners and the losers in this sport, the heroes — those contestants who can slit their pits more than 45 feet — seem to be blessed with equal amounts of native skill, training, and luck. Age, the cruel arbiter in so many athletic events, plays little or no role in the field of pit spitting.

Former world title-holder Richard Hahn, of Benton Harbor, is a case in point.

The 1978 edition of Guinness lists Hahn as champ as a result of his 47-foot, 7½-inch spit back in 1976. Hahn was then 46. And at 50, he continues to spit long and accurately.

In 1978 William A. (known now as "Pits") Mobley of Findlay, Ohio, broke Hahn's record by launching a pit which landed with a terrific bounce and rolled for a total distance of 49 feet, 2 inches.

Mobley is 30, but the second-place winner whose spit was better than his roll, was in his early 20s.

Even much younger contestants have done well, and Hahn's 12-year-old son Dennis has held the junior (12 and under) title for two straight years.

Like most top contenders, the Hahns and Mobley confess to a long history of family spitting.

Mobley, by birth a Mississippian, says that in his youth he never thought of spitting cherry pits —

Photo Courtesy of Michigan Farmer

The tongue's the thing as world record holder William ("Pits") Mobley launches the whopper that won last year's contest at Eau Claire.

for there were none around. Instead, he honed his skills on a local abundance of watermelon seeds.

In fact, watermelon seeds may provide a better training aid than the sweet cherry pits he uses for spring training, Mobley insists. Sweet cherry pits are bigger and heavier than tart cherry pits, he explained in an interview, and so they spit farther and thus give the spitter the illusion he's developed a bigger spit than he really has.

The regulation pits used in the Eau Claire spit are Montmorency cherries, a tart variety with a small, lightweight pit. Since they too are lighter and smaller, Mobley argues that using watermelon seeds during his youth gave him a closer approximation to the real contest pit during his youthful expriments.

But watermelon seeds do have a drawback, he concedes. They are flat, and they don't give the aspiring distance spitter a chance to practice the all-important tongue curl.

And without the curled tongue, the aspiring spitter might as well hang his cherry pail on the nearest bush, for his great expectorations will come to nought.

What, exactly, is the tongue curl?

"Well, first you put the pit on your tongue," says Dennis Hahn. "Then you roll your tongue around it, like a gun barrel, and give it a hard blow. It'll shoot out the end."

As an afterthought, Hahn the younger said, "You've got to have a tongue that will roll."

The suggestion that a certain shape of tongue — one that will roll around the pit — is needed

The path to glory is strewn with countless pits, and the taste of victory can be sour.

for good spitting supports a theory held by Richard Bartz, a football coach in nearby Berrien Springs. Not only are good spitters endowed with rollable tongues, but the ability to spit great distances "is all just innate skill," Bartz says.

Bartz placed first in the finals in 1977, but his pit dropped a few inches short of Hahn's 1976 record — thus losing Bartz the coveted mention in Guinness. And in 1978 the entire field was eclipsed by Mobley's breathtaking spit which rolled just a few inches short of the 50-foot mark.

Bartz says he intends to enter the contest again this year, but he takes a rather uncoachlike stance when it comes to training.

"Practice didn't help me any last year," he says. "I'm just going to go in cold."

"You just have to be gifted," Bartz concludes — and his contention that the ability to spit far is hereditary gains some credence from the fact that like the Hahn father-son duo, Bartz is not the only member of his family with a twist to his tongue.

He has two spitting images in the form of his 12-year-old son Kevin, who was a winner in the junior contest last year. And his four-year-old son Danny has also got a mouth for spatial relationships, spitting 20 feet in practice sessions.

Is is true, then, that champion spitters are born, not made? Maybe — but when pressed, Bartz laughingly says he got plenty of early experience when he was a boy.

"My folks have a small fruit farm, and I used to stand on the back of a trailer and spit pits at my brother's head."

Just like riding a bicycle, Bartz says, once learned, the ability to spit true never leaves you.

While coach Bartz is waiving spring training, Mobley says he is spitting 100 pits every day, and the nearly exclusive diet of sweet cherries has brought him down to spitting trim. He has come from 235 pounds to 220, and at the same time he is perfecting his top-spin — the vertical rotation which causes the pit to bounce and roll when it hits.

There is no doubt that Mobley is master of the roll, but reports coming from Wisconsin indicate an unofficial challenge to Mobley's Guinness record — from none other than former champ, Richard Hahn.

Hahn says he went to an indoor meet last February and spat a cherry 56 feet 6 inches. And, Hahn says, Herb Teichman, organizer of the Michigan event and owner of the Tree-Mendus farm where the spit is held, "was hotter than heck." Hahn says Teichman immediately discredited the Wisconsin spit, calling it an indoor event.

Meanwhile, Mobley remains unperturbed by his adversary's spit. Champion spitters in the Michigan competition, Mobley says, pits are spat from a stationary position, while in Wisconsin contestants are allowed to take steps towards the line, thus giving them added propulsion.

Of course, there will always be spit fans to maintain that Mobley's attitude is nothing but sour — well, sour cherries. But rolls and unfair propulsion aside, the most crucial factor in any outdoor spit is wind.

"If we ever spit into the wind, there will be no records," says Bartz.

Reprinted courtesy of The Grand Rapids Press and Michigan Farmer.

Point that out. Get the South Bend Tribune editorial (about secession). What does Lansing think? Indianapolis? Get into neighboring Berrien County attitudes. Likely to join or not? Prospects of exercise — rural vs. urban — say that — when secessionists held a rally midweek, they were joined by UP (Upper Peninsula) representatives. Decades of history of independence movement. Entire event emerging as strong anti-urban. Numbers of (participants).

"Flesh that out in a maximum of 800 words."

"Use lively quotes, but don't succumb to 'quotitis.'

"Strive for breathing with people.

"Write it by Friday (tomorrow) evening and we're in good shape.

"If you get it in and they ever free up more money, I can keep rolling with you. I don't know how much money you will get.

"Call me Friday, either at the office…or at home… Call collect all numbers. Call the recording room…open to 11 p.m. When they answer, tell them who you are, what city you're from, that you want to dictate a story for the National Desk. The slug is SECEDE, your name is Joel Thurtell, attention Martha Miles, your telephone number is…paragraph, dateline, comma, date, dash, say there's a secessionist movement afoot, once through, punctuation, period, when through, say period, paragraph, end it, thank you, good-bye.

"Once you've filed the story, call the desk, leave word for Martha Miles that the story is in the house, where you can be reached. I should be in tomorrow. Call before filing."

Whew!

Can you imagine cramming all that information into 800 words?

Can you imagine GETTING all that in just a few hours? I was given one day to report and write. Luckily, I'd done much of the reporting beforehand. That's the beauty of query writing — you do most of the reporting even before you get an assignment.

After 30 years, one thing still puzzles me: What did Reggie mean by "strive for breathing with people"?

As for those middle initials, relax. Get a copy of today's Times, and count how many — or rather, how *few* — names contain middle initials. Maybe in 1979, they had a rule about middle initials, but if it still exists, it's being ignored big-time. At the South Bend Tribune, we didn't often bother with middle initials, nor was it a fetish at the Detroit Free Press, where middle initials would have been considered a "speed bump" — a mental and visual obstacle that slows down the reader.

Even so, I can think of situations where a middle initial would help. Frequently used names, like John Smith or Jim Jones, might be made more specific with use of a middle initial or even a middle name. But hey, those are copyediting issues, and this is NOT a book about editing.

Sitting behind his desk in the Times bureau on the eighth floor of the Free Press building in Detroit, Reggie Stuart reeled off a no-tuition lecture on how a Journalist should frame questions, collect details, and he outlined — in case I had trouble with beginnings — how to start the story, how to keep it running and how to get out of it.

Sitting at the other end of the line in my chair in the second-floor garret of our little rented house in Berrien Springs, I wrote down exactly what Reggie said and began to panic. How could I possibly wedge all that information into a story of 800 words?

I planned to reprint a 1979 article I wrote for The New York Times, but the Times wanted me to pay them $520 to reprint a story they paid me $75 to write. Didn't seem right. While the story, *as it appears in the Times*, belongs to the newspaper, the actual text that I wrote, *under no contract with the Times*, belongs to me. To avoid reproducing anything the Times might claim as theirs, I rewrote head, subhead and dateline, retyped the piece and set it in three rather than six-column spread. I am reprinting, on the next page, the wording of my story.

The New Yawn Tripe, Sunday, November 11, 1979

Secession try 'just too far out'

Special to The New Yawn Tripe

EDWARDSBURG, Mich., Nov. 10 — "And who would cut up Michigan?"

That line from a song briefly popular during an even briefer Michigan border war with Ohio, back in 1835, might well be sung today, although it is quite clear who wants to carve Cass County from Michigan's southern boundary with Indiana.

A group of 13 businessmen from this town of 1,107 have called for Cass County to secede from Michigan and join with Indiana, where the economic climate for small businesses, they maintain, is healthier.

The campaign is unlike the "Toledo War" of the last century, which punctuated Michigan's rise to statehood in the 19th century and pitted Michiganders against Ohioans in a contest that determined the ownership of Toledo and the Maumee River's mouth. The hostility in the current border controversy is directed against the home state.

The movement, which calls itself Citizens For Secession, has as its principal spokesman a former marriage counselor who has a University of Detroit master's degree in theology and who has practiced law in Cass County for the last two years. Before that the spokesman, William LaBre, was a lawyer in Mishawaka, Ind., a suburb of South Bend.

Bad for business

Mr. LaBre accuses the state's legislature of ignoring the needs of its country cousins. "Unfortunately," he says, "the Michigan Legislature is approximately 65 percent big-city oriented and will in all probability remain so. Over half of the Michigan House of Representatives are elected from Wayne, Oakland and Macomb Counties, which is the Detroit metropolitan area."

The Citizens For Secession vice chairman, Richard L. Christiansen, 42-year-old owner of Dick Christiansen Industries, Inc., in Edwardsburg, points to himself as a prime example of a Michigan businessman who has been victimized by a state government unwilling to deal with the problems businessmen have when competing with their cohorts just a few miles south.

Workmen's compensation payments run six to seven times as much in Michigan as they do in Indiana, Mr. Christiansen says, and his company, which produces aluminum parts for the recreational vehicle industry focused on Elkhart, Ind., cannot compete with Indiana-based plants working on comparable contracts.

The Cass County secessionists have picked up momentum, drawing 50 people to their most recent meeting — including six representatives from the Upper Peninsula who want that region to become the 51st state, to be called Superior.

In Lansing, the state capital, Paula Holmes, 27, assistant press secretary to Gov. William G. Milliken, said, "I think we very much want Cass County to remain a part of Michigan, but we will try to address their problems."

The issue is to be brought before the Cass County Commission Tuesday, but no decision is expected. The commission itself can schedule a secession, or the residents may obtain a vote through petition. If the county approved secession, the move would then have to be adopted by both the Michigan and Indiana legislatures.

Cass County Commissioner Johnie A. Rodebush expressed the more or less prevailing sense of loyalty to Michigan in practical terms: "It's just too far out. Every doctor, lawyer, mechanic, and other professional person would suddenly find themselves without a license."

chapter 16

beating a dead horse

John Campbell is no Journalist. At the time this happened, around 1979, John was a teacher at the juvenile home where my wife also was a teacher of delinquent kids. But you may get a sense of John's business acumen when I tell you that he went to auctioneer school and eventually started running his own antique sales. Before that happened, however, he was sitting in the living room of our little rented house listening to me tell a story about a story.

It started with a yarn told to me by Scott Aiken, about the Morris Volunteer Fire Department, an independent fire company. These firemen (and believe me, they were always men!) had contracts to provide firefighting service to small towns in the area. They supported their department with money they raised from pancake breakfasts and using their tanker to fill or empty swimming pools.

They took no tax money. Not a dime.

Not a dime? Wow! That was my lead! Taxes are always a sore point, and a story about a service normally provided by government that took no tax money would catch eyes. If I wrote it right. I made sure I made that point in the first line. Bill Sonneborn, the Tribune's Michiana Magazine editor, bought it. I shipped it down to Bob Kirk at the News and he bought it.

(Lo these many years later, I realize the Morris volunteers WERE TOO taking tax money, though indirectly, through contracts with nearby towns.)

At that point, more important things took over my life, such as the birth of our first son, and I filed the story away for future reference. Like my Ponte Vecchio story, this is one that probably could sell today, with some tinkering. If any of the people I quoted are dead, I'd want to know it and say so. But if the Morris fire department is still putting on those pancake breakfasts and filling pools, that story has legs.

That is what prompted John Campbell to say, "Man, talk about beating a dead horse!"

If that dead horse can still be ridden, why not?

2-B—THE DETROIT NEWS—Friday, December 22, 1978

PHOTO BY JOEL THURTELL
Two-stall firehouse of Morris Volunteer Fire Department near Niles.

Town's dinners keep fire engines running

By JOEL THURTELL
News Special Writer

NILES, Mich. — In an age of inflation when wages, prices and equipment costs spiral upward like a house ablaze, can a rural fire department provide adequate service without asking a penny of taxes?

From a statistical standpoint, the Morris Volunteer Fire Department, Inc., faces a virtually impossible task. But they do get the job done, somehow.

The Morris Volunteers, operating from a two-stall station just outside Niles, form one of the last private fire departments in Michigan. The 30-man unit is not subject to — or supported by — local government, but by state and federal rules for nonprofit organizations.

HOW DO THEY raise a $4,000 annual budget to remain independent?

"It takes plenty of pancake dinners and back-breaking work," said A. L. Dulin, 68, who has been a member since the Niles Township Fire Department voted him out in 1948 because he moved from the township into the city of Niles.

The Morris Volunteers, who have no residency requirements, quickly recruited Dulin.

The force was founded in 1941 by the late E. M. Morris, who owned a 1,000-acre farm in the area and supported the volunteers until his death in 1951.

Morris, who made most of his money as head of a loan company called the Associates, purchased the property in the Depression-era 1930's when public services were sparse in this area.

What Morris and his neighbors lacked most, however, was security from a destructive fire.

SO MORRIS BUILT a small firehouse on his land in 1940 and underwrote the expense of a volunteer department. He began by ordering a Dodge truck and had an 800-gallon water tank mounted on it along with a 90-gallons-per-minute pump.

When their patron died, the Morris Farm Volunteer Fire Department faced a crisis. They would continue to serve without pay, but could not sustain their equipment or other needs.

So they registered as a nonprofit organization and became the Morris Volunteer Fire Department, Inc.

Now the pancake dinners and related self-help projects began. For example, the tanker truck was used to empty swimming pools in the fall and refill them in spring.

Eventually the old Dodge was replaced by a 1946 radio-equipped model, later supplemented with a fully equipped 1967 Ford tanker. Currently, the volunteers are converting a second-hand utility truck into a second tanker.

Eight veterans of the early days still sign on the company's roster.

A charter member, Howard Nieb, remains active on the unit's roster at 84 and several retired professional fire fighters from Niles have joined.

Reprinted courtesy of The Detroit News.

chapter 17

cops & robbers

The jangle reverberated through our little house in Berrien Springs. At three in the morning, a ringing phone would jolt us out of our sleep and frighten us with thoughts of tragedy. Family tragedy? Bad news, it turns out, was what this call was about, though nobody we knew was involved. I scrambled out of bed and made for the phone.

"The Apostolic Church is up in flames!" a man shouted. This was Lyle Sumerix, veteran reporter in the South Bend Tribune's Niles bureau. Except Lyle wasn't in Niles. He was home in Buchanan, where a police scanner or maybe a fireman buddy had let him know that a church in Berrien Springs — my beat — was on fire.

If I'd thought my new reporting career would focus on meetings of government bodies and cute features, I was mistaken. And I HAD thought just that. I wanted to pick the cherries from the low branches.

Turned out there was gravel with the gravy.

I hopped out of bed, searched for my trusty Alpa 9d camera. I searched for a roll of film. The Tribune provided us stringers with free black-and-white film, lots of it, but I hadn't bothered to keep my camera loaded. That was a habit that would soon change. Anyway, I loaded the Alpa with film and remembered to put some clothes on.

By the time I got to the church, it was no longer in flames. In the time it took me to find film, wind it into my camera, toss on some clothes, look up the church's address in the phone book, and hit the road, volunteer firefighters had quelled the flames. Nothing but charred lumber to take a picture of. I took that picture, because when their backs are to the wall, editors sometimes will run anything.

Later that summer of 1978, a fierce wind swept into the valley of the St. Joseph River, knocking down trees and damaging houses. Another call from Lyle and I was on my way. This one was so close, I could walk, and a good thing, because there was no place to park my old Plymouth Valiant slant-six. Police events are great tourist attractions. The babble at the scene was about tornadoes.

Tornado! Well, there was then and ever will be debate over whether this particular high-velocity wind was actually a twister. But who cares?

The mere suggestion, even when larded with doubt, certainly juiced up the top of that story.

And so it is for stringers: The gravy of the meetings and features routine is now and then interrupted by the grunt work of heading out at ungodly times to cover awful events.

Homicides. Train derailments. Car wrecks. Car-train crashes. Double homicides. Bank robberies. House fires. Cattle rustlers. Pot busts. Triple homicides, aka triple-baggers. Floods. Windstorms.

I admit it: I thought at the time that writing police news was a royal pain in the ass. At the time, I was writing a novel. Please don't bother me with trifles.

Literature!

This cop stuff was pretty lowbrow, seemed like. Stuff of supermarket tabloids.

Think again.

I did.

Covering cops and fires is the most basic reporting there is. And it is absolutely necessary in a democracy that these agencies be covered, and covered well and thoroughly. And I gotta say that in that day, and in this one, that job was and is being done at best in a half-baked way.

Often, reporters cozy up to cops and prosecutors, because they depend on officials to feed them their news. It's a lazy way to work, but it happens at the best of newspapers. Now, The New York Times admits it dropped the ball and relied too much on biased government sources during the run-up to the George W. Bush administration's invasion of Iraq in 2003. Well, the same bad things can happen when reporters give public safety officers a free ride. In the 1980s, I worked in a Detroit Free Press bureau alongside two ace reporters, John Castine and Dennis Niemiec, who were assailed by many police officers for uncovering and reporting a series of pathological lies and cover-ups by cops in suburban Detroit.

Back in my day in southwestern Michigan as a South Bend Tribune staffer, I wrote about seven firefighters in the town of Decatur who, for a lark, were setting fires to buildings, then going back to the firehouse to wait for somebody to call in the blazes that they then swooped down on and extinguished. Dangerous fun. Felonious fun. They wound up with jail time. What made them think they could get away with it?

Here's one possibility: Lax coverage by local news outlets.

Here's a story you could probably write today: Beer in the firehouse.

Yep, Lyle himself told me many of the fire halls in that day had kegs in the fridge, so that hot and tired firemen — always men — could relax with a cold one after putting out a fire. Heroes deserve a break, right?

Except that in one town, the keg was being drained BEFORE the fires, and firefighters were drunk at emergency scenes. I did not write that story. In conversations with colleagues, I sensed that this particular story would be pushing the envelope a bit too far. I had a publisher once who contended that the fire hall was the most democratic institution in the land. Might as well attack apple pie and the flag. I wish I'd written that story. The problem was getting sources. The person who told me was a firefighter who feared the social consequences — ostracism in a small town — that being my source would have meant for him and his family. I could deal with being persona non grata, but for someone with roots in the community, being a news source is fraught with risk.

Still, I regret not finding a way to write that story. We should not be letting any institution that is fundamental to public safety skate free.

Writing the cop story, even the shortest of cop stories known as a "brief," is Class 101 in the Shoestring J School.

Often, it's a simple thing to collect the "who, what, where and when" of a story and pump all those facts into a single-sentence lead. Or is it? Ever seen a police report? In a few, very few, departments, report-writing has been elevated to an art, and sergeants play a dual role as English teachers, enforcing good grammar and cogent storytelling. More often, reports are rife with misspellings and errant logic. It is the Journalist's task to make sense of the basic police report. But we are not alone. Think of the county prosecutor whose job is making enough sense out of cops' reports to convince jurors that a defendant is guilty.

Most of the time, the basics will wind up being the top of your story. Such a story might start like this:

BERRIEN SPRINGS — Police arrested three St. Joseph men at 5 a.m. Sunday after they fled from the Fill & Spill Gas Station without paying for five gallons of fuel.

There is much to be said for using the good old inverted pyramid to write most cops stories. The idea is that the basic and most important facts are carried in the first lines of the story. That way, if editors need to trim for space, they can cut from the bottom and, if the news hole is really tight, let the first sentence stand. If well-written, the lead will make sense all by itself.

If there is nothing outstanding about the tale, there likely won't be any way to eke a funny or even suspenseful yarn out of the police blotter's humdrum list of facts. So the who-what-where-when lead will work best. But sometimes, a lead is all it takes to induce a chuckle, which happened to me when I found my little June 11, 1982, South Bend Tribune story:

VANDALIA — Two Niles men were caught Thursday while allegedly attempting to steal a 390-pound hog from a farm near here, according to the Cass County sheriff's office.

Some reporters like to take laptop computers to the cop shop and write their stories directly upon first reading of the police reports. My approach was different. I liked to read the reports, take notes or get photocopies of the ones that intrigued me, and then ponder them on my way back to the office. Or if I took notes by phone from a desk cop reading the overnight reports, I'd think about the stories while sipping a cup of coffee. Sometimes, upon reflection, I'd see a better way to write the story than simply reverting to the old inverted pyramid formula.

For instance, there was the May 18, 1981, story I wrote about a state legislator who smashed his car into a tree while making campaign rounds.

Hmmm. Well, I could have just said that, but the story would look like every other reporter's story. One thing I learned from stringing — if my stories read like everybody's stories, they wouldn't stand out. Unlike a staffer, the stringer doesn't get paid unless her or his work is used. A staffer gets paid anyway. So, if I want to sell a story to an editor, I MUST make it appear different. Enticing. Amusing. Worth paying for.

There has to be spriteliness, there has to be zest, there has to be a gleam in the eye.

There has to be FUN in our stories. Learn that behavior as a stringer, and it will serve you well even if you are so unwise as to take a staff job. Did I have fun writing this one?

VOLINIA — In his campaign for the 4th District Congressional seat, state Rep. Mark Siljander was on the stump again Tuesday—this time literally.

The 29-year-old candidate was riding in a car bound for Dowagiac on Marcellus Highway one-quarter-mile east of Decatur Road when at about 9:32 a.m. the vehicle crossed a patch of ice, slid, and struck a tree head-on, according to Cass County sheriff's deputies.

Siljander and the car's driver, Michael Ridenour, 24, of Alexandria, Va., were treated and released from Lee Memorial Hospital in Dowagiac.

Nancy Claire, 23, of Mount Pleasant, who was riding in the back seat, was not injured in the crash. The automobile was severely damaged, a deputy said.

The accident happened about seven miles east of Dowagiac.

I find myself nitpicking retrospectively at this story. "About 9:32 a.m."? That's pretty precise to be "about."

And maybe I should have inserted the seven-mile distance from Dowagiac higher in the story.

Always easy to second-guess deadline writing. I picked this one up from a desk sergeant in Cassopolis, who read the dry-as-bones press release ("Cass County Sheriff James Northrop reports that...") to me over the phone somewhere around seven in the morning, and within an hour I'd written that story and others gleaned from phone calls to the Cass County Sheriff's Department, Michigan State Police post in White Pigeon and various village police departments. I wrote them in my own way and sent them before the 11 a.m. deadline to South Bend.

If you can eke a little humor, a bit of irony, out of a seemingly boring report, go for it. Warning: Not all editors will accept it. But it's always worth a try.

Cops briefs can be fun.

Oh, yes, and poking fun at people — even cops — is part of the fun, as in this Tribune story I wrote in the early 1980s.

LAWRENCE — Policemen here are learning first-hand what it means to walk a beat.

A part-time officer in the Lawrence Police Department early this morning wrecked the town's only squad car.

But cops reporting is not all fun and games. Much of it is deadly serious. And when it's serious, when people are hurt or killed and tragedy overshadows the story, the tone can never be tongue-in-cheek. The job then is to wrap the facts into a lead that sums up the essence of the story. While humorless, there's no reason why the story's top can't be compelling, or ironic, as in this depressing story I wrote for the June 20, 1981, Tribune.

BENTON HARBOR — A man who called a crisis hotline early this morning and threatened to kill himself carried out his promise a half hour later, but apparently by accident.

Benton Twp. Police said at 2:12 a.m. they received a call from Help

Line, a St. Joseph crisis intervention center, reporting that Larry Joe Burns, 31, of City of David, Cabin 184, had called to say he had a gun pointed at his head and he intended to shoot himself.

Officers Keith Diamond and Ronald Kinzle of the Benton Twp. Police Department went to the scene and found Burns in Cabin 186. According to police, Diamond and Kinzle had nearly convinced Burns he should seek counseling at the Riverwood Community Mental Health Center when Burns said he wanted to talk once more with the person on the crisis line.

Burns still held a .22-caliber rifle aimed at his head, and officers reported that as he reached for the telephone, his hand accidentally pushed the trigger and the rifle discharged.

The bullet hit Burns in the head. He was dead on arrival at Mercy Hospital here.

Police said the shot was not intentional.

Mostly, the police beat will bring you sad, sad stories. It's one of the reasons I cringed at the thought of working the cops beat. Life is tough enough, why ask for more sadness?

Yet, we stringers learn from the troubles of others. I'll never look at an open can of soda pop on a hot summer day without remembering how a slug of soda ended a life with a wasp sting on the inside of the throat. Or the woman who learned that all snakes are not garter snakes when she moved one from the path of her lawn mower and found out that drop for drop, a Michigan massasauga's venom is more potent than that of the much bigger western diamondback rattler. And there is the subject of loaded pistols — how easy it is for them to wind up in the hands of kids lacking a sense of what harm bullets can do. Stories I'll never forget.

A stringer is not a specialist. Neither feature stories, nor investigative reports, nor meeting write-ups, nor cops articles are the stringer's single fare. EVERYTHING that needs to be reported, and this includes death reports, should be fair game. The stringer has to be ready for anything.

chapter 18

sniffin' stories

I was reading over a yellowed newspaper clipping, getting ready to pontificate about the virtues of enterprise and imagination, when I saw something that really made my blood boil.

What? No photo credit?

Gross incompetence!

I can't believe it. What I'm looking at — had dug out so I could, as I say, pontificate about it — is what I consider to be the first of what true Journalists call "enterprise stories" that I ever wrote. I was a brand-new stringer with the Tribune, and the story is dated July 13, 1978. By "brand-new," I mean I'd been writing for the Tribune for all of about three weeks, maybe a month if I was lucky.

Doing what big-city reporters look down on as scut work. Covering school board and township board meetings and sitting through two village council meetings a month. It was at one of those meetings, possibly the first one I ever attended, where I introduced myself to Edgar Kesterke, the village president, and Wade Gorham, the village clerk, then took a seat and pulled out my notebook. If the meetings started pushing towards 10 o'clock, I'd shut my notebook and amble on home. Ten o'clock was when my favorite television program came on. "Lou Grant." About another newspaper called the Tribune, a fictitious paper in Los Angeles. Ed Asner played Lou Grant, the no-nonsense, feisty, full of common sense city desk editor of the LA Trib. Remember I said I never took a Journalism class in my life? Well, "Lou Grant" is the closest thing to a Journalism course I've ever had.

It was during one of these village council meetings that the town's public works manager, Cleon Reitz (and I didn't make that name up), stood up and warned council members the town had best stop burning rubbish at Shamrock Park down by the St. Joseph River. Burning within 1,000 feet of village limits is illegal, Cleon said, and the Michigan Department of Natural Resources guy had warned him to quit doing it. Cleon added that he was headed out for a week or two of vacation.

A couple of days later, I was pedaling my trusty Schwinn over the U.S. 31 bridge that spans the St. Joe River when what did I smell? Yes, literally sniff out? And then what did I see? Why, billows of white smoke

Chapter 18

Reprinted courtesy of the South Bend Tribune.

coming up from Shamrock Park and making a nice thick white blanket over the river and the bridge.

Wait a minute, I thought, as I braked my bike. Doggonit, they aren't supposed to burn! I waited and watched. Sure enough, it was a big brush fire, just what Cleon said the DNR didn't want. I turned my bike around and pumped hard for home. I ran inside and found my trusty Alpa 9d 35-millimeter single lens reflex camera with the Macro-Switar f 1.8 lens I was so proud of. Wouldn't be needing the macro feature for this picture. I made sure I had film wound into the body and pedaled back to the river. Hope I didn't miss it! No worry. If anything, the smoke was even thicker. I shot a few frames, then headed back home, where I traded the Schwinn for my old 1965 Plymouth Valiant with the slant six engine. Front end very shaky, but still working. I drove it and my film down to Niles, Michigan, where South Bend Tribune reporters would leave their film at the Michigan State Police post so someone — I never learned who — could pick up the film and have it in the photo lab's hands in time for the afternoon paper.

And this is why I'm so bent out of shape today, more than three decades after I wrote that story and took that picture. No photo credit! Doggone it, I went to a lot of trouble to take the photo and then get the film where the paper needed it. I phoned them a cutline for the photo that said, "SMOKE OVER THE ST. JOSEPH — Berrien Springs village employes burn brush by Shamrock Park, where a state investigator has ordered all burning to cease."

The story, under the headline "Burning resumes despite order," reported the defiance of Clerk Gorham, who told the state to fly a kite.

Next time I stopped in to cover a village council meeting, things were a bit frosty. You get used to that. They do their jobs, I do mine.

But here's the neat thing: Having sat through that meeting, I was aware that burning was a no-no. Therefore, the town's defiance, once I literally sniffed it out, was a surefire story.

Believe me when I say that there were weeks in that little town when I couldn't smell anything of news importance. Certainly not by, say, big-city standards. A few miles west, Benton Harbor was always in financial trouble, somebody was always suspected of rigging the books or some factory was moving out or somebody was getting shot or knifed. All of which made work for reporters.

I got my brush story one week, but there were a lot of weeks in that town of 2,000 people when nothing of consequence happened. Or so it would seem. Sometimes we have to shift our standards a bit. Again, it pays to look and listen.

One day, a secretary from the village offices a couple of doors down from The Journal Era dropped off a legal ad. It was a warning. The village was going to start enforcing its noxious weed ordinance. Got poison ivy? Better kill it, or the village will fine you. Tough stuff.

Now it happens that I grew up next to a huge state forest. I spent a lot of time in the woods. Sometimes I feel like I never came out. But I know what poison ivy looks like. Those three leaves are a giveaway.

I knew I had a good little story for that week's paper. I took my old Alpa 9d camera down to the other village park, known as The Grove, where huge old oak trees gave lots of shade for picnickers — and vines as thick as your wrist clung to the trees and ascended out of sight into the tops of those oaks. What kind of plants were those vines?

Reprinted courtesy of The (Berrien Springs) Journal Era

Poison ivy!

The village was in violation of its own noxious weed ordinance, as I pointed out in the caption of the photo I took of a triptych of giant green leaves.

Okay, so I'm a smart-ass. You wanta sell papers?

Publishing that little piece was a two-step process. First, I had to have the village's ad copy that was the warning. Something official was afoot.

What we call the news peg.

And we duly published that warning and were paid for it.

The village did not pay us for the little afterburner we gave their ad by way of my sarcastic poison ivy photo.

But to do this story, we needed that official warning, and we needed for me, or someone, to know that the village was cultivating a poison ivy patch of its own.

What more did we need?

Well, friends, I can tell you there are many small and some large papers that wouldn't have run that smart-ass piece for fear of pissing off village bigwigs. Here's some arithmetic: When my friends John and Pat Gillette bought the weekly, the circulation, although this fact was hidden from them, was 700. Seven hundred people were paying to have the paper mailed to them. Pitiful. When I left a year and a quarter later, we had 2,000 paid subscribers.

People don't like hypocrisy. People who read newspapers expect the editors and reporters to expose double standards.

So here we are — no news, nothing to write about. Time to change the standards. No, we don't make up the news. We redefine it.

Poison ivy, city-sponsored, is news.

The St. Joe River was a regular source of stories and photos. Some situations are win-win. Driving alongside the St. Joe one spring day, I noticed what looked like suds on the surface of the river. Brownish-white foam — lots of it. Somebody had mentioned it to me. Could there have been a chemical spill? Maybe somebody's emptying their laundry into the river.

I went down to the river, took some photos of suds. Then I called the Department of Natural Resources. No, I was told, what you're seeing is no spill of man-made contaminants. It's a naturally occurring phenomenon. Nature's acids — called tannins and lignins — come from leaves and branches and downed trees that submerge in the river. The water leaches the acids out of the wood or leaves and makes foam.

Darn, someone said, no story.

M-1 The South Bend Tribune, Sunday, March 11, 1979

Brown suds likely to be nature's brew, DNR says

Foam on the rivers

By JOEL THURTELL
Tribune Correspondent

GRAND RAPIDS — A state water quality expert here Friday said the brown foam visible on several Michigan rivers is probably caused by soft water from melting snow and rain runoff combined with acids from decaying plants.

But he added that the Michigan Department of Natural Resources (DNR) is now investigating complaints of river scum on a case-by-case basis.

Reports of a brownish foam on stream surfaces came last week from Watervliet concerning the Paw Paw River, and from Berrien Springs by the St. Joseph River. A similar frothing condition has been observed along the Kalamazoo River, according to James Turk, DNR water quality specialist.

Turk, who is based in Grand Rapids, said he relies heavily upon telephone reports about river conditions from citizens and government authorities in the southwestern part of Michigan because his office is too far from those areas for him to make frequent on-site checks. But the brown foam, which sometimes collects in small coves or around floating tree limbs and may puff up to heights of more than a foot, is not an unnatural occurrence on many rivers at this time of year, he indicated.

One cause of the foam is soft water flowing down hills and through streams into the relatively hard water of rivers in southern Michigan, Turk said. While water in northern rivers is soft and therefore shows little effect from the influx of heavy springtime feeder streams, the soft rain and melting snow waters create foam when they contact the hard water of the southern Michigan river.

"We get the foaming quite often in Grand Rapids when we get a snow melt or a rain," Turk observed.

In addition to the action of soft water meeting hard water, Turk cited the presence of natural soaps formed from decaying organic materials such as dead fragments of trees, weeds, and leaves. These decaying materials are washed into rivers during the spring. Two results of their decomposition are the natural acids tannin and lignin which cause the brown color which can be seen both in the surface foam and in the river itself.

Although these organic acids do not change the chemical composition of the water, their "staining" effect is behind the muddy appearance of lower Michigan rivers in the spring months. During winter, when these acids are absent from the water, the rivers are "crystal clear," Turk said.

Turk said the DNR will work on the assumption that the foaming and discoloration stem from natural causes unless its representatives find evidence of a "point source," or specific spot on a river where contamination materials are entering the water.

All reports of foam on rivers are investigated, Turk said, and DNR staff workers are even now trying to identify the causes of recent sightings of river scum.

SUDS ON THE ST. JOE — Foam, seen last week at different points along the St. Joseph River, is due to "natural soaps" caused by decaying plant material washed into the river, as well as soft water from rain and melting snow as it mixes with the relatively hard water of the river, according to Michigan Department of Natural Resources officials. This view of the suds was taken at Berrien Springs below the I & M dam.
Tribune Photo by Joel Thurtell

Reprinted courtesy of the South Bend Tribune.

No story? You kidding? Why, people were calling to tell me about some chemical spill. They need to know that there's nothing wrong. And the explanation about tannins and lignins gives reporters a chance to teach a little and maybe show people that not everything they read in the newspaper is about something dreadful.

Besides, bottom line, I'm a stringer and I get paid for producing copy and photos. I don't get paid if I shrug and say there's no story. You can be pretty sure that if I spend time on it, this will be a story.

Puts me in mind of the time Charlie Mierau called from Stevensville on the coast of Lake Michigan to report there was a hole in the Indiana & Michigan Electric Co. dam a mile or so from our newsroom in Berrien Springs. Charlie had sold the weekly to the Gillettes, but still owned the Lakeshore Courier, which covered Stevensville although it was put together in our shop.

A hole in the dam!

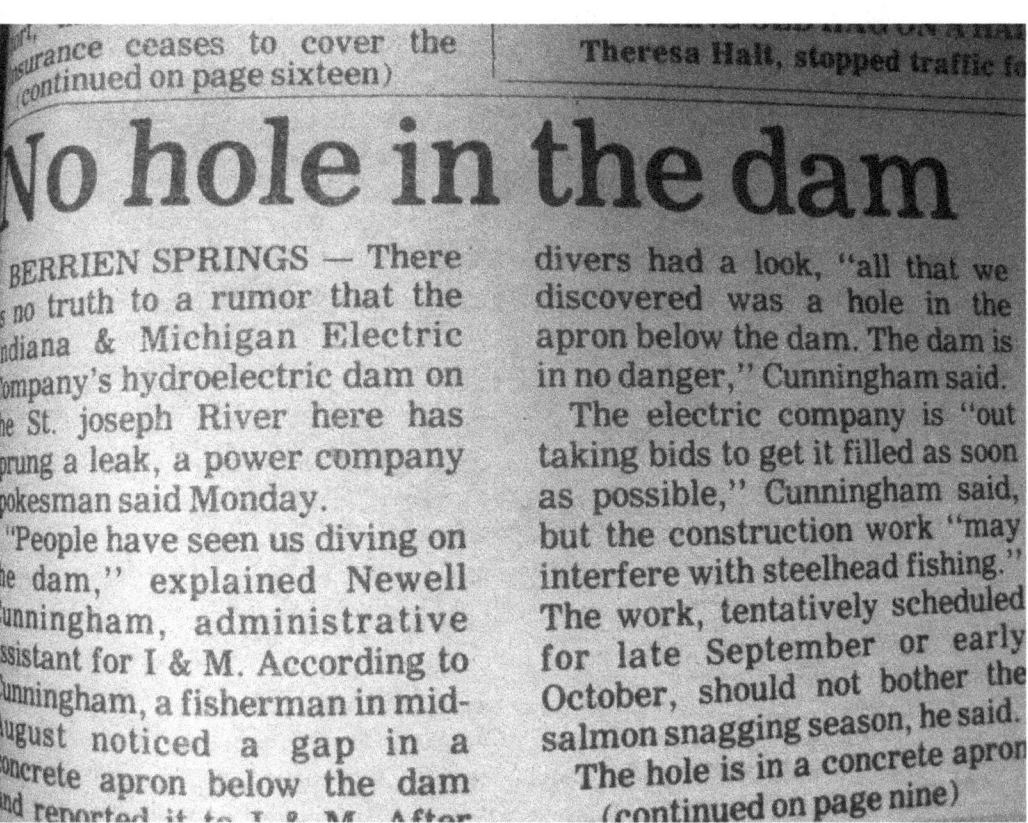

Reprinted courtesy of The (Berrien Springs) Journal Era

The story was making the rounds. Sounded like baloney to me. If there was a hole in that dam, water would be rushing through. The U.S. 31 bridge might be in danger. But no water was rushing anywhere. I called the power company. Divers, it turned out, were inspecting the bottom of the dam. Eyewitnesses, putting two and two together, came up with five and started the rumor that the dam had blown.

Story?

Absolutely.

See what I mean?

Who says nothing happens in a dinky little burg?

At one of those village council meetings, the sessions that could run so long and be so boring, I heard something which, taken by itself, was unpleasant and nasty — a mean-spirited attack on a widow who kept a bunch of cats whose presence offended a neighbor.

The two opponents were both shopkeepers. John Weakley ran the Continental Barbershop and he wore a star — he was the elected constable of Oronoko Township, a political entity that surrounded and took in the village of Berrien Springs. Ruth Johnson owned a newspaper store — she sold newspapers, magazines and candy. She lived in an apartment above her store, and she liked cats.

Too much and too many, said Weakley, who reported to council members that he was having trouble with cat poop. According to my September 10, 1980, story, "Council acts on Weakley 'fecal matter' complaint," city officials could have forced Ruth to reduce her cat population to five, though apparently they couldn't stop her from feeding cats outside. Ruth told me she had nine cats.

"Off the record," Weakley said in the public meeting, "It was 38 one time."

By the way, "off the record" in a public meeting? What arrogance! All words uttered in a public meeting are on the record by definition. I put that quote in the story.

Ruth Johnson didn't attend the meeting.

The next day, I walked over to her shop and asked her about the cats. She reported having a conversation with the barber-constable that went this way:

Weakley: Your cat shit on my doorstep.

Johnson: Well, take some warm soapy water and swish it away.

Weakley: Is that what I'm supposed to do?

Johnson: Either that, or you can step in it. Just be thankful it wasn't an elephant.

To me, Johnson said, "At least the cat had the right idea — picked

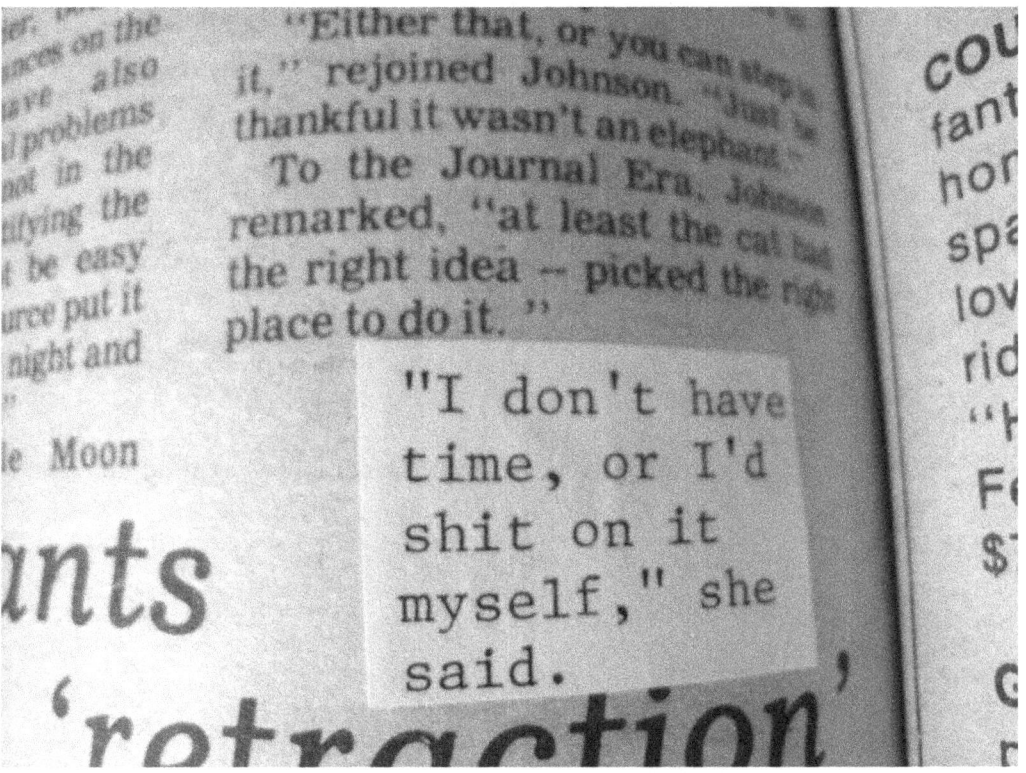

I restored the kicker to my copy of the paper.

the right place to do it. I don't have time, or I'd shit on it myself."

Now I have to tell you something. That is exactly what she said. But there was a battle royal in our newsroom between my publishers, John and Pat Gillette.

No way did Pat want the word "shit" to appear in her newspaper. John thought the whole series of one-liners was hilarious. This was a huge argument between spouses. Karen and I have never argued, of course, but when we do, I like third parties to remain neutral. Therefore, I stayed out of the Gillettes' fracas. In the end, Pat won, sort of. They agreed to lop the last sentence off the story: No more would the line, "I don't have time, or I'd shit on it myself" grace the end of my story. Yet John and I won, too, because we still had Weakley telling Ruth, "Your cat shit on my doorstep"

I don't recall ever getting "shit" into the Free Press, but I managed to get "fart" in. That's a story for another book. Back to my original report of illegal burning. Can you believe those knuckleheads not giving me credit for that "Smoke over the St. Joseph" photo? I hustled for that story and drove the film all the way down to Niles.

More than three decades later and I'm still pissed. A wise old reporter once told me, "Joel, never look at your stories in the paper. It will only make you unhappy."

Newspaper people will talk about certain towns (Detroit is one) as great news cities. That's because they produce lots of murder, mayhem and scandal. But what if you live in a town that's kind of short on corruption and violence?

Hey, the crime stuff is actually easy. It comes looking for you. But in a place that's supposedly dead, you have to go hunting. Tune your ears. Somebody complaining about cat shit? Talk to the cats' host.

Hey, talk to the cats!

Wonderful, even funny, stories are waiting for those who can see or hear them.

chapter 19

get rattlesnakes!

There are editors who will tell you no story will work without a so-called "hook" to hang it from. They want some action, something going on, NEWS, in the narrowest sense, before these editors (and of course, I have names in mind!) will approve a story. I lived through a phase in the newspaper biz when many wonderful stories either didn't get written or were done by the competition because of one editor's prejudice against what generally are called feature stories.

What is a "hook"? Well, my little story about illegal brush burning had a hook. What was happening? Brush fire. What else? State warned village not to burn. What else? Village burned anyway. And more — I caught it as it happened, with my camera. Can't have a better hook than that.

But what if there are no hooks? No news, right?

Are you sure there's nothing going down? If it's a small town you're covering, try driving slowly along streets looking for something interesting. A photographer once closed her eyes and put her finger on a map. Where her fingertip landed was where she went. There was a quickie oil change shop at the corner, so she took pictures of oil being changed beneath a car. She made a photo-story of the goings on. There was no news, but the photo along with a caption told a tale. Incidentally, she placed names and faces of the oil changers in the paper, which is always a nice thing to do and helped sell a few copies.

Okay, what if there really is nothing, NOTHING, going on. I have an idea for you.

Get rattlesnakes.

That's right, this one will always be good. In fact, it's time it was done again. I did it a good 20 years ago. Do you live near a zoo? Or maybe a research university? You will need some help.

Actually, what you'll be needing is someone who knows how to handle venomous reptiles. That is very, very important. Maybe you'd want to sign up for a good life insurance policy, too.

It came about like this: I told a magazine editor a story about a guy who nearly died from the bite of a rattlesnake in southwestern Michigan. The editor was not aware there were venomous snakes in Michigan.

SNAKES ON SALE

Florida company flies deadly goods to catalog shoppers

BY JOEL THURTELL
Free Press Staff Writer

Big black handprinted letters on the box warned, LIVE POISONOUS SNAKES.

Inside the double-boxed crate lay two large rattlesnakes and a thin, yellow-eyed Asian pit viper neatly coiled in cloth bags and waiting for release.

A fast, tireless ratcheting sound, like a child's windup toy that won't run down, gently vibrated the box's plywood top.

With help from a University of Michigan herpetologist, a fat, 3-foot-long Eastern Diamondback rattlesnake slid out of a sack and onto the concrete floor of the University of Michigan's Natural Science Museum.

The rattler flicked its black forked tongue. Its tail was a clattering blur.

"Can you believe you just bought this with your Mastercard?" asked Dan York, a PhD candidate in biology.

Last week, York helped the Free Press prove that anyone with a telephone and a credit card can buy poisonous snakes, regardless of their training or reason for possessing the deadly creatures.

The Free Press snake purchase — $105, plus $31.92 in air freight charges — was made from a Florida dealer who advertises by direct mail and listed 51 poisonous species for sale in a July 1988 catalog.

See SNAKES, Page 13A

A close view of a 3-foot Eastern Diamondback rattlesnake, one of three poisonous snakes the Free Press purchased from a Florida company. The firm lists 51 poisonous snake species in a catalog.

ALAN R. KAMUDA/Detroit Free Press

Reprinted by permission of the Detroit Free Press

The snakes arrived as freight on a Delta Air Lines passenger flight. In Delta's freight depot, a woman read the crate and quickly backed away, gasping, "Oh, my goodness!"

The U.S. Postal Service forbids shipment of snakes or poisonous animals through the mail, according to Don Rouse, a supervisor in the Dearborn Post Office, so reptile dealers often ship by air freight.

Delta air freight worker Jerry Bigelow said, "Most of the people who handle them here do not like to. If I didn't have to handle them for my job, I would not."

From Metro Airport, the vipers — all three snakes fit that scientific category — rode in a reporter's hatchback to Ann Arbor. Earlier, York, 33, placed one restriction on the experiment.

"I'm a coward herpetologist," he explained. "I'm scared of snakes, so I won't work with cobras or mambas — they're just too dangerous. . . ."

But the purchase could easily have included cobras and mambas. The dealer lists a West African green mamba for sale at $275. The list also includes Egyptian cobras at $65 each, monacle cobras at $40 and several other cobra species, as well as bushmasters, kraits, gaboon vipers, puff adders and Florida cottonmouths.

"Fun for the whole family," the dealer's catalog

remarks about its 5-foot West African spitting cobras, $55. Spitting cobras eject venom at their victims' eyes, and have caused blindness in some people who were not immediately treated, according to Dr. Findlay Russell, who wrote the textbook, "Snake Venom Poisoning."

"I'll tell you, I think this whole thing is horrible," said Detroit Zoo Director Steve Graham. "I don't believe in exotic pets at all."

Graham is convinced that most poisonous reptiles are bought for private home collections. He favors a state ban on keeping any kind of wildlife as pets.

But the dealer, Chris McQuade, said, "Where do you draw the line? Do you give somebody a written examination or an oral examination to see if they have the ability to adequately handle the animals? Putting a pit bull in the hands of somebody who doesn't know how to handle it is equally as dangerous."

Graham said owners of exotic pets "want to draw attention to themselves. A pretty green snake with blue stripes is one thing, but the real macho is to have a poisonous snake."

Graham admitted that occasionally the Detroit Zoo buys from the same Florida dealer, but said zoos are minor players in the poisonous snake trade.

"The last time the federal government did figures on animals imported into this country, they found that about 60 percent went to the pet trade," he said. "Thirty-five percent of the animals went to biomedical research, and less than 1 percent went to zoos."

Of the animals destined to be pets, "My guess is that the majority didn't live one year," he said.

Not everyone who keeps poisonous snakes survives, either.

Russell, a physician at Tucson's Arizona Health Science Center, said he received 15-20 reports last year of bites from exotic snakes, including a San Diego collector who died after his albino cobra bit him. And snakes can be used as weapons, he said.

"I have testified on three cases in which people have attempted to commit murder with snakes," Russell said.

But the snake dealer countered, "Anybody who would try to commit a murder with a venomous snake is kind of ridiculous."

Contacted after the snakes arrived, McQuade said, "If you're 21 and you live in an area where the possession of the venomous animals is not restricted or prohibited, there is nothing that would prevent us from selling the animals to you."

The Free Press order was filled by a salesman named Eric. While taking the order, he didn't ask how the snakes would be used, if the buyer knew how to feed and care for them or whether proper snakebite medications were available in area hospitals.

York, who is experienced in handling vipers, made sure that the appropriate remedies were nearby.

Eric said his firm could supply a bamboo viper for $20. Also in stock was an emerald pit viper, $75.

"They're real, real docile, but they have a hell of a long strike range if they decide to hit you," Eric said.

The decision was made not to buy the emerald pit viper. The less-expensive bamboo viper was selected.

Next, an order was placed for a rattlesnake that would look good in photographs — a 3-foot Eastern Diamondback priced at $45.

Eric said he could offer a reduced rate — $30 — on a 4-foot Western Diamondback rattler whose lighter brown and tan coloration would contrast nicely with the Eastern's black-brown-and-cream pattern.

It was agreed. Eric would throw in the Western Diamondback.

"Hey, just as a joke, tell your friend who's going to handle these that you bought an 8 1/2-foot black mamba," Eric said. "You open the cage and they'll shoot out over your head, and it's not like you live if they bite you."

The black mamba "can strike so quickly that the victim may be unaware he has been bitten," Russell wrote in "Snake Venom Poisoning."

A large black mamba can strike 5 or 6 feet and hit a human above the waist, Russell said.

One study reported a 100 percent fatality rate from black mamba bites.

Eric said his firm sells black mambas for $300 to $500, but doesn't often trade in them because they are very rarely allowed out of their native African countries.

Her disbelief, and my efforts at convincing her that there are rattlers in the Lower Peninsula, made her want to know more. Piquing her interest was, of course, what I was trying to do. I'd wanted to write an article about massasaugas ever since an acquaintance took that nearly fatal dose of venom decades ago. In the meantime, I'd written news briefs about other people who were bitten — kids at one of the Detroit-area metroparks, a neighbor in southwestern Michigan who played chicken with a baby rattler and lost, a woman who tried to move a rattler from the path of her lawn mower.

Finally, I had an editor who was interested not just in a brief, but in an all-out, well-researched article about massasaugas. By research, I mean that I drove to St. Joseph on the opposite side of the state, in quest of court records in the medical malpractice case of the fellow who nearly died, and I pored through old news and medical records, finding reference to four people who had actually died of massasauga bites. This was important, because there were — and are — people who will tell you the bite of a massasauga is no more dangerous than a mosquito bite.

I enlisted experts, one of whom was a doctoral candidate in biology at the University of Michigan whose dissertation topic was pit vipers. Rattlesnakes are pit vipers, meaning they have infrared sensing organs that can "see" in pitch darkness. I was interviewing the expert at the university's Natural History Museum when he showed me a mail-order catalog for a business in Florida that sells every imaginable species of snake, including cobras, kraits, gaboon vipers, mambas, both green and black, and yes, rattlesnakes.

Mail-order rattlesnakes. I was amazed. Using my credit card, my expert told me, I could order any of these snakes and have them shipped by air freight. That was a story separate from the magazine story about massasaugas. My expert, Dan York, offered to accept any venomous snakes I purchased over the phone, as long as they were pit vipers and as long as the university hospital had the proper antivenin on hand.

I got to work. That is to say, I picked up the phone, dialed the store in Florida and ordered 1) an eastern diamondback rattlesnake, 2) a western diamondback rattlesnake and 3) a bamboo viper. I paid for the snakes along with special packing first in cloth bags and then in a wooden box, plus shipment by Delta Airlines, giving my credit card number.

There was one bad moment when the western diamondback got loose and headed straight for me. I was armed ineffectively with a broom. The photographer, laughing, snapped away.

Page one story. Made quite a stir. State legislators huffed and puffed and introduced bills to regulate shipments of venomous reptiles into Michigan.

That was before the day of the Internet. Now, you could order the same kind of "product" via the Web. You'd need an appropriate person or organization to receive it, such as a researcher like Dan York, or a zoo looking for a free reptile acquisition.

No reason why some intrepid stringer couldn't do the same story. Several could do it in different towns. The combined power of all those stories might actually force some kind of regulation of the trade in venomous creatures.

It's a story that could be written anytime. No hook or peg needed from outside. It's kind of a do-it-yourself hook, with the writer doubling as actor and creating the need and hopefully the market for the story.

Give it a try.

Just don't pet the snakes.

chapter 20

addicted

Ain't it great to see your name over a newspaper story?
Watch out!

If your purpose for becoming a stringer is to survive as a writer of non-news stuff — novels, short stories, poetry, historical research, literary criticism, music theory, you name it — then stringing can become a pitfall, a barrier.

If you aren't careful.

Beware of becoming addicted to the sight of your own name in print.

As nice as it is to produce regular news articles and see your name over a body of text that didn't issue from your own printer, don't let that pleasure become an obsession. If you have long-range writing plans — a book, an ambitious magazine article or an unfinished doctoral dissertation — it can be easy to put the big project on a back burner while rolling with the excitement of covering daily news.

Believe me, I know. I've let it happen too many times. Covering the murder du jour can be a heady thing. Not just your name, but your reporting, is in the eye of the public. Important people — the judges, prosecutors, police detectives, defense attorneys — plus the public at large are reading what you have to say about the case. But just remember: Daily news is dead tomorrow. People house-train their puppies with your stories.

I find that a schedule helps me stay on a long-term track. If I'm writing a book, chapters are fine milestones; it's easier to feel good quickly about finishing a chapter than to sit and think about all the horrendous work left to be done before the book is finished. What time do you start working for the newspaper? Are you a morning person? Can you rise at five or six in the morning and squeeze out a half hour, an hour, maybe more time, for the Big Project before starting your cop calls?

Remember the Big Goal: surviving as a writer. Now, it's very easy to say to yourself, Well, Self, I AM surviving as a writer. I'm writing for one, two, three, or a multitude of newspapers. Their paychecks don't bounce. That is fine. And if that is your ultimate goal, great. But if you entered this story as someone who wants to support yourself financially AS A WRITER while working on some visionary piece of literature, then it's important not to lose sight of that.

For many writers, stringing will be a path, not a destination. I'll go even further: It might appear that because I became a full-time staffer that I have given up on my long-term goal of writing fiction. I have to confess that for long periods, I did indeed fall away from those outside projects. Yet even as my wife and I raised two sons and even as she attended medical school, became a physician, a resident and an assistant professor at the University of Michigan Medical School, I wrote two novels in addition to the one called *Stringer* that I wrote while I was — guess what — stringing. Add those three to the long one I wrote in the Peace Corps and later as a farmworker, and that comes to four novels. I've also written short stories and four children's books. But one of those novels, come to think of it, I wrote while on strike. And this very book, *Shoestring Reporter*, lay unfinished for more than a quarter-century. I began writing it and made a comprehensive outline even when I was stringing. The birth of our first son and child-care duties still left me time for that. What derailed the project? Taking that full-time reporting job.

In 1981, I made lots of notes and an outline. Twenty-six years later, I discovered somebody had done much of the work.

Me.

chapter 21

getting hired

Okay, you want a job stringing, right?

You're dedicated to the proposition that you should make as much money as possible while spending as little cash as the real world allows.

Working on a shoestring, in other words.

How do you get somebody to hire you for a job that isn't really — in conventional terms — a job?

Here's what you do. Wherever you are, be it big city or little town, grab as many area newspapers as you can find.

Do any of those papers use stringers?

They won't be so gauche as to call them "stringers," of course. Look for telltale words like "correspondent," as in "Joel Thurtell, Tribune Correspondent."

Another giveaway is the word "special," as in "Special to the Free Press by Joel Thurtell." When the News ran my stories, they printed "News Special Writer" under my byline.

Jot down the names of these "correspondents" and "special writers." Note also what towns they write about.

Don't be discouraged if your town already has a stringer. Remember that there is always more work than any one, two or more people can do. If there isn't room for two people to string where you live, you can always hunt for stories in other towns.

Having made your list of towns with stringers, note which towns don't seem to have a reporter.

Read the stories. Are some writers more interesting than others? Who seems to be doing the most thorough job of reporting?

Make another list of the best of the stringers.

Choose the name of a stringer some distance from you, just to avoid any threat, you know, any semblance of competition.

Be sure that you've read this person's work. Give that stringer a call, and introduce yourself as someone interested in breaking into the stringing line of work. You might add that you've been reading the work of various stringers and admired this person's work. Use your judgment, of course, but don't hesitate to lay on the flattery. Reporters take a lot of heat from readers and editors, so they're eager to hear kind words about their writing.

During the conversation, you would like to learn how many papers this person strings for. You'd also like to find out which papers pay the most and which pay the least. Are some papers slow to pay? Are there chiseling editors and if so, who are they?

It's always better to elicit answers without asking direct questions, though direct questions are okay if there's no other way to get the information.

A few months after I retired from newspaper work, I read a news story about grafting fruit trees. Now, that is something I'd like to do. The story was written by a stringer. Her contact information was in the tagline at the end of the story. I gave her a call. What I really wanted was to learn how to contact the subject of her story. It happened to be a story that interested her greatly, too, so we had a good conversation during which I mentioned I'd been a reporter.

Oh, wow! she said, and went on to explain how I could get work stringing for her paper, which was in need of stories from an area not far from where I live. She gave me the editor's name and phone number and urged me to call her.

Easy! Except I haven't made the call. Too busy working on this book!

Now, pick up those newspapers again. Look for the names of staff writers who cover your own geopolitical area. Make a list of their names. Getting phone numbers is easy these days, because the papers often print contact information at the end of articles.

Call the staff writers and introduce yourself just as you did with the stringer. But this time, you don't need to worry about being a threat. A staff writer isn't going to feel any rivalry from a lowly would-be stringer.

What you want to know now is whether, in the staffer's view, the paper needs more coverage in your area. This is critical information, because some newspapers have a policy similar to "redlining" by banks and insurance companies that deny service to people in certain areas — usually economically poor areas. Some newspapers refuse to assign reporters to write stories about areas where they have few or no advertising customers or where they simply refuse to deliver the paper. The Detroit dailies have excluded huge areas of Detroit and many suburbs from regular coverage.

You wouldn't want to pitch a story about an area the paper doesn't cover, would you?

Actually, I find the practice of redlining offensive. As a staffer at the Free Press, I sometimes found ways to cheat. I'd write about proscribed areas by simply inserting a character from a coverage area into the story. For instance, I was told not to write about Southwest Detroit. Okay, but I could write about an affluent town like Grosse Ile. I'd find someone from Grosse Ile who was working, say, as a volunteer in Southwest Detroit and write a story that mentioned the Grosse Ile person even though it focused on the Southwest Detroit subject. That was hard for editors to refuse, and I got away with my little scam.

As a stringer, which is to say, a writer of lower status, you will find it hard to pull stunts like that. If you can do it, great. But you need to know where the red lines are.

Very important: Who is the editor who supervises stringers? A staffer will know this.

Now it's time to draw all this intelligence into a coherent picture. Find a map of your area and make an X over any town where a stringer is needed. If you are looking at working for more than one paper, then you'll need to devise a more complex code. Maybe one X for your favorite paper, XX for the next choice and so on.

How many of these symbols are near or in your own town?

Now you have, literally, a road map to your future as a stringer.

Next step: Write a letter to the editor in charge of stringers. Be careful. This letter is actually going to be a sample of your writing abilities. It needs to be good.

No, it needs to be perfect.

Length — no more than half a page.

You can let your first draft flow, but once you're finished, it's time to rewrite and condense.

Don't use the word "stringer." Use the polite term "freelance."

Tell the editor you are a freelance writer living in, let's say it's Crawdad Junction. You would like an opportunity to work for him/her as a correspondent.

In reading the Daily Bazooka, you have noticed little news from Crawdad Junction. You would be willing to attend village council, school board, township board and any other meetings the editor might like to have covered. If the editor would like to purchase feature stories about Junctionites, you can supply those, too. Along with photos.

Yes, for sure, mention that you own a camera and know how to use it and how to transmit digital images to the newspaper, if needed.

Briefly list any academic credentials. The more you have, the better. But remember that academic degrees don't guarantee you can be a good stringer. Editors know this all too well. The most important thing is letting the editor know you are willing to work and to meet deadlines.

Is that it?

Definitely not. Most likely, if you now sit back and wait for a call, it will never come. Wait a week, then call the editor. Did he or she receive your letter? Just wanted you to know I'm still interested in reporting for your newspaper. What if the editor would let you attend a meeting and file a report as a tryout?

If the editor insists that you work exclusively for that one paper, my advice is to move on to the next publication. At least, I'd advise that you don't agree to work exclusively for one paper unless the pay is really substantial.

When I was trying to string for the Tribune, the editor wasn't getting back to me. I'd leave messages, but no callback. Weeks passed. What was going on?

My wife worked for newspapers and actually studied Journalism at the University of Michigan. "Be persistent," she advised me. "Reporters have to be persistent to get stories. Editors want to hire people who are persistent. Keep calling him."

Now, that doesn't mean I called him every day. Too much persistence turns into another "p" word. Know what I mean? Don't be a pest!

Eventually, the editor called me. He didn't need to see me. He didn't ask about a camera. He had one question for me: Had I ever covered a meeting?

I told him how I'd worked for a year at WMUK-FM. I told him how I would have the Portage City Council agendas mailed to me. I'd write a short advance story and have it recorded over the telephone to play the day of the meeting. Then I'd go to the meeting, listen to the business, take notes, go back to the radio station late at night, sit down at an IBM Selectric typewriter and write a story. I tried to make it amusing as well as enlightening. Didn't want to put people to sleep. Then I'd read it into a tape recorder under the watchful eye of an engineer. The next day, I'd hear my voice reporting on the meeting.

Reporting on the meeting. That was the key information the editor wanted from me. Could I cover a meeting? Yes.

You're hired.

He gave me a list of five meetings per month that I was to cover, with pay at $25 a meeting for every story I phoned in.

That was it. By telephone. A letter, no résumé, and a phone interview.

A job!
I was a writer. A *professional* writer.
You can do it, too.
Good luck!

chapter 22

you're fired!

"Due to the cyclical nature of the auto industry, we have had to dispense with the services of our freelance writers."

That note from a Detroit News editor was a real kick in the pants.

In my then short career as a stringer, I'd been earning a reliable $400-$600 a month from the South Bend paper. Those were 1970s dollars. Take the average, $500, and it would have been worth more than $1,400 in 2007. Not too bad, huh? Then on top of it, for shipping to the News my already-printed Tribune stories, I'd collect another $75. In 2007 dollars, that's $212. Like interest on principal. Frosting on the cake.

Except suddenly, the frosting was gone.

Fired.

But I had my Tribune work. I had my check from The Journal Era. I had checks coming in sporadically from the Free Press, The New York Times, Time, The Indianapolis Star, Planning magazine, The Progressive and other publications.

A few years later, I discovered the News had a new state editor and was paying not seventy-five bucks, but $175 to $200 for stories. Two hundred bucks in 1984 would be almost $400 in 2007.

Again, they were stories I'd already written for other papers. Think about that — we live in a time when newspapers are laying off staffers. With one's eggs all in one basket, the staffer can be devastated at the loss of a job. The savvy stringer just rolls with the punches. In fact, the staff layoffs can mean more work for stringers. That news hole is still there. The editors still need copy. Who's going to write it?

You!

I'll say it again: If you double-dip, you have a cushion against unemployment.

So getting fired may be not so bad. It can even be good.

I've been fired four, maybe five times. Once was by the U.S. Postal Service, for filing a Freedom of Information Act request. My FIRST FOIA request! Post Office — worst job I ever had. I'll discuss that in more detail in *Shoestring J School*. But the other times involved irregular or stringing jobs at newspapers. Why, I was fired from one newspaper twice! Some members of the Kalamazoo College Student Senate didn't take kindly to my sarcastic reports in the Index. My depiction of their organization as a "dead body" annoyed them. I was relieved of my duty to cover their meetings. It was not a loss. I'd rather be shoveling waterlogged, stinking beans in a burned-out elevator than sit through the maunderings of self-important student politicians. Really, the arrogance! The senators sat around a table, and the ones with their backs to the audience blocked our view of the ones facing us. You could barely hear them. As I say, not a loss. But my relief ended when the editor decided I could not possibly get in trouble as the Index music critic. Think again. Getting the boot had no financial edge, since we student reporters worked gratis.

Yes, stringing can be unstable.

Another time, when an editor departed, I too got the heave-ho, though not immediately. In 1979, it seemed too good to be true that I actually had an in with an editor at the Detroit Free Press. This editor liked my work, and over lunch she assigned me several stories. This was a Big Deal. She invited me, and I drove all the way to Detroit from Berrien Springs.

Hey, fantastic! I've got an in! A nice working relationship seemed to be developing. I sold a major story about Michigan Indian fishing rights and their larger-than-life Upper Peninsula Ojibwa champion, Big Abe LeBlanc. I had another story in the works and a third on tap when one day I got a call from the editor. The FORMER editor. She was actually just a few blocks away, in Berrien Springs on her way to Chicago. We had lunch. She had left the Free Press abruptly and was going to start a PR firm in Chicago.

Too bad for me.

An old Free Press hand once told me, "The next boss is always worse." All might have been well, except that the story I had in the pipeline for the Free Press Magazine was butchered by her successor. He re-characterized my main sources, embarrassing me. My writing didn't turn the new guy on; his high-handed rewriting pissed me off. I stopped sending him stories. That seemed to be the end of writing for the Freep.

But editors come and editors go. As things worked out, I wrote more stories for the Free Press Magazine. As with the News, there would come a time when the Free Press again would become a good place to sell stories.

chapter 23

nuts & bolts

Let's say you browbeat, sweet-talked or otherwise cajoled some editor into assigning you to write a story. A job! Well, of course, it's not a REAL job, is it? You are a mere stringer. I once heard an editor archly proclaim, "We don't EMPLOY stringers." Pretty condescending, no doubt about it. That editor might have paused for a second or two had he considered that NOT being employed by a newspaper, yet being PAID to provide copy for that institution, might actually be the preferred way of life from the point of view of the stringer.

But pretend for a moment that your idea for a story has struck a chord with some person who — whatever he or she might think — actually DOES employ stringers. Pretend that you have a onetime assignment. You might consider yourself a temp. But also consider something much bigger and better: You are a JOURNALIST now. So what if you're not a full-timer? So what if the paper doesn't print "Staff Writer" under your name? So what if the bosses think they don't "employ" you? All they're worried about is whether they have to contribute to your unemployment compensation should they sack you.

Journalist.

That is what you are.

It means a lot of things to a lot of people and to many it doesn't mean much of anything. But to you, it means you have arrived. You are a reporter now.

What do you do with it? Now that you have an assignment, what next?

This is no time to panic, freeze up or back out.

Full speed ahead!

The next step is very important — your first test as a reporter. Chances are, it's completely new to you.

Now that you've been assigned to write something, how do you go about it?

Your fundamental reporting tools are the pen or pencil and steno pad, right?

Not exactly.

The fundamentals: A reporter's basic tools are eyes, ears and even the senses of smell and taste and touch, together with your brain, which compiles all the information. Steno pad and pencil are mere extensions of your brain's logic and memory. One of the greatest things about reporting is the total lack of need for any equipment other than one's senses. I've often watched photographers lugging their heavy bags of equipment, and television cameramen with even bulkier baggage. And there I am with a pad and pen, both of which I can do without if circumstances eliminate them.

Incidentally, let's take a break to consider why I'm compressing all this advice into one measly chapter. I wondered about it myself, but decided one chapter for the nuts and bolts should do the trick. In this chapter, I'm relating the basic mental and physical tools you will need to be a stringer. To work as a newspaper reporter. If you can learn all you need to know from one chapter in a book, why would you plunk down tens of thousands of dollars to enroll in college or university Journalism classes? You might ask, too, why you'd pay the price of an entire book when only one chapter gives you the tools to do the job?

The answer is that a huge proportion of college Journalism instruction involves tutoring the uninitiated in the rites of passage mandatory to people who work in newspapers. These cultural oddities, partly linguistic, partly political, are the core of the fraternity-style, closed society that envelops newsrooms everywhere. J school mainly helps you navigate the treacherous shoal waters of the newsroom. Most of the remainder of this book coaches you in the same way that a J school might — at best — help you understand the sociology of newspapering. Except that the book is cheaper.

Okay, back to class.

First, in spite of what I said about needing only your memory, a good reporter knows the limits of memory and enhances those limits by taking notes. That means writing down on paper, or in this day and age, possibly tapping down on a laptop the words that people say. You can practice this: Try summarizing conversations you have with friends. Or take notes while talking on the telephone. You can do this by writing on a pad of paper, or you might try typing as you talk. If you are a fast and accurate typist, the keyboard might be the best way to go. However, remember that you are making an impression on someone at the other end of the line. Will your tapping be audible? Will it inhibit the other person? Or will it inspire more talking? You will have to judge these things yourself.

If you can take down quotes verbatim, great. If you're not that fast, don't worry — make sure you write down the essence, the crux, of what you hear. But if you hear something that really sums up the idea, get every word, if you can. You'll want some direct quotations, and you can't make up what you don't have on paper.

Now for a confession. I'm nearly 65 as I finish this book. For years, my handwriting has gotten worse and worse. I couldn't seem to make it better. I blamed my poor writing on stress, and I'm sure tension has something to do with it. But my writing was not always terrible. It has gotten so bad that I prefer interviewing people over the telephone so I can type my notes. But in the past few years, tapping the keyboard has gotten harder. What gives?

A couple years ago, I went to a surgeon to have a cyst removed from the joint of my left index finger. The doctor inspected both of my hands and casually remarked that I have arthritis in my fingers — all of them. Suddenly, I understood why my writing has gotten progressively worse, and why I couldn't make it better. Arthritis — that explained why typing also got harder.

What to do? I take my time. I ask people to repeat so I can catch up on my notes. If someone makes a snide remark about my handwriting, I just say that I have arthritis. If they feel embarrassed for having made a cutting remark about a physical condition, good! They should feel bad!

No doubt about it, shorthand helps. In my 30-plus years of reporting, I met only one reporter who knew shorthand. It was a tremendous help to him, and by all means if you can afford the time and money to learn this skill, go for it. But if you can't do it, don't despair. You can create your own shorthand.

When I was a student in Germany, listening to lectures in German, I found that I could more speedily write down notes if I didn't try to translate them into English. I could take notes even faster if I shortened some of the most-often-used expressions. One example: The word "between" seemed to pop up often. In German, "between" is "zwischen." Instead of writing the entire word out, I abbreviated it to "zw." I still use that code notation to signify "between" in my note-taking. "For example" in German is "zum Beispiel." In my notes, "zB" signifies "for example." These are just zBs zw you and me. You can concoct similar foreshortened code signs known only to yourself. That is enough. Just be sure that you remember your special ciphers when the time comes to decode.

I mentioned earlier that it's a good idea to find writing models — good stories in premier publications that you can study to learn how fine writers and editors structure their work. It's not enough to read the glitzy Page One news and feature stories. As a stringer, you will be required to do the nuts-and-bolts writing, which includes police and fire reporting. Therefore, look for stories written by veteran cops reporters. I'll deal with this topic more completely in *Shoestring J School*, because I believe writers often lose great opportunities for storytelling that come straight from the police blotter.

In the cops stories, note how often writers use the so-called "inverted pyramid" to organize their article. Who, what, where, when, all lumped at the top. Works pretty well, doesn't it? Yet there are other ways to organize stories that differ from the tried-and-true inverted pyramid. Again, I'll deal with this in far more detail in *Shoestring J School*.

There's one kind of story you won't often find in the elite newspapers: the meeting story. Yet this is your real bread-and-butter work.

Covering township board, school board, village and city council meetings. Sounds like a bore, right? Well, your job is to stay awake. And then some. Many things happen at these meetings that go unreported by conventional reporters. Your job is to monitor the nuts-and-bolts pieces. Okay, the planning commission has just approved a new shopping center that will add so-and-so many dollars to the tax base, hire so-and-so many workers but ruin a wetland that extends to a popular hiking park. There are enough elements here to keep you writing for a long time.

That $25-a-meeting promise is just a baseline. Milk more stories out of a meeting in addition to the basic meeting summary and you will accomplish two things. First, you will alert people about issues they need to know about. Second, you will add more money to your bank account.

How can you lose?

Well, you can lose if you write a report that is inaccurate.

I don't care if you write an article that makes people angry. That is part of the territory. But make sure what you report as fact is indeed a fact.

The first time can be intimidating. Most likely, you've never been in this government building before and most likely all the elected officials are strangers to you. I suggest making a road map in your notepad, a list, going from left to right, of the elected officials sitting behind the board table. Often, there will be name placards to help. A left-to-right drawing is also a good idea. Soon enough, you will know the players, but right now they are strangers to you and you are a stranger to them.

Make sure you grab a copy of the meeting agenda as you walk in. You are not required to sign in, but it's a good idea to fly the flag and let people know you are the reporter from the Daily Bugle. Make sure beforehand that you know how long the story should be. Your editor may have an idea what the hot topic will be. If a controversial issue is on the agenda, this may be the only thing you will write about. But often, your editor will trust you to figure out what is the story and what is not a story.

You have been given, in a very offhand way, a position of public trust, since it is your judgment that will be selecting the news that people will read.

Note-taking is absolutely essential, even when the issues are mundane. Why? In my case, it keeps me focused on the meeting. Otherwise, my mind might wander until suddenly I realize the officials are in the middle of discussing something important and I've been daydreaming for the last 10 minutes. But more importantly, my memory simply won't play back for me all the details that people discuss in a meeting, especially when issues are complex. But my notes prod my memory, and together they help me put together an account of what happened.

Keep agendas and minutes and any other printed material you can lay hands on during these meetings. Read this stuff later — there may be future stories lying there.

What if there are no name tags? No problem: Just write down in your notepad distinguishing things about the speakers. "Guy with white shirt," or "Black tie," or "Baldie." Later, you can ask the clerk to help with names to attach to your on-the-fly labels.

What if there's no printed agenda, and there are no name tags to identify the participants? These unstructured and very informal meetings are often the ones that stretch on for hours and try the patience of outsiders. These are the public meetings that truly resemble fraternity meetings, when the only audience is the panel itself and maybe a lone reporter. There are at least two dangers here: Sleep is one problem, and the other is the temptation to depart before the meeting ends.

You see, the long-winded monologues may be designed to wear down the audience of one — the reporter — so he or she will decamp, enabling the officials to enact something in private that may or may not be reflected in the clerk's minutes of the meeting. It is at these clandestine "public" meetings that the presence of a reporter is very important.

Sorry to say, you gotta stay. To the bitter end.

chapter 24

the pack-a-day gang

I had just pushed the SEND key on the old Tel-E-Ram, commanding the suitcase-style computer to transmit my story to the newsroom through an earmuff on the telephone handset. Suddenly, the old hand, the veteran Tribune cops reporter who thought he was going to "edit," meaning quash, censor and otherwise delete, the top of my story, demanded to see it.

I'd been a stringer on the SBT for three years. This was my third day as a full-time staff writer. For the first five days, I was supposed to get my news from my beat, Cass County, but report to the Tribune bureau in Niles for "help" in learning how to work these cantankerous old Tel-E-Ram writing machines. That was my understanding, but one of the veteran reporters interpreted "help" to mean he could oversee my reporting and bully my writing. So, when he asked to see the police report I'd just written, I told him, Sorry, it's already there. Already being read by real editors. He was miffed. Later, when the presses were running, I let him see it.

Okay, let's interrupt my story right here. What can you learn from my experience? That other Journalists are not to be trusted. Hold your cards — and your stories — and your story IDEAS — close to your vest. Not only will other writers steal your ideas, but they will try — subtly or with crude force — to change or kill them. It's all about CONTROL. In this case, while there are many different ways to write a police story, the veteran cops reporter knew only one way — the inverted pyramid. Who, what, where, when, how and why in the top graf — yes, Journalists love to say "graf" for "paragraph." Had he seen my story before I transmitted it, there would have been a battle imperial as he sought to censor me, simply because I didn't follow his tried-and-true formula.

Cardinal rule: Don't reveal what you're working on, or how you're writing it, until it's complete. Then it's best to show your work only to the person or persons who will actually decide whether and how it will be played. Now, back to the show.

When my would-be mentor read my story, he was even more annoyed. I had NOT used the inverted pyramid model imprinted on his brain in J school. All those W's, what, where, etc., crammed into the first sentence so the reader can skip the rest of the story and move on to the ads. If you want people to read your story, folks, the inverted pyramid is guaranteed NOT to be the best way to write. It's a tried and true turnoff. You want to tickle your readers' curiosity, tease the readers into reading more...and more...and more...until you hit them with your little surprise at the end.

Frankly, I would not have let him read my story before I sent it no matter what the content. It was a matter of principle. I was a new reporter, but this old fart did not outrank me. He was arrogant to think he could dictate how I wrote. But I also knew that he'd never have agreed with the way I wrote that story.

Here's what happened. It was February of 1981. I sat through a morning meeting of the Cass County Board of Commissioners my first day as a staffer. There, at the press table, I met the editor of The (Dowagiac) Daily News; the reporter from WDOW-AM, the radio station in Dowagiac; and a stringer from The Elkhart Truth. Four of us sat at a table watching the meeting. When the commissioners broke for lunch at noon, I was invited to go with the other reporters to John's, a bar restaurant. We walked out of the county building into a heavy snowfall. As we approached John's, you couldn't see half a block for the snow. But we noticed something you couldn't miss: a crowd of people on the street, and lots of cop cars. Flashing lights. Some guy had just shot up the bar and was still holed up inside. Minutes later, cops stormed the bar and dragged the shooter into a squad car.

This was our story. Far more interesting than anything the county board might do. Sticking together, the reporters went to the village police station, then to the county courthouse and the sheriff's office to get their story. The official version of the story. Now, I was used to working alone in that garret. I watched the Cass reporters troop from one office to another, collecting their information ensemble. This was my introduction to the pack approach to reporting. I would learn over the months that these reporters shared tips and information, and a couple of them wrote stories in tandem.

Together, they shaped their interpretations of what happened and then shared them with their readers or listeners. You could call it a team approach to Journalism, but it seemed more like herd behavior. It was insurance against the scoop. There was a tacit agreement that by sharing, they would ensure that all the stories looked the same. That way, nobody looked bad. Tacit agreement: No scoops. Nobody would look bad in the eyes of editors. And nobody looks great, either.

I moved away from the pack. When I was certain they weren't watching, I went back to the bar and found the one man who had stayed put when Jimmy Lee came in and started shooting — the one man who was the lone witness.

Here's the lead that so irritated my wannabe mentor:

CASSOPOLIS — Marvin Burns took a look out the window of his home here Tuesday morning and decided the snow was falling too heavily to drive a truck to Grand Rapids.

Instead, Burns walked over to John's Bar at 135 S. Broadway and sat down for a quiet beer. The coast-to-coast truck driver never finished that drink.

If I'd let the veteran have a peep at that non-pyramidal lead, he would have fought — and probably won — a battle to replace it with something that would have read like this:

CASSOPOLIS — A 22-year-old Cassopolis man was in custody Tuesday after firing six shots from a .38 caliber revolver in John's Bar at 135 S. Broadway. Nobody was hit, but police officers were injured while making the arrest...

See what I mean? You read that and know all you need to know about this little news item. As a means of persuading readers to finish your story, the inverted pyramid won't do the trick. Once you start your story this way, it's very hard to shoehorn in such interesting details as Burns' remark to me that Lee turned over his table, and "I didn't even get a chance to finish my beer."

It's the difference between bean-counting, a real bore, and having some fun. The inverted pyramid was invented for economy, not storytelling. My new friends on the beat were pursuing the inverted pyramid. They didn't need color. The more their stories resembled each other, the better, from their point of view. None of them thought to look for a Marvin Burns to add detail to their story because when you write a lackluster news story following standard formulas, the last thing you need is to paint a picture. It would require explaining things, and that would mean stepping outside the formula. The last thing conformist reporters care about is convincing readers to READ their stories.

In a staff meeting a year or so later, my editor made some remark about me and a textbook. I didn't follow the gist until he handed me a photocopy of a book page. Turns out my fatal glass of beer story was reprinted in a Journalism textbook published by Harper & Row: *Reporting*

From *Reporting and Writing the News*, by Warren K. Agee, Phillip H. Ault and Edwin Emery, Harper & Row, 1983: *Instead of using [a] flat approach, The South Bend Tribune reporter wrote the story from the point of view of a tavern customer, supplementing information on the police report with facts and quotations obtained by interviewing persons present during the shootup. The result was this lively, detailed account:*

He sat down for a quiet beer and...

By JOEL THURTELL
Tribune Cass County Bureau

CASSOPOLIS—Marvin Burns took a look out the window at his home here Tuesday morning and decided the snow was falling too heavily to drive a truck to Grand Rapids.

Instead, Burns walked over to John's Bar at 135 S. Broadway and sat down for a quiet beer. The coast-to-coast truck driver never finished that drink.

Out front, a man, later identified by Cassopolis village police as James Lee, 22, of Hilton Street Apartments, Cassopolis, swung a .38-caliber revolver at the thermopane windows of the tavern, breaking two panes before he entered the building.

Burns said that moments after entering the bar, Lee fired six shots from a .38-caliber revolver. Nobody was hit by the bullets, but three police officers were hurt while trying to wrestle the gun from Lee's hands. Burns, who was one of the few people who remained in the bar during the incident, recalls that a waitress shouted, "He's got a gun!" Many of the bar's patrons quickly ran out the front door.

Waitresses estimate about 65 customers were having lunch at 1:10 p.m. when James Lee entered the bar.

Lee came to Burns' table, and, recalls the trucker, "He asked me what I was looking at."

Burns said nothing, and Lee turned over his table. "I didn't even get achance to finish my beer," said Burns. Burns rose and stood in a corner opposite the bar's shuffleboard game. He was the only one who remained in the rear area of the bar.

Burns said Lee then tipped over the shuffleboard game one-handed and began firing the revolver across the bar.

"I thought he had just went on the nut," said Burns. Burns said Lee was not aiming at anyone in the bar.

A waitress said lee tried to force open a door leading to a rear room where she and others were hiding.

A police witness, Captain Paul Parrish of the Cass County Sheriff's Department, said he heard four shots, a pause, then another pair of shots.

From inside, Burns said a waitress shouted that the gun was empty.

Parrish and Cassopolis Village Police Chief Frank Williams ran into the bar and rushed Lee. Parrish said he and Williams wrestled Lee to the floor and disarmed him, although both officers were struck in the head as Lee fought with them. Several policemen then carried a kicking and cursing lee to a police cruiser.

The episode lasted about 25 minutes, according to a sheriff's department dispatcher.

Lee was lodged in the Cass County Jail on charges of assaulting a police officer, careless use of a firearm and malicious destruction of property.

Reprinted courtesy of the South Bend Tribune

and Writing the News by Warren Agee, Phillip Ault and Edwin Emery.

My story appeared in a chapter called "The Feature Approach," under the heading, "Ways to use a 'soft' style."

"Telling a story from the point of view of a participant is one method of featurizing the news."

The authors then rewrote my story in a hard-news style. Before reprinting my story, they wrote, "Instead of using this flat approach, the South Bend Tribune reporter wrote the story from the point of view of a tavern customer, supplementing information on the police report with facts and quotations obtained by interviewing persons present during the shoot-up. The result was this lively, detailed account."

Wow! A "lively, detailed account"!

Better than winning a Journalism award! I felt as if I'd hit the jackpot. Words of high praise from Harper & Row.

Had I not pushed the SEND button, had I let someone with a narrow vision of Journalism censor me, I never would have had the honor of seeing my byline in a textbook on Journalism.

Think for yourself. Don't show other people your work in progress.

Use your own judgment.

Avoid group reporting and group thinking.

Trust yourself.

Be independent.

chapter 25

"never lead with a quote"

"Never start a story with a quote," I was told by someone who had actually studied Journalism in college and even worked for a newspaper. (Shhh! Please don't tell anyone, especially her, but that advice came from my wife!)

It was early in my stringing days, and my experience as a newspaper writer was close to zero. Karen had actually written for a newspaper, The Ann Arbor News. She was high school editor and later a reporting intern there, and she knew plenty about how newspaper articles ought to be written. I was lucky to have a writing coach living with me.

But I'd had a somewhat different experience, because I'd written radio reports. In the 1970s, I was an unpaid volunteer for the Western Michigan University radio station in Kalamazoo. I put together my own feature stories for WMUK-FM and for about a year I made a weekly trek to Portage, a big suburb south of Kalamazoo, where I would sit through city council meetings, take notes, go back to the station, write up a report and read it while an engineer tape-recorded me.

Storytelling was the key to writing — and voicing — a meeting report that would not put listeners to sleep. Sometimes, the best way to open a story was with a direct quotation from someone who spoke at the meeting. Not that I tape-recorded those speakers. I didn't. Instead, I'd use my own voice to dramatize what they said.

"We need a new canoe!"

I opened a report with that line, enunciated with lots of histrionics stressed into my voice. A Portage council member named Don Hinga had used that line to draw attention to his idea for changing a city policy. It worked. People sat up and listened. I figured if it worked for him, it would work for me, besides giving a colorful reflection of what had happened in an otherwise dull meeting. So I led my report with an imitation of the councilman: "We need a new canoe!"

At least one person loved it: He was Tony Griffin, the station's news editor. If I was going to please or amuse anyone with my antics, it had to be Tony. He knew that if my stunt got a laugh out of him, it would get yucks in radio land. I followed with context, explaining that the comment came from a councilman who wanted a new policy on this or that.

This or that policy would have bored listeners. The new canoe caught their ear. Once I had their attention, I could launch into a short explanation of the issue.

As I stewed over the writing of one of my first Tribune meeting reports, I decided to use a quotation in my lead. I read it to Karen. Not done in newspapers, she warned me. But I recalled how it had worked more than once at WMUK. Before that, I sometimes used direct quotes to start chapters in history papers. Why? Well, academic historians can be pretty dry, too. So much so that a convention of historians once erupted in flames from spontaneous combustion. No, just kidding!

The key point to remember is that the quote must be more than euphonious. Not only should it roll off the tongue, but most importantly, it should illustrate whatever point or theme you want to make. If it's to work, it has to be relevant.

I used a quotation lead once, and the Tribune copy desk let it stand. Well, well. I tried it again. What do you know, I got away with it! I didn't do it for every story. I did it when it would help propel a story into its plot, and I did it only when there was a quote worthy of top place.

I did it, but I didn't see anybody else — full-time staffers or stringers — doing it. It stood out, stylistically. That was not bad. But those were the early days of Journalism for me, and I sometimes felt my lack of formal Journalistic training.

One day, I got my first assignment to write a story for The New York Times. A radio-style lead popped into my head. The story was about a lawyer hungry for some publicity who proposed that the border county of Cass should secede from Michigan and attach itself to Indiana.

While researching the issue, I found that there was a skirmish between Ohio and Michigan in the early 19th Century over a contested bit of geography that included the city of Toledo. I wanted to point out in my brief story that while border disputes may be unfamiliar to modern readers, they are not new. So I borrowed the opening line of a song from the Toledo War and made it my lead.

I learned that there are no real fixed rules about writing. I learned that I should be skeptical of anyone who tries to prescribe "thou shalts" and "thou shalt nots" to writers. I learned that if I follow my own judgment, things will work out better than if I let my writing be shaped by the prescriptions of others.

A few years ago, when the Free Press was still paying top writers to coach us on the finer points of our craft, a New York Times reporter gave us a tip on tuning up our style: Never, never, end your story with a quote. She said it's a cheap way to conclude a story, foreclosing a thoughtful ending.

Hmmm. Well, at least she didn't ban quotes in leads. Remember how I quoted a song from the 1835 Toledo War in a feature I wrote for her very own paper? Yes, the Times copy editors approved a quote lead in my yarn about the proposed Cass County secession from Michigan that went like this:

"And who would cut up Michigan?"

chapter 26

jump-starting with papa joe

It's a bit after six in the morning, I'm brewing coffee, reading the Times and writing up my day's "to-do" list. When I get to a dozen entries, my head starts to spin. Which one do I start on first? But wait—I'm retired! No deadlines! Well, forget that. I'm so busy in my so-called "retirement" that I'm more beat at the end of a day than if I'd been grinding out cover stories for a newspaper.

Retirement is a dirty word, as far as I'm concerned. I haven't needed so desperately to organize my time since the days when I was a stringer for a daily while editor of a weekly and father of a newborn son. So many demands, so little time. In the midst of it all, I needed to write, write, write, but often there were half a dozen projects big and small competing. Which to start first? How to get started writing at all?

I'll say it again. There is no such thing as writer's block. I love the old Brenda Starr comic strip where the reporter, sitting at a keyboard, stammers, "I-I've got writer's block." An editor nearby replies, "Writer's block is for writers. You're a Journalist. Type on!"

Nonetheless, getting started can be hard. I love mornings for writing, even in Daylight Saving Time when it's dark. The house is quiet; it's a great time to concentrate. But those to-do lists can be unnerving. Best to leave the list-making for later in the morning. At night, before hitting the hay, I try to outline my first writing project for the next morning. That way, I at least know where I'm headed when I start the day.

More and more, I'm forcing myself not to open e-mail in the morning. Nothing derails last night's vows about work faster than unanticipated e-mails. Leave them till later.

What about that coffee high? More and more, I'm drinking less and less coffee. If my to-do list is piling up on me, caffeine only makes my stress worse.

There is a better stimulant than coffee. I need a strong countervailing force here. But I know what to do. Head for the CD player. Choice of music is critical. You want to jump-start the day, don't play dirges. Know what I mean? Something constantly upbeat, imbued with heavy doses of musical energy, that's what I need. Man, that will get me moving.

Here's what I'm spinning these days: First, Franz Josef Haydn's piano sonatas. My CD is called "Haydn: Klaviersonaten Nr. 32, 47, 53 & 59" and it has Emmanuel Ax playing on a Sony disc, SK 53 635. Solo piano, great melodies and always upbeat. No adagios, please!

Haydn gets me moving away from the heavy op-ed columns in the Times and all that depressing world news and straight into my own writing. Key words: "Allegro," "Presto." Quick melodies that make you want to dance. Why, the middle movement is marked "Menuet."

Once I'm in the swing, whacking away at writing, I need a change of pace. Musicians call this "modulation," I believe. Fancy way of saying what we writers call "transition." What I do, see, is modulate from Papa Joe Haydn to Grampa Bach. Good rousing Bachian organ music really gets me stirred up. My favorite CD for this is "The Biggs Bach Book," with organist E. Power Biggs at the keyboard on a CD by CBS Records, MK 30539. Nothing beats Bach, but he has his match in Georgie Boy Händel, so once I'm working really hard, nobody around except Patti the dog, I crank the volume up and spin my way into a three-disc set called "Händel: Complete Organ Concertos" recorded by the English Concert directed by Trevor Pinnock with Simon Preston on the organ and Ursula Hollinger playing harp. It's an Archiv set, Digital Stereo 289 469 358-2 and it will keep you hopping for all of 199 minutes.

By the time Papa Joe and Grampa Johann and Uncle Georgie have spun their course, it's time for lunch. Maybe a snooze. I am retired, you know. I've actually been playing this same lineup for weeks, and it's nearly time for a change.

Need some get-up-and-go? Try Papa Joe!

chapter 27

are newspapers dead?

From all the hype, most of it generated by newspapers themselves, you'd think that the newspaper biz was a dying industry. Seems odd, because newspaper profits until recently were higher than that of many other industries. Grocery stores are lucky to earn 4-5 percent for their shareholders. Newspapers typically earned 15-20 percent, sometimes more. But the Internet has plowed a huge furrow into such standard money machines as classified advertising. As I fine-tune this manuscript, four newspaper companies are in bankruptcy court and others seem headed there.

For you the prospective stringer, is this a dead or dying business not worth jumping into?

Am I steering you into a dead-end career?

Ever hear of the liar who believed his own malarkey? Beware of theories masquerading as fact, and be careful about swallowing the negative hype the papers are feeding themselves. Part of their malaise is delusion.

Self-delusion.

Moreover, much of their trouble right now is self-inflicted.

But these are rough, uncharted times. Historians may well call this period the Panic of 2010. More newspapers may go down. Does that mean you can't write for them? Yes, it does — if they truly disappear. But if they migrate to the Internet successfully, profitably, there will be lots of work for stringers. If not, you will find Internet outlets willing to pay for the same skills and independent thinking I'm preaching in this book.

One example: A friend (not a J school grad) quit her full-time job at the Free Press and now strings for WebMD, an online medical advice Web site. As the monopoly power of newspapers wanes, there will be an explosive movement of readers to online news services, often highly specialized, and the demand for writers who are thinkers will explode.

But let me chat for a few minutes about what I see as the plight of newspapers. Wait a minute. What do we mean by newspapers? Are we talking about newspapers that are printed on actual, real, feel-it-and-the-ink-slides-off-on-your-hand paper? Or are we talking about this newfangled gizmo, the electronic, or digital, whatever — computerized Internet news that has no connection to paper at all? I'm going to assume we're talking about both — the whole kit and kaboodle.

Great. Now, who am I to talk about such a weighty topic? What is my expertise? I was just a beat reporter. Some days, with all these electronic advances, with audio and video recording and when my cheapskate Gannett e-mail would jam because somebody sent me a graphic that was too big for the tiny allotment of space the company apportions to reporters, and I couldn't reply to readers, sources or editors, which is considered in Corporate Journalism a must-do — well, I would feel real, real beat. If we're talking about the future of newspapers nationwide, or worldwide even, I don't know much. I'm not teaching a class on the topic. Hey, I'm a guy who never took a J school class, period. So who am I to talk about the future of newspapers?

Well, not having formally studied the topic, it's possible that I might see things somewhat differently. I do believe that what we are talking about is a very simple thing: how to persuade people to buy newspapers and how to persuade those people and maybe others as well to purchase advertising in our papers. Paper or electronic, it doesn't matter. Unless we're being subsidized by some rich foundation, we need to sell papers as the vehicle for the ads that we also sell, and together, that is what ensures that our paychecks don't bounce.

A long time ago, in 1979, I became editor of a very small weekly newspaper. It circulated with a very weak pulse to begin with in two towns in southwestern Michigan. Being editor meant that I reported

Reprinted courtesy of The (Berrien Springs) Journal Era

Subscription: $4.50 Per Year in Berrien County
Subscriptions: Out of Berrien County $5.00 Per Year
Second Class Postage Paid at Berrien Springs, Michigan 49103

Editorial
Public meetings should be open to public

Towards the end of the Berrien Springs Board of Education meeting Thursday two members of the public arrived and asked to address the board about a change in school bus and wrote all the news, wrote editorials, an occasional column, and features; I took the photos and developed the film, printed the negatives, laid out the pages, answered the phone, sold an occasional ad and watched the publishers cull deadwood.

Right, deadwood — freeloaders. People who received the paper without paying. The owners were slowly figuring out which subscribers were on the mailing list simply to puff up the circulation figures for the former owner so he could defraud my bosses when he sold the paper to them at an inflated price. It's a good thing we didn't know at the outset that only 700 people thought enough of our paper to pay for it. In a little over a year, we had pumped the numbers up to a real 2,000 paid subscribers.

A 186 percent increase in a little more than a year.

How did I figure that? Well, the change in circulation was 1,300 (subtract 700 from 2,000 and you get 1,300). Divide 1,300 by 700 = 1.86 = 186 percent. See my chapter, "What's the Percentage?"

How did we manage a 186 percent increase? We had some things going for us. First, we lacked credibility in the beginning because the former owner had squandered it. This was good. As we struggled to regain what the previous owner had frittered away, people slowly realized we were different. We created our own identity. The contrast was dramatic. He looked bad, so we looked better. Better is good. Good is great.

People came to trust us.

Credibility. Very important.

Another thing we had going. We were curious. If it seemed interesting to us, we would find out about it and write about it. No matter how goofball the topic. None of us were trained Journalists, so we didn't know what was the norm for news.

We had courage. We investigated and broke stories that made life uncomfortable for some people, including us. We alienated neighbors and bigwigs who benefited from secrecy.

We had flexibility. We could try something one week, see if it sold papers. If it didn't, we could stop it pronto, no recriminations, no bad performance reviews, no mass firings.

A 186 percent increase. Pretty heady. I felt like a dragon slayer.

Now around that time in Detroit, in 1981, the paid daily circulation of the Free Press was said to be 622,129. I joined that paper as a reporter in 1984. I had great ideas about how I could make a difference. Detroit — wow! This was the great newspaper war. I sent a memo to the executive editor, Dave Lawrence, outlining my plan for printing on the presses of out-state dailies and really eclipsing our archrival, the News. I quoted Ulysses Grant on the art of war. Find the enemy, hit him fast and hard and move on.

There was bitter rivalry between those papers then. I worked hard to break hot stories. It was not as easy as it was at the weekly, though. It was weird. It was supposed to be war, but it seemed as if we pulled our punches. There were committees of editors who could blunt a story or stop it entirely. Once, I had a story that showed how the News had published a phony report. My city editor told me he wouldn't run it. "We're not gonna piss on the News," he told me.

Wait a minute, this is war? Sounds like a permanent truce to me.

By 2007, Free Press circulation was 318,000. That's a decline of 49 percent from 1981. (Take the original number, 622,129 and subtract from it the new number, 318,000, which is the 2007 circulation. 622,129 minus 318,000 = 304,129. Divide 304,129 by 622,129 and get .49, or a drop in circulation of 49 percent.)

Man, I feel like a failure. I'm kidding, of course. Back in '84, Dave Lawrence had listened politely and then explained why each of my ideas was harebrained. Notice, however, that out-state dailies are now printing the Chicago Tribune and The New York Times. Are those papers harebrained?

As I write this in summer 2009, the Detroit Free Press is no longer a daily newspaper, nor is the News, at least in terms of home delivery. Respectively, they have gone to three and two days of home delivery. On the other days, if you want the paper, better go to a gas station — or read it on the Internet for free.

I'm trained as a historian, not as a Journalist. Historians are loath to predict the future. But I believe that if we look at the past, we can learn some important lessons that may help us understand where we are headed. If we ask the right questions.

There is too much generalizing about the future of newspapers. Their general demise is prematurely predicted. The general does not explain the particular, nor does the particular necessarily explain the general.

Certainly, the experience in Detroit is unique. In that span of time between 1981 and 2007, we have seen major disruptions. The Internet is blamed now, but these events had nothing to do with the Web. First, there was the Joint Operating Agreement in 1989. Gannett at the News and Knight Ridder at the Free Press actually had an amazing situation: Forty percent of readers took both papers. And the companies wanted to get rid of the duplicate readers. Circulation declined after the JOA, directly because of the monopoly and its lunatic policy of killing off dual subscriptions.

Self-inflicted injury.

In 1995, the companies provoked a strike. Circulation went down by roughly a third and stayed that way. Self-inflicted. I still find people who refuse after all these years to restart their Free Press subscription. Recently, circulation at the Free Press and News has plummeted. The Free Press went from 342,000 readers in January 2006 to 318,000 in January 2007, a 7 percent decline. The News went from 217,000 to 193,000 in the same period, an 11 percent drop. One year!

With the threely and twoly (in 2009, the Free Press dropped home delivery four days out of seven and the News dropped home delivery five out of seven days) delivery schedule, it's impossible to compare then and now. But wherever I go, people tell me they're cutting off their subscriptions. Nobody says they're starting the paper.

The JOA and the strike carved huge numbers of readers away. So it would seem. But we have to question everything. Remember that deadwood I mentioned at The Journal Era? When I came to the Free Press in 1984, I was shocked to see the News telling advertisers it was selling 1,000 copies a day in Berrien County. I knew that was a lie. I used to string for the News, and I couldn't even buy the paper in Berrien Springs. I had to drive to St. Joseph, where a handful of copies sat in one newsstand only.

After I came to the Free Press, I heard tales of whole semitrailer loads of the News being dumped daily, of huge quantities of the News being found in ditches. Sure, they had a big press run, but they were literally ditching the papers. I was sure they were lying about their numbers. I was outraged. In my Ulysses Grant memo to Dave Lawrence, I urged the executive editor to investigate the fraud at the News.

A pal at the Free Press laughed at me. He predicted nothing would be done. Why? Because, he said, the Free Press was fudging its numbers, too. This was the Great Newspaper War, remember. In 1981, both Detroit papers were claiming a combined circulation on Sunday of more than 1.5 million copies. By 2007, the lone Sunday paper, the Free Press, claimed 631,000 subscribers. A 58 percent loss. Wow. But what if that 1981 figure is bogus? If those earlier numbers were inflated, that means the decline in circulation now being lamented was not nearly as dramatic as it's being portrayed.

Some PhD candidate in history would find a very interesting dissertation topic questioning the very foundation of our fears about newspapers. What if the baseline for our grief over newspapers' demise turned out to be a mirage? It's hard to talk about the future if we're glimpsing the past through a thicket of misconceptions, misinformation and lies.

Nowadays, it seems that the big downward driving factor for circulation is the Internet. Right? Nobody talks about JOAs or strikes or mendacious circulation claims.

I wonder. At the Free Press, I listened to editors lecture us in meeting after meeting on how important it was for us to somehow attract young readers. I know young readers. I have two 20-something sons. They read newspapers. They even subscribe to them. Online. Free.

Are we wasting time trying to attract readers we don't have, never will have or already have on the free Internet while shortchanging readers who are actually paying for the paper? I hear from middle-aged and older people now that they are freeloading online, too. Deadwood. Nobody is forcing us to ramp up the money-losing Internet while undercutting the for-pay product.

I think about the publishers of The Journal Era back in the 1980s as they cut off the freeloading subscriptions. Why pay to print and mail papers to people who were draining the paper's assets? Today, newspapers are seeking out deadwood as if it would somehow pay. They behave as if this idea of giving their product away is inspired behavior. Newspapers are putting more and more effort and time into online reports. Not only are they getting no reimbursement for the news, they're having a hard time selling ads online. The New York Times in September 2007 announced it was dropping its profitable TimesSelect pay-to-read offering in order to generate more free hits that would make ad sales more lucrative. (In January 2010, the Times announced it would again be charging people to read its stories — sometime in 2011.)

In 2008, nationwide, online advertising accounted for only 5 percent of newspaper ad revenues. The print papers still produce 95 percent of the revenue, yet those readers are being shortchanged by increasingly smaller news holes and stories that are hastily reported. Readers know this. Could a decline in quality explain why people are canceling subscriptions? If so, the fault may not be the Internet. Once again, self-inflicted harm.

I actually have hope for the future of newspapers. Journalists mostly lack originality. They follow the leader. If the decline is more apparent than real, they are not likely to see it unless somebody at a bigger paper begins to say it.

The future of newspapers, whether paper or digital, may well lie with those owners who are able to fine-tune their operations without bullying from Wall Street and institutional investors. The future of newspapers will be with those editors and publishers who can think independently, separate their decision-making from the pack mentality and find flexibility to experiment and change quickly.

One thing is sure. If newspapers are to survive, whether paper or digital, they need to find more good old-fashioned credibility, curiosity and courage. Forget pandering to age groups or other special interests. Good stories appeal to everyone. If they don't, people will see no reason to pay for them.

Now, where are they going to find the credibility, courage and curiosity? Not in the J schools. You, the stringer, may be the salvation of the newspaper industry — if you can bring fresh, credible insights and fresh, credible ideas for stories that matter to readers.

chapter 28

a new journalism

Shoestring Reporter is just another how-to book. Right?

I hope not. True, I'm trying to show how YOU can report and write as well as the pros who are churned out of the nation's myriad academic Journalism programs. Actually, I believe YOU, my readers, collectively can do a much better job. And THAT is my real purpose in writing this book.

There is a problem with Journalism in America. A serious problem. It is a craft — I will not dignify it by the term "Profession" — plagued by seemingly self-imposed limitations on its own freedom of thought and expression. It is beset by a groupthink that I believe is imposed in those Journalism classes that you and I happily missed out on.

Censorship is a bad thing. Self-imposed censorship is worse. I began to catch onto the molded thinking of my fellow academically trained Journalists soon after I started stringing. There was a mini-scandal that had reporters in the South Bend chapter of the Society of Professional Journalists in a big lather. A reporter for a radio station had been voicing radio advertisements. Note that reading for ads was part of his assignment at the station. But the purists didn't worry about that. This guy, in their estimation, lacked credibility and could not be a full-fledged Professional Journalist, because he was straddling that divide between business and editorial operations. Somehow, voicing ads was tainting the objectivity of his reporting.

I listened to this discussion and was temporarily influenced by it. Gosh, a Journalist should not be tainted by the business side of his or her news organization. The time came when I was editor of the weekly Berrien Springs Journal Era. Occasionally, I sold an ad over the phone. I shot photos for ads. I thought about the SPJ thing. How my fellow reporters had discussed what sanctions they might be able to mete out to teach the miscreant radio reporter a lesson. There were none, of course. How could someone without the power of signing his paycheck punish a guy for doing his job? But they could talk, and yammer they did. Among the elect, the guy was a pariah. Somehow, he survived.

Years later, a friend of mine who was a reporter put up a yard sign favoring the Democratic incumbent for state senator. Down the street lived another reporter who began self-righteously running her mouth about the audacity of any Journalist who dared to express his political sentiments. Compromising his objectivity and that of his newspaper and similar pseudo-intellectual gunk.

It shows you how stupid Journalistic ethics debates can be. The advoicing issue is actually trivial. How about this one: As you work into stringing, you will eventually meet a Journalist who will piously tell you that she or he does not vote, because voting would compromise her or his objectivity.

Now I could tell you that I'll deal with "objectivity" in a future chapter, but in fact I wouldn't waste my time. There is no such thing as "objectivity," and anyone who believes in it is naïve at best and brainwashed at worst. We are all biased. Each of us was born, had parents, siblings maybe or not, grew up in the world; each of us has been hurt and helped and each of us has learned to cope with the world using knowledge based not on statistics or science but on subjective criteria. Gut reactions. This works for me, this does not. I like this, don't like that. Plain and simple. And those judgments form decisions we make about everything in life, including which stories we find interesting and which stories we wouldn't touch with radiation-proof gloves on.

Somehow, though, Journalists have come to view themselves as some kind of super beings with powers of objective reasoning that ordinary mortals lack. Nowhere in the Constitution does it state that there is a special class of human beings exempt from the duties and freedoms of citizens, yet Journalists will tell you with a straight face that they must not participate in politics, sometimes to the extent of refusing to vote; they will tell you that they should not be compelled to testify in court trials. And they certainly should never take a stand on any political issue.

This is hokum, folks. You wonder whom it benefits. Not Journalists, who are hamstrung politically, and gleefully join in the pseudo-intellectual hog-tying frenzy. The beneficiaries are the owners of newspapers who blithely donate their millions to politicians so they'll enact newspaper money-making machines like the Newspaper Preservation Act or in the case of broadcasters lighten the obligation to be fair and not to monopolize a market. Too many "bona fide" Journalists ignore these disparities. We need people who can see through the scams.

What we need is a new kind of thinking in Journalism. We need new Journalists who can look at the state of this craft and say honestly that Journalists have been censoring themselves often more severely than their editors and news organization owners censor them.

How often do the newspapers you read write about labor unions? Until recently, how often did they openly discuss issues like national health insurance? Yes, I said openly, meaning with an open mind. That would mean looking at national health insurance as more than a cash cow for private insurance companies. But until the Obama administration, the idea of a government-run national health insurance program for everyone was rarely discussed, and when the topic comes up now, it is called "Socialism," a negative label Americans have been trained — by the media — to think of as a Bad Thing.

How often do the media comprehensively discuss their own sacred issue of objectivity? Count how many of their articles are official-driven — that is, inspired by press releases or tips from government officials or allied nongovernmental organizations, charities, cultural institutions and businesses.

Here is where a stringer can shed new light. The stringer is not molded in the crucible of newsroom opinion. Yes, it may be an uphill battle to convince editors you have a new approach to an old story, but remember, you don't have to rely on relationships with editors at just one news outlet. You can play the field. And if you can find new ways of looking at age-old issues, you could brighten, enliven and rejuvenate Journalism.

chapter 29

never too old

I got my first stringing job over the phone. The editor who hired me couldn't see me. He based his decision entirely on the way I responded to his questions. Or not.

Because there were some things he didn't ask me. He didn't ask me if I had a J school degree. I didn't tell him that I lacked that piece of paper. Equally as important, he never asked me how old I was. I was 33 at the time. Now that may seem young to some of you nonagenarian or centenarian wannabe stringers, but the thirties can actually seem aged if your prospective editor is a 20-something. So it was good that age could not easily become a factor in my editor's decision to hire me.

He hired me because he needed someone to phone or mail copy that would fill his daily need to stuff that gaping news hole. No extraneous factors, like age, got in the way. This is one of the advantages of being a stringer. Invisibility. If you are perennially at the end of a phone or an e-mail line, your bosses can't see that maybe your hair is gray or that you rise from your chair with the help of a cane. This stuff shouldn't matter. And while I was a stringer, it didn't. Many months passed after I began sending stories to the newspaper before I met my editor. I was the one who initiated the meeting. Had I chosen never to meet Tom Gruber in person, we would never have seen each other. That is the way of stringing.

Since I aspired to become a full-time staffer, it was important to me that I meet the people I worked for. I had nothing to hide. So I thought. But once you enter the world of the staff writer, even as an outsider striving to enter it, the rules change. Age, race and sex, as well as personal appearance, become major determinants. Think hard before you start transforming yourself from stringer to staffer.

Think being in your thirties is no big deal? Remember what happened when I applied for that European Union fellowship to Paris? I wrote about that in Chapter 10, "Checkered Career." When I was 37, the French thought I was too old for a mid-career fellowship in Paris. I'd argued that in fact I was just beginning my "mid-career," having begun my pro Journalism career at the age of 33 1/3. But it turned out "mid-career" was a smoke screen, and age was the real determining factor.

Joel Thurtell

Employment

Detroit Free Press reporter since 1984; Two-year hiatus 1995-1997 while on strike as member of Newspaper Guild Local 22
South Bend Tribune reporter, 1981-1984
South Bend Tribune stringer, 1978-1981
Berrien Springs Journal Era weekly newspaper editor, 1979-1981
Detroit Sunday Journal, union strike paper; reporter, book review editor, 1995-1996
Freelance writer for TIME, New York Times, Detroit News, Planning Magazine, Detroit Free Press Magazine, Indianapolis Star Magazine, National Fisherman, The Progressive, Grand Rapids Press, 1978-1984
Technical writer for amateur radio magazines QST and Electric Radio 1971-present. Currently have the cover story in January 2003 QST; Author since 1999 of monthly column on wooden boat restoration for Flashes, a publication of the International Lightning Class Association
Author of book about wooden boat restoration, "Plug Nickel," published by Hardalee Books in 2001.
Author of four novels, three children's books and several short stories
Founder in 1995 and CEO of The Radio Finder, an internet company dealing in antique amateur radio equipment. Website: www.radiofinder.com
Belt sander, Landscape Forms wood shop, Kalamazoo, 1977
Belt sander, Watervliet Foundry, Kalamazoo, 1976-77
Farm worker, Hood Orchards, Paw Paw, 1974-76
Rural letter carrier, US Postal Service, Paw Paw, 1975
Peace Corps Volunteer, Togo, West Africa, 1973-74
Owner-driver, Ann Arbor Yellow Cab # 58, 1972
Research assistant, William L. Clements Library, University of Michigan, 1968-70
Belt sander, Newell Mfg. Co., Lowell, Michigan, summer 1967
Bean packer, C.H. Runciman Co., Lowell, Michigan, summer 1963, 1964
Blackboard washer and john cleaner, Kalamazoo College, Kalamazoo, Michigan, 1963-67
Printer's assistant, Lowell Ledger newspaper, Lowell, 1961
Carrier, Grand Rapids Press, 1957-1961
Farm worker, Rev. Norman Woon's onion farm, Lowell, Michigan, mid-1950s

Education

University of Michigan, M.A., 1968, in English Constitutional History with English literature cognate; Ph. D. Candidate, 1970, Colonial Latin American history with anthropology cognate
Rackham Prize Fellowship, 1970-71 for year-long dissertation research in rural Mexico
Kalamazoo College, B.A., 1967, history major and German minor

My "real" résumé, ca. 2003.

Foreign study at university in Bonn, Germany, 1965-66
Intern in Washington, D.C. office of U.S. Rep. and House Minority Leader Gerald Ford, 1965
Senior thesis research in British Museum and Public Record Office, London, 1967
Graduate of Lowell High School, Lowell, Michigan, 1963
Exchange student to Germany, 1962

Union

Tenants Union, Ann Arbor, 1968-69; took part in rent strike
Newspaper Guild Local 22, steward, ca 1987-present
Guild Salary Committee, Chairman, 1994-1995
Actively involved in recruiting new members, 2002-2003

Family

Married to Karen R. Fonde. M.D.
Sons Adam, 23 and Abraham, 20

Hobbies

Licensed amateur radio operator since 1959; Sailing and restoring wooden boats

---

At 37, I was too old. Elsewhere, I mentioned the editor who thought my age — 37 at the time — was too old for a rookie reporter on the cops beat. And there was the Free Press editor who "complimented" me on having such high energy at age 45.

A couple of years ago, as I was approaching 60, I applied for another "mid-career" fellowship in Journalism, this time at the University of Michigan. A reporter who actually got the fellowship I applied for told me later, "You would have been a great Fellow — too bad you're too old."

An old friend and terrific Journalist, Jeanne May, who was inducted into the Michigan Journalism Hall of Fame, never would tell people her age. Jeanne had battled another discriminatory barrier in Journalism — sexism and the idea that Journalism is a male-only club — and had learned that the less editors know about your personal life, the better.

Do the best work you can, but keep your age to yourself. You are never too old to be a stringer, but you are never too young for a biased editor to use your age against you.

chapter 30

brainwashed

It's taken me years to formulate a few key secrets about Journalists and the J schools that spawn them, and I'm going to reveal these secrets to you so you can avoid making some of my mistakes.

I admit it: For a time, I was deluded about my status in the community. I thought because I was a Journalist that I had certain rights and duties that made me better than my neighbors. But unlike the vast majority of Journalists, I never let myself be conned into thinking that I gave up some rights when I became a Journalist.

It's important that you know that most Journalists believe they have given up their rights as a citizen to take part in political discussions and to participate in politics. I don't have stats for the following, but I'm convinced the vast majority of Journalists believe that unlike John Doe next door, they don't have to obey the law when it comes to answering a court summons, either.

It's one thing for people to believe in myths. So long as you can avoid subscribing to the shibboleths, it's the lookout of the benighted, not you. But beware of deluding yourself. I'm convinced that the prime myths of Journalism originated with publishers in an effort to control Journalists. Here's why: Journalists find out things that ordinary people, even newspaper publishers, wouldn't otherwise know. Often, if it's something to do with government or police, it doesn't affect the publisher. We can pour out ink by the tanker-load on cops-and-robbers stories, or bad-guy politician stories that don't affect us directly. But what if a publisher has an interest in something going on in government? What if the publisher is trying to persuade local elected officials to steer government legal advertising — worth lots of money — to his or her paper?

What if a newspaper is trying to persuade a mayor and a city council (this actually happened in Detroit) to grant the paper a tax abatement for construction of, say, a printing plant?

Or what if a pair of newspapers decide they could make more money if they were not competing but instead joined in a normally illegal monopoly? What if such monopolies, prohibited for other businesses by federal antitrust laws because they fix prices and screw consumers, were made legal by Congress through something euphemistically called a Newspaper Preservation Act that was enacted because of lobbying by newspapers?

Wouldn't the newspapers want to control what the public understood about their attempts to influence events in which they have a big self-interest? Wouldn't they want people to think they were and are great altruistic institutions in quest of higher truths instead of the grubbers after the almighty dollar that they really are? Then they would want to control what is reported about those undertakings. Do you think they would play fair and allow the Journalists whose paychecks they sign to report honestly about those affairs? Do you think there is green cheese on the moon?

Or what if a media giant was concerned that federal communications rules might force it to sell some television stations because it had dominated a local market or two beyond the already high level allowed by the government? Rupert Murdoch wouldn't try to influence reporting on his manipulations involving the Federal Communications Commission — would he?

Major media corporations spend millions on lobbying and campaign contributions in hopes of getting their way with government agencies. There is nothing objective about this. And nobody says they don't have a right, like any other business, to influence events that affect their profits. Why, that would be their right under the First Amendment, wouldn't it?

But the same First Amendment would seem to preserve the right of Journalists to investigate these behaviors and expose them. Who are the best people to out them? Who are the people who delve into business and government doings? Journalists. An independent Journalist can be a dangerous thing. But if those theoretically independent Journalists can be muzzled, the story of media influence on politics can be stifled. Publishers can easily muzzle reporters — it's done all the time. Kill their stories. Cut their copy to ribbons. Forbid them to write about uncomfortable — to publishers — topics. What if a reporter is revealing unsavory facts about a local congressman with the power to investigate the legality of the Detroit newspaper monopoly? Hey, maybe the answer would be to transfer the reporter from investigations to writing suburban features. This is done all the time, but for publishers it isn't enough. They have sought to persuade Journalists to censor themselves.

What better method for controlling reporters than persuading them to stifle themselves? What if you as a reporter know some bad things are going on, but you are not allowed to write about them? You try to peddle your story to other news organizations, but are forbidden by your editors, who speak grandiosely if vaguely of conflicts of interest. Didn't our Detroit monopoly come about because a Supreme Court justice recused himself due to contact with one of the interested newspapers, thus giving us the Joint Operating Agreement on a 4-4 vote?

So you decide there is another way to put your knowledge to use: You will donate money to a political party in hopes that through the electoral process you may indirectly achieve positive change. Isn't this the same thing publishers do?

Yes, it is. But woe unto the working Journalist who tries to do it. The Journalist must be Objective. He or she must not be tainted by the smell of political opinion.

Let me tell you what happened to me. In the early 2000s, I learned that a powerful Member of Congress from Detroit, John Conyers Jr., had for years been abusing his paid congressional staffers by forcing them to campaign for him and other candidates, including his wife. He made them do it on government time. That is illegal. They used government offices, government phones, fax machines, copiers. All illegal or unethical. When I first proposed doing the story, I was turned down.

No surprise.

An inside source in Conyers' office had given huge amounts of documents portraying Conyers' behavior to the FBI and they showed no interest, either. At the time, Conyers was the ranking Democrat on the House Judiciary Committee. Even in the minority, he had tremendous power. In 2008, he was chairman of the committee investigating the Bush administration's handling of illegal wiretapping and the Bush administration's firing of U.S. attorneys who wouldn't prosecute Democrats for sham offenses.

There is another area of federal law that few people notice. Certainly it doesn't get ink from Detroit newspapers. It is the fact that in 1989, the federal government allowed the Detroit Free Press and the News to operate a monopoly in which they combined their businesses and set prices. Normally, this would be illegal under antitrust laws, but the 1970 Newspaper Preservation Act allows it if one of the papers can be shown to be "failing." Ostensibly, this was to preserve two "independent" newspaper voices in Detroit, one owned by Knight Ridder and the other owned by Gannett. Today, Knight Ridder no longer exists, Gannett owns or controls both papers, along with a large chain (recently made smaller) of suburban Detroit papers, and the question of whether those multiple ownerships in one market constitute a monopoly contrary even to the permissive Newspaper Preservation Act is never raised.

Or is it? I didn't write about John Conyers anymore in my last couple of years at the Free Press. I didn't write investigative reports for the Free Press at all. I was assigned to write features exclusively. It was suggested to me that my last assignment may have been related to my age. One young reporter, hoping she wouldn't be picked for what appeared an ignominious fate — writing for weekly feature sections rather than the supposedly more glamorous life of the guns-and-mayhem Metro Desk reporter — suggested managers might want to assign "elderly" reporters to the features beat so the oldsters could "coast to retirement."

Others linked my features assignment to my reporting on Conyers. Did John Conyers threaten the Detroit newspapers, maybe suggest he'd mount an investigation into the legality of the current monopoly if they kept on publishing stories exposing his abuses of congressional staffers? Or did newspaper executives fear that might happen and stop me from writing about Conyers as insurance against retaliation from the congressman?

This is all speculation, of course. At the bottom end of the food chain, a staff writer is often kept in the dark about the motives of higher-ups. My proposed explanations are what historians call *hypotheses* — theoretical explanations that have to do until more evidence is uncovered. A hypothesis may well be contradicted; it may be replaced with one more accurate; it may be replaced by one totally different. I don't know. All I know is that I was stopped from writing about Conyers, and my editors forbade me to write about him in other forums.

In 2004, I contributed $500 to the Michigan Democratic Party. Nothing to do with Conyers. I wanted to help oust George W. Bush from the White House. Three years later, when editors of the Free Press learned of my largesse, they read their own ethics policy and realized I had not violated it. So they rewrote the paper's ethics policy to prohibit campaign contributions and threatened to fire me if I gave any more money to political parties.

A reporter who knows too much about a powerful Democrat is prevented from reporting further on that congressman. In the name of objectivity, the reporter is threatened with dismissal if he takes the story somewhere else. When he gives money to the political party of that very congressman, he is warned that it was a no-no even though it was not. And he is threatened with firing if he gives money to political parties or candidates in future.

My mind is boggled. Even felons may donate money to politicians. Newspaper oligarchs like Rupert Murdoch may lobby politicians. Murdoch, Gannett and other media corporations may routinely lobby Washington for favorable treatment. Media outlets may routinely manipulate reporting; they may publish editorials for or against politicians, but they forbid their employees to give money to a candidate or even place political bumper stickers on their own cars.

The weird thing about all this pillorying of Journalists by other Journalists is the failure to perceive that in giving money to a politician, the Journalist is trying to influence events. What is wrong with that? Now, if the money flowed the other way, and I TOOK money from some organization that I wrote about, that kind of behavior should be condemned. In that case, it could be reasonably argued that my influence as a reporter was being bought.

Now for the real whammy. In denying my union's grievance protesting the Free Press' threat to fire me if I exercised my constitutional right to take part in the political process, brass at the Free Press actually wrote on paper the statement that I, as the employee of a private institution, have no First Amendment rights. See how it works? The First Amendment was made for newspapers, not for news workers.

What does that boil down to? An argument for being a stringer. This is a case against being a full-time Journalist. Not all media organizations ban political giving by staffers. Time magazine does not. The New York Times does. Most news organizations do. On one end, they lobby, they publish reports and editorials that favor their business interests and on the other end they censor the Journalists who work for them, preventing them from spilling what they know about the bosses' business interests.

To be truly independent, you not only must not BE a staff Journalist, you must refrain from SEEKING full-time employment. Even so, stringers will find editors trying to force their so-called Ethics Policies onto them. But as a stringer, an independent contractor, you are free to reject those policies. It may mean giving up some income. It may mean turning down work from employers who insist on imposing their repressive policies on you.

Such is the price of independence.

Now more than ever we need independent Journalists!

We need YOU!

chapter 31

bait & switch

It was seven in the morning. I was still in bed when my wife roused me. It was my editor at the Grand Rapids paper. Groggy, I picked up the phone and realized that the person speaking was not "my" editor after all, but his replacement. As a stringer, you learn quickly that the newspaper business is never static: Staff turnover — "churn," some call it — is a fact of life.

In this case, "my" editor had left the paper, and his successor was calling to "adjust" the fees his predecessor had agreed to pay me for a series of travel stories I had already — key word, *already*, — written, submitted and seen go to print. I was supposed to receive $70 per story. Not big money. But too big, it seemed, for the new guy. So here I am at seven in the morning standing in my PJs listening to this turkey telling me seventy bucks was too much and he was cutting the fee in half. Thirty-five bucks seemed fair to him.

But to me it didn't. I told him so. A deal is a deal. I upheld my side of the deal. We had agreed on the price. I reported and wrote the stories, submitted them and they were found acceptable and ran in the paper. Now is no time to renege on the fees. Seventy bucks, I said. I hung up and headed back for bed. The phone rang. I picked up. My new editor had a change of heart. Seventy bucks was okay after all.

I tell the story to illustrate how untrustworthy editors can be. Not all of them are like that. But there are enough liars and cheats in the newsrooms that I feel it necessary to warn aspiring stringers to be careful. Try to get conversations about fees, deadlines, story lengths and other specifications in writing. E-mail is wonderful for that. Paper trail.

Now, you might ask, why did the editor come so quickly to agree with me? I don't know, of course, but I can guess that he decided it wasn't worth the $35 to run the risk that I would call his boss and report his chiseling.

It pays to understand that newspapers are organized loosely along hierarchical lines. There is a chain of command. You may also be interested to know that newsrooms are getting less and less pleasant; there is more anger, far more ass-chewings going on now, because the incessant news about layoffs and firings has placed everybody's job in jeopardy. People are scared, and that includes editors. The last thing a mid-level manager wants is to have some lowly stringer bad-mouthing her or him to the bosses. If there is an ounce of credibility to the complaint, it can hurt; even if the complaint is bogus, it can be used to enforce discipline.

What that means for the stringer is this: Keep a clipping of the masthead staff listing handy. Know who the top editors are — in other words, know who's boss over your editor.

But remember, if you use that ploy, it likely will be the last time you work for that editor — and maybe the last time you work for that paper.

PAGE TWO   THE

The Journal Era

P.O. Box 98, Berrien Springs, Michigan 49103

BERRIEN SPRINGS OFFICE - 119 W. FERRY ST.

The Journal Era (USPS 277-700) is published weekly for $4.50 per year by John W. Gillette, 119 W. Ferry Street, Berrien Springs, Michigan 49103.

John W. and Patricia V. Gillette...................Publishers
Joel Thurtell ....Editor

-TELEPHONE-
Berrien Springs 473-5421

PUBLISHED EVERY WEDNESDAY

Subscription: $4.50 Per Year in Berrien County
Subscriptions: Out of Berrien County $5.00 Per Year
Second Class Postage Paid at Berrien Springs, Michigan 49103
Member of Michigan Press Association

Reprinted courtesy of The (Berrien Springs) Journal Era

chapter 32

first thing we do...

"...is kill all the editors."

Shakespeare, right?

Okay, I know. It's "kill all the lawyers."

And just as there are fine lawyers who sometimes save our butts, so there are fine editors in the world.

Having said that, let me warn you about another Bait & Switch ploy I've heard too often. It's the false promise of 1A, as in, "Hey, Joel, they're talking about your story for Page One. So we need it fast and make it REALLY good."

There's a double insult there. First, I ALWAYS make my stories REALLY good. I don't need some penny-ante editor to motivate me off the dime to write well. Fact is, most of my stories never got close to Page One, but that doesn't matter. I report and write them as well as time and my limited talents allow.

The second and bigger insult is the very idea that I might be motivated to do better by being lied to. Or just considered a chump. Placement of stories is a moving target. Editors may talk about putting a story on 1A, and seconds later — maybe there's a triple homicide or the mayor's been indicted — that 1A story is slated for a spot next to the death notices.

From the writer's point of view, that Shakespeare quote might well be from an editor: "The first thing we do, is kill all the stories."

For staffers, it doesn't matter. Oh, sure, we get bent out of shape when our stories are cut or killed. I bellyached about this to an old-timer early in my career. Woe is me, they've spiked my story, I lamented. "So what?" the old hand said: "You get paid the same."

He was right. I'm on salary. The story dies, but my paycheck won't be docked. Not so for you, the stringer. I'm recalling a time early on in my stringing when I thought I'd really hit it big. The Chicago Tribune was going to publish a story of mine. I was very excited. It was a timely story, meaning it had to run on a certain weekend or it was dead. The editor told me it would run on a Sunday. My wife and I decided to spend that weekend in Chicago. I looked forward to the glory of seeing my byline in the venerable Trib.

I bought several papers that Sunday. No story.

On Monday, I called the editor. So sorry, she said. We ran out of space. And that was it. No story, no pay. Which brings up the dismal subject of death once again. I learned the hard way that death should be mentioned early on when dealing with editors. If your story should die for any reason, you are entitled to collect a "kill fee." The kill fee won't be as high as the fee they agreed to pay you upon publication, but it should be a good portion of it. After all, you worked on the piece, and it's not your fault if the newspaper suddenly runs out of space. Actually, you can bet it's poor planning on the editor's part. So the editors shouldn't cringe at spending part of their budget on a story they didn't use. Besides the money, there's another benefit: If you secure the promise of a kill fee, an editor will be less likely to actually kill your story.

Why? Because whether or not they run your story, it will nick the paper's budget and the editor will have to explain to his or her bosses why the story didn't make the paper. Smacks of negligence. Editors are evaluated, and as oxymoronic as it may seem, like "military intelligence," there are occasions when editors actually think ahead. Committing money for a story and not using it is bad planning. Unless there is a good reason — like maybe you screwed up the reporting, did a sloppy job of writing or simply blew deadline — the editor won't want to make excuses and most likely will make sure your story — well-reported, beautifully crafted and submitted well ahead of deadline — makes the paper.

chapter 33

not well paid, but...

I was going to be a teacher, but something happened.
Something called Journalism.
I know plenty of high school and college teachers. About all I envy in their lives is the long summers off with pay. What a deal. There have been times when I've actually looked into what it would take to get back on the teaching track. Eventually, we concluded that, first, it would cost too much money and take too much time either to be certified as a public-school teacher or to finish my doctoral dissertation and secondly, compared with what I'm doing, teaching would be — sorry to say it, teachers — a great big bore!

There's more money and better benefits, I grant you. But think of the downside. Lesson plans? My God, you'd have to outline what you were going to teach for an entire year, then stick to it. Teaching would be the antithesis of Journalism, where the lesson plan changes not daily, not hourly, but every minute. One of the maddening and exciting things about Journalism is the simple unpredictability of it.

Am I admitting to a strong streak of attention deficit disorder? So be it. Now, I'm not saying a Journalist is disorganized. Many are, of course. And the process that passes for thinking is more Pavlovian than process, by which I mean Journalists often move ahead in a series of knee-jerk, me-too motions diametrically opposite to thought. Teaching — my God, you'd have to put up with sniveling, middle-class brats belonging to somebody else! No thanks.

There is something akin to true freedom in Journalism — for the stringer. Not so much for the staffer. Staff writers are slaves to hierarchy, lackeys of careerism, either their own or their editors', and often have no choice about what they write, and how.

Let me give you one lurid example. I will never forget this experience. On March 24, 1987, a regent of the University of Michigan committed suicide by jumping off the campus bell tower. An editor called me and ordered me to phone the regent's husband for comment. I was not happy about this assignment. No way did I want to phone the dead woman's husband. However, I was an employee of the Free Press. That means that the editors command and I obey. Or else.

I'm not kidding. Neither are the bosses. Reporters have been fired for refusing to obey editors' orders. Also, while foul language is fairly normal in newsrooms, beware of smart-ass remarks to editors. I know a reporter — rather, a *former* reporter — who was fired for saying "Fuck you!" to her editor at The Detroit News.

Insubordination.

In the case of the regent, I called the husband. He was himself a newspaperman and knew, I'm sure, that I was calling under orders. But he made it clear he wasn't happy at being disturbed as he offered his "no comment." I hated doing that and I hated myself for having done it.

If you're a stringer, ladies and gentlemen, you don't have to make those calls. Tell them to order a staffer to do their dirty deeds. They can't fire you, because they never hired you. They might cut your workload to punish you, but if you are a good writer and dependably help them fill their news hole, believe me, their revenge will soon lose its sweetness and they'll be back knocking on your door for more of their beloved copy.

Meanwhile, back to the benefits of Journalism, which beat teaching, selling insurance or just about any other occupation I can think of. Yes, as I mentioned before, I got to fly in a Navy F/A-18 Blue Angels jet fighter. I've flown with Detroit-area traffic reporters, watching the streets from 500 feet up in a helicopter. I got to fly in a World War II AT-6 training plane like the one my dad flew. I wanted for years to find out what it's like to fly in a blimp and finally I arranged it and wrote an article about it.

What's it like in a blimp? Kind of like a boat. It rocks!

Speaking of boats, I stood on the bridge of a U.S. Coast Guard icebreaker knocking floes off the Detroit River; I persuaded editors to pay me and a photographer to take a five-day canoe trip up the Rouge River through the heart of crime-ridden Detroit, an adventure that so far nobody has wanted to repeat.

I wondered what it would be like to blow glass, so I did it, with the help of a local glassblower. I carved a dolphin out of a 300-pound block of ice, coached by an expert whose story I wrote. And so on. Curious about how some job is done? Do it, then write it up for the paper!

You see what I mean — I pretty much write my own leads. I concoct my own story ideas, then find ways to produce them. Some are complex, others are fairly simple. All are fun.

And you can do the same thing as a stringer. And unlike me, you can sell and resell those stories for years to come. Think of it as investing in the stock market.

The stock is YOU!

chapter 34

censorship 101

Ever find yourself reading a newspaper and sensing that something is missing? That's because usually something *is* missing. Articles often stress one or two angles, but seem to ignore others. As you read, questions may rise in your mind to which there are no answers. At least not in the papers.

There is a reason for this. It's called censorship. Much of it is self-imposed not only by newspaper owners and their editors, but by reporters themselves — upon themselves.

Here's one way it happens: Say you are assigned to cover a beat. Maybe it's county government. The county executive issues a press release. It highlights issues that make him or her look good and downplays or ignores the negatives. Do you dig around to find the downsides and write a balanced report? A good reporter would. But there are reporters out there who would be satisfied to parrot what the officials tell them. They, like their editors, fear the news hole, and they depend on government sources to help them clutter the paper with boring government-focused claptrap. Small papers seem especially guilty of this practice, but it happens even at the hallowed Times.

The problem with writing the balanced report is that it might piss off somebody with the power to exclude you from those press releases, press conferences and other freebies that grease the news machine and make a reporter's life oh so much easier.

Recall Times reporter Judith Miller, who went to jail supposedly to protect a government source? Eventually, we discovered that Miller was viewed by government officials as a "friendly" reporter, and in fact she was writing biased reports that helped mislead the United States into the Iraq war. What I am discussing is bribery. By accepting the payoff — a leak, maybe, or an exclusive interview, you are agreeing to float a one-sided report. If you allow this subtle form of bribery to order your reporting, you have effectively agreed to be censored.

It can happen in many ways. When I was editor of the weekly, a delegation of important people, including the school superintendent, visited the publisher and me and invited us to join the Rotary Club. Somebody else invited us to join the Lions Club. Worthy organizations. We declined. I was plenty accessible without having lunch once a week with people who want to use me to get their names into the paper. Worse, I can imagine the pressure that would bear on an honest reporter who started writing stories questioning a member of his or her service club. There would be tremendous mental pressure simply not to do it. No, thanks.

Since retiring from the Free Press, I've joined a Rotary club. But at this point in my life, I'm not writing local stories in a newspaper, and a service group is one way I can help do good work in my community.

Fear of pissing off government officials is a major mental liability that many reporters and editors harbor. Here's another example: A government official leaks documents to you that give you a scoop and you beat other reporters on a story. Hey, great, you're one up on the competition. But what if you suspect that government official of being a cheat or liar or thief? Do you report it and thus risk being cut off from your little underground news tip gravy train? If you hold back, once again you have agreed to be censored. Nobody has to kill your story. You simply don't pitch that story. Happens too often.

It's in our heads. How do you beat it out of your brain? Here's my solution: You are the Journalist. Ask yourself, Who is my boss? Is it this government official who's feeding me juicy tips? Is it the sheriff — and this actually happened to me — who blacklisted me on breaking crime news because he didn't like my stories?

Is it my editor? Is it the owner of the newspaper?

The answer to all these questions is NO.

My bosses are my *readers*. If I can stay true to the people who truly appreciate what I do, if I can remember that they are the ones who finally will judge my work, then it's much easier to gather the strength to do the right thing.

We don't write for government functionaries, for business cronies, for editors or even for other reporters. We write for one audience: the readers who trust us to write fairly for them.

As a stringer, you have a luxury that eludes most staff writers. You have independence. You can write the truth as you see it. If an editor assigns you to write something that is false, you can simply say NO! But the staffer who says it risks being fired. You can be fired, too, but if you have several employers, you can afford to say adios to one or two who ask you to do things that are offensive.

Your independence is not complete, of course. You can write a story and see it in print, and it may read quite differently than you intended. The nice word is "editing," but the reality is censorship. You can squawk about it, and should. If the bad editorial behavior continues, start selling your stories to the competition. Or just stop submitting them. Unlike the staffer, who loses health and pension benefits by quitting or getting fired, you aren't getting the candy, so they can't take it away.

chapter 35

page one envy

"The most powerful tool newspaper owners have for socializing reporters," a veteran newsman once told me, "is Page One."

Certain kinds of behavior are rewarded with this seemingly rich plum, and other kinds of behavior are discouraged by denial, again of this supposedly enviable prize. In a minute, we'll think about how rich this plum really is, but for now it's important to recognize that the front page of the newspaper does not necessarily showcase the best and brightest writing on a newspaper's staff. Oh, sure, editors in their meetings may pretend that what they're pitching for 1A is the paper's best offering. But underneath and behind the scenes many political considerations — unspoken — are the powerful moving forces that determine what you read on the front page of tomorrow's newspaper.

It's not really democratic. It's not really based on merit. It's based on a system of rewards and penalties, unwritten, unspoken, but nonetheless potent.

It's not completely true, but close enough for newspaper work, that editors have dumb story ideas. At a top-down, editor-driven paper like the Free Press, where editors too often are not tuned to the ideas reporters pitch, but prefer seeing their own inspirations in print, certain tools are needed to make this happen. One of the best tools for putting ill-considered claptrap into the paper is the compliant reporter.

A reporter who thinks independently and speaks his or her mind would be a poor tool for an editor who has the brilliant idea of chasing a day-old crime story that has been thoroughly beaten into the ground by radio and TV.

A good reporter would say, "Bullshit!"

But what if you have an inexperienced, preferably single, young, recent grad from J school with little self-confidence, zero experience with any work outside newspapers and a marked inability to hatch original story ideas? In a meritocratic system, such a reporter would be headed for failure. But sometimes editors feed their lame ideas to an untalented reporter, all the while complimenting and stroking him or her, massaging poorly written copy until it meets minimum newspaper standards for grammar and construction, placing it on Page One. Presto! A star is born. Yes, it is not only possible but actually done very often — manufacturing stars.

When I first started reporting for the Tribune, I was disappointed that my work rarely appeared on Page One. I thought it might have something to do with the fact that I was a stringer, not a staffer. I was probably correct. When I became a staffer, I thought that would change. Here I was, writing investigative reports, writing controversial stories, yet I rarely made Page One.

It was disappointing and baffling. A meagerly reported boring story about a school board in Berrien County would make the front page while my revelations about commissioners in the county next door was played inside.

What was going on? Eventually, I figured it out: Marketing. There were far more readers and advertisers in Niles than in Cass County. The quality of the writing, the depth of the reporting and the impact of the story were less important than playing to the market that was dominated by that little Michigan border town adjacent to South Bend.

The playing field is not level. Editors will discriminate against stringers. The unfairness is practiced against staffers, too. Get used to it. Make sure you get a paycheck. Hang up your ego when you log on. Remember this: Page One looks good in a clip portfolio, but it doesn't pay bills any better than a story that ran on Page 13.

That's right, Page 13. That page has special meaning for me. It taught me that if your story is truly important, readers will find it no matter how deeply buried it is. I learned this in 1980 when I wrote my first real investigative story about a juvenile court judge who freed a socially well-connected boy who had raped a woman at knifepoint. Staff at the juvenile center argued the kid was a danger and should be kept behind bars, but the judge let him go. Soon, the kid had raped and murdered a classmate. The girl would have been alive if the judge had listened to the staff instead of to the boy's dad. That was my story. Pat Gillette, copublisher of The Journal Era, was offended by this story. She didn't want to use the word "rape" in her paper. John Gillette, her husband and copublisher, persuaded her that the story with the word she disliked could run, but on Page Three. Okay. But somehow the printers misunderstood. The story ended up on Page Thirteen. Didn't matter. Readers found it. It was explosive no matter where it played.

Report your story as well as you can, write it as brilliantly as you can. Don't worry about where it shows up in the newspaper. If it's important, it will be read.

Pity those people who constantly make Page One. They are the darlings of editors only as long as they behave themselves. Disobedience will be punished. The reporter who sucks up for Page One is a weak reporter. The reporter who keeps his or her own counsel, persists in reporting good stories even though editors show little interest and even though the articles run deep in the paper — that is a strong reporter. Demeaned, yes, but actually more powerful than the lackeys of Page One.

So don't envy the Page One writers. Feel sorry for the suckers. Then ask yourself: As a stringer, how can I make this work for me?

Well, as those editors and fair-haired reporters are scrambling to subdivide the scarce Page One real estate, there is a crying need to fill the inner pages of the paper. You aren't going to be paid more for a story that runs on Page One, and given the internal politics (which you, as an outsider, a mere stringer, cannot even know), the chances of making it are slim. Concentrate on writing fine stories and don't worry about where they land. Remember, you are needed — not on Page One, but where it counts, within the paper. Readers will find you even if the Page One folk don't.

Here's another reason it's good to have your copy buried: What the big bosses don't read, they won't mess with. Page One gets microscopic scrutiny from all the Big Egos who want to think that but for them the paper would never be printed. They don't pay nearly as much attention to what appears inside.

There is freedom in being a back-pager.

chapter 36

why are editors dumb?

That is not a fair question.

I'm sure that at least some editors came into the world as intelligent life forms. They may have remained smart through school and college. Where they went wrong — where they got dumb — was in the newsroom.

Recall a previous chapter called "The Pack-A-Day Gang"? Reporters, even ones from rival papers, will band together to collectively protect themselves while out on the beat. Nothing wrong with this. In fact, it makes sense. From whom are they protecting themselves? Not their sources. Not the cops or judges or government officials they cover. No, nine times out of 10, they are cooperating to ward off the excesses of editors who have just leaned back with a fresh cup of coffee and terrific ideas straight from the latest television newscast.

But cooperation has ill effects. By collaborating, reporters often blunt their own ability to ask questions. They tie their brains to those of others, they become dependent on others for information and they let others filter out potentially important facts. The biases of other people become their biases. As Journalists let this happen, they allow themselves to lose mental power. They get dumb.

Well, editors and reporters band together in the newsroom, too. They will unthinkingly support one another's prejudices and biases. Hey, if I'm prejudiced against Judge Bang-Bang and you hate Mayor Punk, let's combine our displeasures for more firepower. Honestly, the collaborative bile that flows through newsrooms and news bureaus is very potent, if ugly, stuff. It can make and unmake careers of those who unwittingly allow themselves to become targets of Journalistic venom. This is part of what I mean about becoming dumb by stepping into a newsroom. It is also a form of subtle bribery. I'll hate your enemy if you'll hate mine.

You, the stringer — and more so the staffer — can be hurt when these machinations are going on. It happened to me a few years ago when I was caught up unintentionally in a feud between staffers and a county prosecutor. I'll delve into that more deeply in my chapter called "Struck Out."

There is the desire to be respected for news judgment. This is a hard one. If you're an editor, you aren't as likely to actually FIND a story, compared, say, with a reporter who's out roaming and talking to actual people who may know actual facts. The next best thing to a source in the field is radio, TV and now the Internet. So what if you're not mixing with real people? There are real ideas on the Web, aren't there? So what if they're ideas that have been chewed on by local, regional and national media? You can make yourself look smart by assigning a reporter to "localize" an idea you cribbed from the Times, say, or Newsweek or Channel 7, which no doubt stole it from some local reporter in the first place.

As a stringer, an independent observer and thinker, you can offer fresh ideas, unthought-of perspectives, to editors who may themselves be struggling against the forces of numbness pressing on them. The beauty of stringing is that if one editor rejects your idea, you simply peddle it to another. Before I was hired full-time at the Free Press, I would offer story ideas to that paper before pitching them to the News. Mostly, Free Press editors rejected my ideas, whereupon I'd send the story to the News and see it published.

One of those rejected-by-the-Free-Press, published-by-the-News stories stands out in my memory. I learned of a group of elderly Potowatomi Indians, all of whom had been taken from their families at age five by the federal government and placed in a school for Indians where it was drummed into their young minds that it was bad to be Indians. They were not allowed to speak Indian languages or take part in any activities related to Indian culture. They were to be "assimilated" into American society. Late in life, having retired from their White Man's jobs, they got together and started weaving baskets of black ash made as best they could recall according to the Indian techniques that supposedly had been expunged from their minds. One of these people, Mark Alexis, intrigued me in particular because he had managed to build a birch-bark canoe based on his recollection of how he'd watched his father do it.

The story ran with my photos in the Tribune. I sent it to an editor at the Free Press. No dice, he said. After striking out at the News, I waited and, when they got a new state editor, I sent it to him. Dave Good ran it, along with several of my photos. It had one of my favorite leads: "Mark Alexis is trying to remember what it was like to be an Indian." Dave Good had payroll mail me a check for $200. Not bad for 1984 (when two hundred bucks was worth $394 in 2007 currency).

Mark Alexis gets his Indian woven baskets ready for sale.

PHOTOS BY JOEL THURTELL

Potawatomi basket weaver Julia Weesaw.

Indian, 68, hunts roots

By Joel Thurtell
News Special Writer

SISTER LAKES, Mich. — Mark Alexis is trying to remember what it was like to be an Indian.

Alexis, 68, is a full-blooded Potawatomi. But in 1921, federal Indian policy said boys like Alexis, then 6, should grow up to be middle-class Americans — not American Indians.

He was taken away from his family in the Potawatomi community of Toquin, near Watervliet, and sent to a U.S. government Indian school at Mt. Pleasant.

"WE HAD no choice," recalls Alexis. "If you were an Indian, they took you."

From then until he retired as a tool and die maker, Alexis lived pretty much like a white man, working a white man's job.

He left the school at 17, having visited his family twice in 11 years.

"They called it assimilation," says Alexis. "That was the idea, to get rid of the culture."

Continued on Page 5C

Reprinted courtesy of The Detroit News

Retired as toolmaker

Thursday, Apr. 19, 1984—THE DETROIT NEWS—5-C

Indian seeks return to the old ways

Continued from Page 1C

Alexis' parents didn't speak English. They spoke Potawatomi, he says.

The Indians at Toquin were hunters and trappers, and during the summer they gathered berries and fruit. They paddled on the streams of western Michigan in canoes they made of birch stripped from broad trees in the hot summer months.

And there was nothing wrong with any of that, to Alexis' way of thinking.

After he retired from Paramount Die Cast in Stevensville, Alexis started the Black Ash Basket Project. The group met each Saturday during the summer to explore the old ways of basket-making.

THAT WAS three years ago. With a grant from the Michigan Arts Council, the group can now pay to heat the old Silver Creek Town Hall, five miles northwest of Dowagiac on Town Hall Road. Members bought the building, renamed it "Potawatomi Hall" and meet every Saturday, all year.

"We figured we'd get it going so the young people would learn," he says.

But, many of the older Indians hadn't made baskets in many years. First they had to remember how it was done.

"I learned this from my grandmother and mother," says Julia Weesaw, 75, as she scrapes a paper-thin ribbon of wood. "I just learned by watching them.

"WE CHILDREN just made little ones. We sold them at resorts."

Pauline Starrett, Mrs. Weesaw's cousin, is in her mid-50s. She never wove baskets or saw them woven as a child, and only started coming to the Saturday sessions about six months ago.

"I don't want it lost," Mrs. Starrett says.

Nodding towards Mrs. Weesaw and Mark Alexis, Mrs. Starrett observes that "when these people go, basket weaving will go. There's nobody else to do it."

BUT, MAYBE there is some hope, she adds: After all, "until they started doing it, nobody did it."

The group sells its baskets at local fairs and Indian gatherings. Their wares bring in anywhere from $5 to $200, with the money going to support the project.

At Potawatomi Hall, the men and women have divided the basket-making work.

Alexis and his friend, Mike Daugherty, drag black ash logs out of the swamp.

"ASH IS more flexible," says Alexis. "We also use swamp oak."

In Daugherty's back yard, Alexis pounds the log until the growth rings loosen.

Using his bare hands, he pries a ring, or "grain," away from the log, pulling off a strip of wood about an eighth of an inch thick.

The men deliver these grains to the hall where the women strip and scrape them into thinner pieces to be woven into baskets.

"IF IT'S TOO thick, you split it," says Alexis. "If it's still too thick, you split it again. You split it till it's like a ribbon."

And, then you scrape it smooth with the knife blade.

Using a small metal ruler, Daugherty's wife Rae, also a Potawatomi, measures the width of the grains she wants. Later, she will slice through the wood to get ribbons of the right size.

The strips of wood are then woven in checkerboard design around uprights laid out in a circle.

WHILE THE women weave, Alexis and Daugherty, who describes himself as "part Choctaw, part Cherokee and part Irish," lecture each other about this summer's project.

"We're gonna make the Indian's Mercedes Benz," declares Alexis. "A Potawatomi lake canoe."

Alexis says he knows where there's a good 12-inch thick birch tree down by a riverbank to supply the skin of the canoe. And, he says he has the cedar planking and black spruce roots for lashings.

"I made little ones out of elm bark as a boy," Alexis says. "I never made one to launch, but my folks used to.

"We've still got the idea we can do it. We can do it, because we're Indians."

DESIGNER DRESS SHIRT MONTH

Some years later, the Free Press editor who rejected my Mark Alexis story became one of my editors on the Free Press City Desk. And the Mark Alexis thing kept reinventing itself. This editor would stifle my ideas. There is a tendency for writers whose ideas are crapped on to convert to the editor's mindset and come to the belief that the idea is indeed crappy. I was lucky to have had this editor kill my idea only to have it resuscitated by the rival News. Because whenever the Freep editor would dump on an idea, I'd just think about the nice play the News gave the Mark Alexis story and, of course, I'd remember how sweet it was to cash that $200 check.

The memory was especially sweet one day in late 1987 when the same editor censored a section of a story that I thought was real dynamite. Years later, for the twentieth anniversary of a horrendous airplane crash, the Detroit-area papers were plowing up the lost lives of the 146 people who had died in the crash of Northwest Flight 255 at Detroit Metro Airport in 1987. It was interesting to see the bylines — at the Free Press, the stories were being written by people who either had not been at the paper in 1987 or had had nothing to do with covering the crash.

There may be a subconscious reason for this. Maybe it was better, from an editor's point of view, not to assign reporters who knew too much and who might dig up unpleasant memories. Newspapers are superficial for many reasons, one of which is that it is easier to be shallow than to delve.

Back in 1987, within an hour of the Flight 255 disaster, I was headed for a hospital to look for survivors. I learned that there was one, a 4-year-old girl named Cecelia Cichan. For the next couple of months, I spent most of my working time at the University of Michigan Medical Center where Cecelia was being treated for burns. I had some strong opinions about how the media around the world were playing that story. The story of the lone little survivor captured people's hearts, especially when it was coupled with the report that her mother — who had perished in the accident — had shielded her and thereby saved her life.

That myth echoed around the globe until one day when a Wayne County sheriff's deputy handed my colleague John Castine a map showing where the bodies of each of the Flight 255 passengers had been found. According to this gruesome map, Cecelia had been found far from the body of her mother. No way could the mom have shielded the child. John and I set about writing that story.

I was curious to learn where the myth of the mom saving the little girl came from. I read many newspaper articles backwards through time and found the first mention of the life-saving myth in an early edition of the News dated the morning after the crash. The article attributed the claim to an emergency medical technician, who was named. I called the EMT, who exploded at my question. She told me she had never claimed that. She said her quotes were made up.

I wrote about that in the article that John and I prepared. I got a call from the editor — same guy who nixed the Mark Alexis story. He complimented me on ferreting out the source of that wild rumor, but told me the Free Press wouldn't print my report on it. "We aren't going to piss on the News," he said. "It might make a good Columbia Journalism Review story, but it's not for the Free Press."

Once again, I remembered Mark Alexis. My Cecelia Cichan story was censored. It was not a bad story. It was a good story. But it was a tough story, and tough stories can be hard on editors. They have to sell them to other editors. This was a story that would force many, many media outlets around the world to ask themselves how they could have run with a fabricated report and whether they were not writing the same kind of fiction every day. It was a bitter pill for our editor to swallow, even if it involved lousy Journalism at a rival paper.

As a staffer, I really had no other big outlet. The News was no option. Sell the story to the News? This was not about aging Indians in a remote part of the state. This was about a great big lie the News had fabricated. Not likely they'd set the record straight about themselves. But if by some odd chance I'd had the story published in the News, the Free Press could have fired me. As a stringer, once my story was rejected by the Free Press, I was free to sell it to the News. As a full-timer at the Free Press, I was forbidden to sell to supposedly competing news organizations.

Once again, the stringer wins, the staffer loses.

chapter 37

it's not who you know

Not one of my newspaper jobs had been listed in a classified advertisement. Not one of my jobs had been posted in any official way. It is important to understand that if you rely on official job listings, you won't find out about most of the career opportunities that are out there.

About my first serious reporting job, working as an unpaid "volunteer" for a university radio station. That sounds easy, doesn't it? Just about anybody could get hired for a job that pays no salary, right? Well, at the time, I was the only volunteer working at the station. Even though I wasn't being paid, the station manager wasn't about to let just any knothead go on the air. You had to be a knothead with special qualifications. It didn't hurt that I had a graduate degree in history. But my entrée to this job hadn't come from my résumé, either.

We'd just come back from Africa and our service in the Peace Corps. It happened that my wife was driving to classes at Western Michigan University and sometimes she'd carpool with a woman who was married to the chief engineer at WMUK-FM. I was writing a novel, working on a farm and trying to find a job. It wasn't easy. It was 1974, and the country — the world — was in a deep recession. Jobs were scarce. My graduate degree in history tended to turn off employers, who assumed I wouldn't be happy in some white-collar job unrelated to teaching history.

I thought about my past. I'd been a ham radio operator since I was 14. I'd studied for Federal Communications Commission exams and passed them. Why not go into broadcast engineering? I could pass those FCC tests. I called Doug Howe, the husband of my wife's friend, and we had lunch.

Doug told me I was barking up the wrong tree. Radio stations were automating their operations and phasing out on-site engineers. The future, Doug told me, was in reporting. After lunch, he led me to the office of Tony Griffin, the station's news director. Tony explained that the station didn't have money to hire a reporter, but I could be one if I'd work without pay. In return, he and Doug would teach me how to run a tape recorder, how to edit tape on a reel-to-reel machine, how to interview people. And Tony gave me a regular assignment — writing and voicing an advance report on weekly city council meetings, attending the meetings and writing reports on the deliberations.

You might say the job was not a job because it didn't pay. But it was a job, because I had responsibilities. I filled a need at the station. In addition to weekly council reports, I found people to interview for features that aired on the station. I learned to find stories, to sense what would interest listeners and to write and edit my pieces so they'd fit into short time slots.

During the year that I was a radio reporter, you could hear my voice broadcast with that 50,000-watt signal and you'd never know that the station wasn't paying me. You'd never know that to make ends meet, I was trimming grapevines in the middle of winter, standing in a vineyard with snow falling or freezing rain, waiting till my feet got so cold they hurt before going into the house, stoking the wood fire and reading *War and Peace*. I was a rural letter carrier for a time while I worked at WMUK. Fellow workers at the Paw Paw Post Office were mystified that this guy whose voice they heard on the air was casing letters in the back room of the post office. They figured anybody who was on the radio was rich.

After about a year of unpaid work at the station, I asked the manager to put me on salary.

No can do, he said.

Au revoir, I said.

Trimming grapes at 13 cents a vine just wasn't paying for the gas to drive 60 miles round-trip to and from the station. Meanwhile, I tried and failed to get a paying job as a broadcast reporter. I decided to hang up Journalism. I finished my novel and headed for Manhattan with high hopes of finding a publisher for *Colima, Colima*, my (first) novel.

When I returned to Michigan, novel still unpublished, it was to Berrien Springs, where my wife had met Scott Aiken, the reporter with The (Benton Harbor) Herald-Palladium who coached me about working as a stringer. Once again, there were no ads to lead me toward a job. Scott explained how the papers relied on stringers to feed them local news. He said neither The Herald-Palladium nor the South Bend Tribune had a stringer in Berrien Springs. Stringers didn't need to be great Journalists, he said. They needed to sit through boring meetings, understanding enough of what happened to write a coherent report. Fact is, he said, it didn't need to be terribly coherent, because the good old H-P had some stringers whose writing was pretty marginal. Anybody who could write intelligently would be ahead of the curve. I've described my meeting with the H-P's state editor and his demand that I write only for the Benton Harbor paper. Once again, I said au revoir.

When I got the call from the Tribune's Tom Gruber, it seemed to make a difference when I said I'd covered those council meetings. That's because he badly needed meeting reports from Berrien Springs — especially at that time, because the rival H-P didn't have a stringer in town. So, that unpaid job worked nicely. It was sort of a one-line recommendation. I was hired.

Note that to this point, I had not sent a résumé or formal application for my jobs. Not for the radio gig, not for the South Bend thing. I was sending stories to the Free Press and News in Detroit. Nobody asked for a résumé. Nobody checked to see that there really was a Joel Thurtell and not just some kook writing spurious junk under a nom de plume. Editors need to fill space. They ask few questions. I was hired, hired, hired. Ditto with Time magazine, The New York Times, The Grand Rapids Press, The Indianapolis Star and so on. This success was happening when I didn't even have much in print to show people. It didn't matter. Fill the paper!

After about a year writing for newspapers, I got a call from somebody named John Gillette, who said he and his wife, Pat, were thinking of buying the weekly Berrien Springs paper. They needed an editor. He'd gotten my name from a stringer who'd started covering Berrien Springs government for the H-P in response to my Tribune reports.

I was known — my byline was running several times a week in the Tribune. Over lunch, my soon-to-be boss outlined the plan: I'd work part-time editing the weekly. I could keep working for the Tribune and other places.

No résumé. No job app. Just an agreement over lunch. The critical factor was having my name dropped by another stringer who didn't want the job. I was known as a Journalist in town and when someone was looking for an editor, my name came up.

It was exciting to be a Journalist. It was exciting to see my name over stories in newspapers. Now that I was editor of the weekly, my byline ran there, too. I was simply having my Tribune stories reset by The Journal Era's typesetter. I didn't bother to rewrite them. What's wrong with plagiarizing yourself? I was also writing editorials and occasional personal columns.

I was getting to know other Journalists. Jan Marsh was a reporter in the Niles bureau of the Tribune. I learned more about the craft by talking to Jan and to Scott Aiken. I got to know Gene Walden, the Tribune reporter who covered Cass County. Gene promised to let me know if he got a different job and resigned from the Tribune. Fantastic!

During this time, when I was writing sporadically for The New York Times (well, I wrote two stories for them) and working for Time (nothing I ever filed with them made the magazine, but they paid me), I decided to try for a job at the Free Press. A letter came back from the city editor explaining that a requirement for Free Press reporters was at least two years of experience working at a daily newspaper, full-time. Sorry, my stringing for the Tribune didn't cut it.

One day, Gene Walden called. He was going to be a reporter in Minneapolis, and he was about to call Tom Gruber to say he was resigning. Wait five minutes, he said, then call Tom. I watched my clock and phoned Tom. My call must have come seconds after he hung up with Gene. Nevertheless, it took the Tribune people several weeks to make up their collective minds to hire me. When they did, so I was told, I was offered the highest salary they'd ever paid a starting reporter. Still, I suspected there was some hesitation about hiring me. Why? No J school, maybe?

But once again, J school didn't matter. I was a full-time staff writer on a medium-sized daily newspaper. Less than four years later, I was hired by the Free Press as a staff writer. Did my daily newspaper experience at the Tribune make a difference? Yes, in the sense that as a Tribune staffer, I was able to report and write some ambitious investigative stories. I also wrote and photographed stories for the Tribune's Sunday magazine. Once I was on the Free Press staff, though, I found out that the supposed two years of daily newspapering experience requirement I'd been told of was a figment of some editor's imagination, because the Free Press was hiring young people straight out of college.

Journalism majors.

True to form, the Free Press job had not been advertised. It hadn't even been posted when I started campaigning for a job. I was under some pressure from home by then, because my wife wanted to go to medical school, and there are two medical schools in the Metro Detroit area.

By 1984, I knew some people on the Free Press staff. Eric Kinkopf was a sportswriter who had been editor of The (Dowagiac) Daily News. Dowagiac is not far from Berrien Springs, where I lived. We'd bumped into each other covering stories. I'd gotten to know Eric, had had lunch with him, so I felt fine about calling him for advice about jobs at the Free Press.

I learned that in spring 1984, there was a freeze on hiring. Don't let that bother you, Eric said. Do these two things: First, write a cover letter to Dave Lawrence, executive editor, explaining who you are and what you've done. Include some strong clips and an autobiography. Next, write a different cover letter to Bill Mitchell, city editor. Include some strong clips and the autobiography.

The autobiography was supposed to be just a few pages, Eric told me. I wrote one that was more than 20 pages long. I included some old family stories and tried to explain why Journalism is important to me.

Make sure the two cover letters are memorable and different, Eric repeated.

The day after I mailed the two packets, I got a call from Bill Mitchell and the following weekend my family was in Detroit having dinner with Bill's family. The idea of a non-Journalism major, a historian and former Peace Corps volunteer married to another former Peace Corps volunteer and prospective physician intrigued Bill. A few days after I mailed the packets, I got an enthusiastic response from Dave Lawrence. Amazingly, to me at least, Bill and Dave had not talked to each other. Soon, I was getting stringing assignments and by fall of 1984 I was on the staff.

That lengthy autobiography? I was interviewed by various editors, including the late Neal Shine, who was managing editor then and later would become publisher. About that autobiography, Neal said. Too long. Then he chuckled. "You ought to have it published."

The advice Eric Kinkopf gave me was invaluable. Do you need an Eric to help you get a stringing or staff job? It can help. But the answer is: No. Just take his advice. If you're trying for a staff job, follow his recipe — send different materials to the top person overall and the top operational editor — and see what happens. Remember how I got that stringing job at the Tribune? I didn't know the Michigan editor, Tom Gruber. All I knew was his name.

That's the formula: Find out who does the hiring. The rest is really up to you.

chapter 38

got the picture?

"What about Art?"

First time an editor said that to me, I was baffled.

Art who? I didn't know anyone named Art.

Turns out Art was not a person. Art was a concept. What the editor really meant was, "Do you have a photographic illustration for your story?"

I was ready for that one. I sure did have a photo. I'd been coached by a pro, a J-school-trained Journalist. It was late winter 1978, and I was getting ready to leave Manhattan after several fruitless months trying to sell my first novel to agents and publishers. I decided to go back to Michigan and try my hand at Journalism.

One of my favorite pastimes in Manhattan was going to off-off-Broadway plays. They were often very good, and if they turned out badly, it was easy enough to walk out at intermission. Admission was cheap. One of the small theaters was running a series of Oscar Wilde plays, and the main female character was played by an actress who was described as having recently come to New York from Detroit. I interviewed her and pitched the story to the Free Press Magazine (now defunct). The editor asked about Art.

Yes, I said, I have Art.

Or thought I did. Problem was, I'd had my subject stand in front of an iron fence in her trench coat, it being Manhattan in March, and I'd stepped back far enough to snap a photo showing her from the top of her head to the tips of her shoes. Not Art. Luckily, the paper's library had Art in the form of a file photo — a head-and-shoulders shot — of this actress from her days on the stage in Detroit.

Why was my photo not Art?

Well, readers really had no interest in seeing this woman's trench coat. Ditto the iron fence behind her. Ditto her shoes. What they want to see is the face of the person featured in the story. And her face in my photo, as it would have shown up in newsprint, would have been about the size of the eraser on my pencil.

"Go as close to your subject as you and the subject are comfortable with," a newspaper photographer once told me, "And then take a step closer."

If that seems too close, use a telephoto lens. But make sure, whatever else you shoot, to get a well-exposed, sharp, close-up photo of the person's face.

Years ago, I worked as a Free Press photographer for six weeks. I learned many tricks from real photographers during that cross-training session, but the one piece of advice that I most often recall came from Patricia Beck, a veteran photojournalist. At the beginning of this experiment, I was assigned to ride with Pat to photo assignments and shoot everything she shot. We were sent to a Detroit elementary school where then-Governor John Engler was making an appearance. We needed photos of kids. I stood by a wall snapping photos, probably using a telephoto lens. I noticed Pat down on her knees and very close to the kids. When shooting children, Pat advised me, always get down on their level, or lower still. Instead of being distant, or even threatening, the photographer connects with the kids. Photos taken from close-up and with a personal interconnection — Pat often chats with her subjects while gently coaxing them, usually making them laugh — are more likely to capture warmth and spontaneity.

Today's stringer has advantages I never dreamed of when I started writing for pay in the 1970s. I was buying liquid chemicals, developing my film, sending negatives or prints to editors, and it was a real hassle. And expensive. I would put story copy and photos on a Greyhound bus headed for Detroit and the News. It was a real time sink.

Now, for relatively little money, say under $200, you can own a digital camera with more features than we dreamed of having on our old film cameras. You can transmit your images by Internet to editors, or post them on a Web site as a virtual catalog.

Amazingly, you don't have to wait until the chemicals have set to see what kind of picture you took. You know instantly, and if it's not good, you can reshoot. But no amount of modern devices can make you ready for the big test. Are you ready? I wasn't.

It was Saturday afternoon on a hot day and I was napping in our bedroom on a hog farm near Berrien Center, Michigan.

The phone rang. Lyle Sumerix. There was a big pileup of cars less than a mile from my house. By now, I knew the drill. I quickly loaded film into my camera and headed for the scene where a car had ignored a stop sign and was struck broadside by another vehicle. Four people were killed, others were hurt.

I sighted through my lens, only to discover the film canister wasn't seated correctly in my camera. I had to rewind, then reseat the film canister. I mentioned this problem to Lyle.

"Always load your camera right after a shoot," Lyle said. "That way, you're ready for the next assignment, no matter when it happens."

Simple, right? Why hadn't I done it? Thereafter, I always kept my cameras ready with film.

Reporting and writing are not only elements of cops reporting. Stringers often need to illustrate their feature stories, and they'd better have a good camera.

And keep it ready.

After that piece of advice from Lyle, I made it a rule to ALWAYS keep my cameras loaded with film.

We don't use film now, but that doesn't mean we can't put ourselves in a self-inflicted jam.

Are your data cards cleared for action?

Did you recharge your battery?

If you want more pointers on taking pictures, there are many books on the subject. I am no expert. I know one thing for sure: Photos sell stories.

Got the picture?

chapter 39

byline fever

Got a long-range writing project in mind? Maybe it's a novel, or a nonfiction book. Maybe you're contemplating a life of stringing as a way of avoiding the nine-to-five pitfalls of regular jobs. Great idea. Beware another pitfall — byline addiction.

People have been known to become addicted to the sight of their own name in print. (I touched on this in my chapter called "Addicted.") How do I know? Let me count the long-term projects I've undertaken for several newspapers. Believe me, when you embark on a controversial investigation of a judge, or a sheriff, or say a county executive, or maybe you uncover a financial scam involving many school officials, bond underwriters and powerful lawyers, you'd better be ready to knuckle down, work hard and come up for air — maybe — when the series sees print.

It can be great work. It can seem like the most wonderful work. Just don't try to write that novel while you're in the midst of a big project. And projects aren't the only dangerous undertakings. Beat reporting can become addictive. I call it the murder du jour. It can be very heady — being in the know about the latest macabre criminal behavior by local bad folks. Finish that crime story, head out to visit with friends and you're suddenly a celebrity. I wrote an article about the disappearance and probable murder of Teamsters union mogul Jimmy Hoffa. Months later, I received a call from a Los Angeles television production company — they sent a crew to film and interview me, the supposed "expert" on Hoffa. Nervous about the interview, I spent several hours in the library scanning books about Hoffa and union history, hoping I could learn enough to appear like the labor historian that I was not. It was a good thing I did, too, because what I knew from the story I'd written wasn't enough to justify the amount of trouble the crew took setting up cameras and lights or the amount of time they spent asking me questions, which ranged well beyond the outline of my little journalistic essay.

But believe me, folks, in my last days at the Free Press, old JT was concentrating on one- and rarely two-interview stories with a fair amount of first-person narrative to fill in for lack of exhaustive reporting, which for the moment I am not inclined to do.

Why not?

Because in those last few years, the newspaper I worked for had become more and more demanding — not in terms of quality, but in terms of story output. I know there are overworked reporters who will laugh when I complain that I was required to turn in five stories a week, but at the Free Press in late 2007, that was a goodly load of work, which by the way had come to include photography.

By writing personal columns, I reduced the need for the kind of thorough reporting I used to do. Instead of making a call to an expert, I could reminisce about some experience related to what I was writing. Since this was a personal column, the need for sourcing was virtually nil. The emphasis was on wit and neat turns of phrase. Isn't that what column-writing is all about?

In truth, there was another reason. I might have spent hours at home doing those interviews that would have inflated my columns into standard journalistic exercises. Why didn't I? Very simple. I was busy at home. I was working on my book, *Up the Rouge!*, and when that didn't occupy me, I was drafting chapters for this book. And I was working on other books and Web projects that didn't relate to daily news reporting. The Free Press wasn't paying me to slave over those five-stories-a-week in my off-hours, so I found better things to do. I've spent days, weeks, months, years on long-term newspaper projects, but now the projects belong to me.

Enough of byline myopia. The murder du jour, geek story of the decade can go to another reporter. Seeing that byline, and now that sig, which is newspaper jargon for my photo with the byline, is intoxicating. Being recognized while walking the dog can be flattering. But I must remind myself that life is short and I still have many books I want to write. Chasing ephemeral news stories doesn't place me closer to finishing those books. I started newspaper writing as a way to make a living. It became a craft, something I did because I loved doing it, but it also became an obsession.

The writing of books is also an obsession. The difference is this: The books are mine. The news stories belong to the paper.

Want an object lesson in byline fever? Take it from me, this very book is that lesson. I started writing a manual for stringers a quarter-century ago, right after I started working full-time as a reporter. I wrote some chapters and an outline, but as I became immersed in news writing, I forgot the project. A couple of years ago, I unearthed the three-ring notebook with my draft chapters and outline. Not bad, I thought. I vowed to write the book, but set it down and left it until, well, until a certain point when I realized I'd better write this before the newspaper industry imploded. Through the summer of 2007, I wrote chapter after chapter. Then, that October, I learned I was eligible to retire from the Free Press. I was offered a buyout. I took it. I began working on book projects in my spare time, and redoubled my efforts on *Shoestring Reporter*.

Wow, what an idea, I thought. I can write about this so much better now, 25 years later, than when I first took it up. Well, okay, except that maybe if I'd written the book then, my life would have changed.

Think about these words. I wrote them around 1981 when I was first drafting this book:

Beware, stringers, of becoming addicted to the sight of your name in print.

As nice as it is to produce regular news articles and see your name over a body of text, don't let that pleasure become an obsession.

In short, if you have long-range writing plans — a book, a magazine article — it can be easy to put the big project off while rolling with the excitement of covering daily news.

But daily news is dead tomorrow. It lines bird-cages, wraps dead fish, house-trains puppies.

Fewer articles which show thought, clarity, good news judgment are better than many, anyway. But some kind of schedule is necessary to stay on the long-term track.

What is the long-term track?

This will sound oddly ironic, since the purpose of this book is to build confidence and get you earning money as a stringer.

The purpose: Survival as a writer.

Stringing is a path. It is NOT an end.

My own goal is to get out of newspaper work, but only by remaining a writer.

Well, I did take that advice, sort of. When I wrote those words, I had written two novels, both then and still unpublished. Since then, I have written two more novels and two nonfiction books, including this one. I've also written four children's books, one of which (*Seydou's Christmas Tree*) was published in 2009. I've also written several short stories and hundreds of essays for my blog, **joelontheroad.com**.

Could I have written more had I not done so many research-oriented news articles? Probably. But consider this: Most of those deeper works of Journalism, along with the reams of notes and documents I collected as background, will be fuel for future books and articles that

I plan to write now that I am finally retired from the newspaper business.

Take your pick: Do your own work and own it, or do work that is constantly scrutinized, controlled, even censored by others, and let the newspaper own it. I've done both, and prefer outright ownership.

I know what my choice will be.

Do you know yours?

chapter 40

what's the percentage?

A few years ago, I worked in a suburban bureau with several young reporters fresh out of J school. Guess what: Not one of them could figure out the rate of change between two numbers. They were clueless about calculating percentage.

Bet you can do it.

If you are considering a life of stringing, odds are that you already have held one or more jobs in your lifetime. Chances are that you know how to figure percentages. Either from work, or as the result of a decent high school education, many people who would want to be writers can do the arithmetic.

How do you figure percentage change?

In these calculations, we have an old number, and we'll call it o. We'll call the new number n. We'll call the number we get by subtraction x.

Here goes. Subtract the old number from the new number:

$n - o = x$

Now, divide that answer, x, by the old number.

x/o = percent change.

Okay, remember when I wrote about declines and gains in newspaper circulation?

When we took over The (Berrien Springs) Journal Era, its paid circulation was 700. A year and a quarter later, paid circulation was 2,000.

What's the percentage change?

Well, let's see:

$o = 700$

$n = 2,000$

Our formula is $n - o = x$, so where $n = 2,000$ and $o = 700$, we get $2,000 - 700 = 1,300$, which is x.

Now, to find the percentage change, we divide x by $o = 1,300/700 = 1.86 = 186$ percent.

Just so there's no confusion, this was a 186 percent INCREASE in paid circulation.

Not bad for a little boondocks weekly whose staff never went to J school, hey?

Let's practice some more. For fun, let's see how the pros, the J school geniuses, have done. We'll work out their percentage. This time, though, we need to be alert. The change, while dramatic, will not be positive.

We know that in 1981, the paid Sunday circulation of the Detroit Free Press and The Detroit News was 1.5 million. How do we know? Well, that's what they claimed at the time. We'll take them at their word, or rather, at their number. By 2007, the Free Press was the only Sunday paper in Detroit. Its circulation was 318,000. That is what's called a DECLINE. But what is the percentage of decline?

Well, $n = 318,000$ and $o = 1,500,000$.

$n - o = x$, so 318,000 minus 1,500,000 = negative 1,182,000.

The answer is negative, because we're measuring a DECLINE.

To get percentage change, divide 1,182,000 by 1,500,000 = .79. That's a decline of 79 percent between 1981 and 2007.

That shows you what trained professional Journalists can do: reduce two fine newspapers to a single mediocrity and run it into the ground.

Tired of thinking about percentages? Let's think about thinking.

chapter 41

think again

When I think about thinking, I really mean two separate but related processes. The first is *deduction*, the mental gymnastics we go through to figure out the answer to a question, and the other is *inspiration*, the series of firings that go off in our minds to give us ideas.

When I first thought about writing this chapter, I was mainly concerned about inspiration, the getting of ideas. You see, it is so seldom that Journalists have real ideas that I thought a chapter devoted to inspiration might work well in what amounts to a handbook for wannabe Journalists. Actually, if you are in the habit of having original ideas, you are far ahead of most working Journalists.

But an experience with readers of some of my Free Press articles convinced me there's a serious deficiency in the way some people, maybe many people, come to conclusions about what's happening in the world around them.

I wrote a feature story about some kids from Detroit who visited a nature area in the suburb of Grosse Ile, an island community in the Detroit River. In passing, I mentioned that part of the river was filled with flowers called American lotus, a threatened species of native plant in Michigan. I wrote that the lotus plants had found their way to this spot near Grosse Ile by natural means.

I received phone calls and e-mails of outrage. I was told that the lotuses were planted deliberately by a local man in 2002. Not only that, but each of my callers had a photo to prove it. In fact, the photo was genuine. It was published in a newspaper. What could be more authentic, right? The man in the photo, shown sitting in a kayak, was indeed planting lotus plants in 2002. That he was not doing it in the area of lotuses I wrote about, and that most of his seeds didn't sprout were facts that didn't concern some readers. Actually, I consider those two factors — that the seeds didn't take and that they were in the wrong place — of less interest than the fact that lotuses were reported growing in Gibraltar Bay (off the Detroit River south of Detroit) four years before the deliberate planting took place. If lotuses appeared four years before the intentional planting, they could not be the result of human effort no matter where the deliberate planting took place. The lotuses got there some other way. There are no photos of anyone planting them in 1999 or earlier. Best bet: They got there by themselves. In fact, it is well-documented that plants have a natural way of doing that. It's called reproduction.

Cause and effect. It is very simple. Causes always precede effects. Period. You cannot do something today that produces a result yesterday.

It seems so fundamental a truth, yet I failed to persuade my critics. I belabor this point because it is essential in thinking through a problem that we not invert cause and effect. Learning to put causes before effects is very important for reporting any kind of story, be it government, business, even features. Often when people present some issue to a reporter, they don't bother to sort out the chronology. Emotions may be in play, or maybe they are deliberately trying to mislead you. Maybe they are just plain intellectually lazy or not very bright. Also, unconscious biases can cause people to withhold or distort information. As a reporter, you may have to do their thinking for them. Establish an accurate chronology of events right during your interview. By pinning people down on precisely when events occurred, you are laying down rules of discourse that say implicitly: Don't try to mislead me; don't lie to yourself; clear up your thinking; I need a concise presentation, not a rambling polemic.

If you think such erroneous thinking comes only from people in the boondocks of the Midwest, I'd like to show you a January 25, 2010, article in The New York Times Book Review that, when it comes to the broad tapestry known as European history, seems clueless. In a review of a book about Henry VIII and Anne Boleyn, the reviewer states, "Henry had fought for years to extricate himself from his first marriage and create a world where he and Anne could be husband and wife; to achieve it, he had split Christian Europe apart."

The pope refused to grant Henry a divorce from his first wife, Catherine of Aragon, so Henry created his own divorce by separating the English church from Rome and then having his own "pope," the Archbishop of Canterbury, grant him the divorce from Catherine. When did this happen? In 1533.

According to Wikipedia, "*The Ninety-Five Theses on the Power and Efficacy of Indulgences*...were written by Martin Luther in 1517 and are widely regarded as the primary catalyst for the Protestant Reformation."

If you read the claim that it was Henry VIII who "split Europe apart," and don't know much about history, you might attribute the Protestant Revolution to an English king. But knowing that the pivotal act propelling this huge turnover in governments and religion occurred 16 years before Henry's famous divorce helps to reveal the Times reviewer's comment as a bald misstatement of history. Rather than being the instigator of the Protestant movement, it turns out, Henry was enabled by Luther's and others' earlier protests to take his bold action. The Reformation was well under way when Henry divorced Catherine to marry Anne Boleyn.

You could even argue that without Martin Luther, Henry would not have dared challenge the pope; he therefore would not have divorced Catherine; minus the all-important divorce, he could not have married Anne Boleyn, who therefore would not have engaged in various intrigues and affairs and quite possibly would not have lost her head to the sword of Henry's imported executioner. In the Times review, we see historical cause and effect inverted with an absurd result.

From thinking during an interview, and thinking about book reviews, let's turn to thinking in the newsroom. As a stringer, you may assume this doesn't apply to you, since you will not be working in the newsroom. But keep in mind that you will be dealing with reporters and editors who work in newsrooms, and their very culture and manner of thinking, their fabric of biases, is bound to have an effect on how you work. It may also affect how *you* think.

Here's an example that seems extreme, but is not as rare as one might think. At lunch with my editor, he outlined what he thought I would accomplish as "his" reporter. Did I think a certain politician was "a crook"? I said I didn't know, because I had no evidence that he was.

"I think he's a crook," the editor told me. "I want to get him."

Setting aside how damaging to a newspaper that kind of biased comment could be if it were ever found out and should that political figure ever sue for libel, that kind of comment illustrates how news reporting can be steered into certain channels and away from others. An editor with that kind of attitude has a closed mind. Be sure that the biases, bigotries and blindnesses of colleagues don't rub off on you.

Now, what about inspiration? I can speak only for myself. I work and think best in the early morning. I try to rise at 6:00 a.m., make coffee, read the papers — in paper form! — and move on to writing. Often, reading the papers gets me thinking about my latest writing project. I try to keep the early morning free of appointments.

Often, stories don't quit playing with my head when I go home from work. My wife gets annoyed with me, because I use up our supply of telephone notepads writing story leads that turn into the entire tops of stories and sometimes wind up finished products. Grab the ideas when they pop into your head.

Ideas tend to come when you're not expecting them. While driving, I mull stories and suddenly will see clearly the outline of a story that eluded me when I was typing. If there's time, I may stop by the road and write. Otherwise, I try to memorize the key lines or elements of the inspiration.

It helps to talk about ideas with other people, not necessarily other Journalists. It's a requirement of the Journalist's craft that we love to tell stories. As you're gathering information for a story, try to think how you would put the facts together to tell a story. Try your storytelling out on friends or family. When you sit down at last to write, your fingers will dance over the keyboard, because your brain already knows what to say.

chapter 42

for the record

Okay, I admit it: There is something in my background that helped me — more than, say, driving a taxicab, delivering mail, grinding castings in a foundry, cleaning blackboards in college classrooms or picking blueberries — and that bit of background is my long training and before that, my natural penchant for history.

I'm steeped in history. As a kid, I loved reading about history. No surprise, then, that I majored in history in college and studied history at the graduate level for several years. Not only do I love to read about history, but I love to learn enough about the past that I can be a historian, writing about things that have happened so that others can read about them.

Does this mean that YOU should suddenly apply to become a student of history at some college? Certainly not. But with a little effort, you can acquire the same habits of thought that help historians puzzle their way to answers about riddles from the past.

But for a few quirks of fate, such as the Selective Service program, aka the draft, in the late 1960s and early 1970s, and my own inability to stay still for long periods poring over tracts in a library, I might have become a professor of history. Instead, through further accidents of history, I became a Journalist.

A Journalist who practiced what he learned in those history classes.

A practicing historian.

I'm starting to outline another book, *Tomatoes and Eggs; Reflections of a Shoestring Historian*, in which I plan to discuss not only how I've used my training in historical research and historical THINKING in my career as a Journalist, but how the products of those techniques — articles about contemporary events, institutions and people — have actually caused changes in the course of history.

Two senses then, to my use of the term "practical historian."

Using the techniques of historians not only to mine information about present-day issues, but to THINK about them has helped me step back from the deadline pressure of the newsroom and look for perspective. It never hurts to ask: What will people think about this story 10 or

20 or 100 years from now? How will it fit into the historical framework?

Moreover, watching the effects of my newspaper revelations work out in contemporary society has been an exciting and gratifying experience. As a graduate student in history, I was well aware that if I followed the conventional path and became a history professor, I'd have to write articles for publication in academic journals that few people would read. No doubt, academic historians sometimes write things that affect their colleagues' way of thinking, and that may even indirectly influence the way people in general think. But nothing can beat the impact of a well-researched piece of Journalism, especially when it reaches hundreds of thousands of tables at breakfast time. Truth revealed in Journalism has the potential of forcing decision-makers and action-takers to change their behavior. It's harder to accomplish change through The American Historical Review.

Historians work in many ways, but the most important focus of the best historians is on what they call "primary sources." Written records are the best window into the past, the best way of learning what shaped events. And since today's events turn instantly into yesterday, they are as much historical phenomena as things that occurred a century or a millennium ago. We can for all intents and purposes consider them the same.

However, the chronicler of contemporary events has an advantage that is also a disadvantage: He or she can actually talk to players, eyewitnesses. Better take good notes. Or bring a recorder. Interviews are the Journalist's stock in trade. They are also the Journalist's Achilles' heel. An over-reliance on he-said, she-said may dazzle the reader if the quotes are spritely, but often the interview is not conclusive. People will sometimes deny their remarks later, or toss out the disclaimer that they were "quoted out of context." That excuse often is meaningless, except that it can cast doubt on the credibility of even the strongest of interviews.

What's the solution? The best fallback is documents. Written records.

Engraved on the face of the University of Michigan William L. Clements Library is the aphorism, "Tradition fades, but the written record remains ever fresh."

More than once, I've been saved from falling into the pit of unreliability by written papers that — unlike quotations from unrecorded interviews — were hard to deny, no matter how much tradition, or traditionalists, tried to make them fade away.

Whenever possible, grab documents when they're offered. If they are withheld, demand them. Use sunshine laws, the various freedom of information and open meetings laws, state constitutions, state penal codes, whatever laws demand that officials disclose records.

It never hurts to have a friend inside an institution who hands you copies of records that are being withheld by officials, often in defiance of laws requiring their disclosure. Just as often, you will find parallel sources of records that are not under control or even in the purview of officials who might be making trouble. A few years ago, I was looking into the finances of a township that I suspected — correctly, as it turned out — was bankrupt. According to the Michigan Constitution, public officials MUST disclose financial records of public institutions, yet the clerk of the township refused to let me have the records. When I attended a public meeting of the township board, I was firmly escorted to the door, even though the meeting by law was supposed to be open to the public. It seems that by dint of asking questions, I was the wrong kind of public. Such behavior by public officials was illegal, and my paper, the Detroit Free Press, sued the township for access to the records.

Meanwhile, I drove to Lansing and visited the state Treasury, where I found parallel copies of all the township's financial records. That was useful, because it took months for a judge to declare the township officials' behavior illegal and order disclosure of the records. By that time, I'd seen everything and written the articles revealing the decrepit state of the local government's finances. Incidentally, the judge also ordered the township to pay the newspaper's legal fees, which amounted roughly to $14,000. Broke, the township wound up paying the law firm on the installment plan.

You just can't beat a good signed, dated document for having what lawyers call "probative" power. You can even reproduce damning records alongside the text of your article for added heft. While paper records are the raw material of the historian, the practicing historian has a way of thinking that is most useful for Journalists. Boiled down, it's understanding the relationship of cause and effect and that causes go before effects. More than once when assembling pieces of a complex story, I've found it helpful to make a time line in my mind, and sometimes even on paper, to help me organize how events unfolded. It also helps in weighing the accounts of various sources for accuracy and credibility.

If you want to be a Journalist, think like a historian.

chapter 43

if you can't beat 'em

Let's say you've taken my advice and buttonholed the editor or editors of your local papers. Hire me as a stringer, you say. No dice. We already have stringers. Or maybe, We don't employ stringers. Oh la-dee-dah! Hoity-toity.

You aren't gonna call it quits, are you?

You have two choices, which you didn't have in the 1970s and 1980s when I was stringing.

One is spelled B-L-O-G.

Or you might start your own rival newspaper.

Here's what you do with the blog: Go to the government meetings that your local paper covers. Or maybe they don't cover them. Anyway, take notes, write a story about what happened and post it on your blog. Write three or four of these blog reports, then go back to your editor and show her what you've done. If you can get some of your blog readers to write testimonials, all the better.

Maybe now they'll hire you.

The answer's still no?

Start a paper and compete with them for readers and ads. See how long it takes before they offer you a job. But maybe by then you'll be earning a little money and tasting what it's like to be an independent newspaper publisher.

Hey, maybe you'll drive the old newspaper out of business!

Sound like a nutty thing to do in this day of waning newspaper circulation? It's a big step from stringing to running a newspaper, and as I say, everybody knows newspapers are dead.

Why, conventional wisdom says if the paper newspaper isn't dead yet, it will be a goner soon, lying supine in the ultimate newspaper morgue.

Who would deny it? It's well known that newspaper circulation is down, down, down. Being driven there by the Web, right? Ad revenues are history, too. Gobbled up by Google, Yahoo, craigslist, eBay and sundry other Web sites.

Anybody who'd START a newspaper, a PAPER newspaper, in these times, why, that knothead should check into the nearest regional psychiatric institution, not so?

Shhh!

Don't tell Greg Rokicak.

Greg, whose last name is pronounced ROCK-a-check and whose nickname in his hometown of Gibraltar, Michigan, is "Rocky," has some news for purveyors of conventional wisdom: Their paths need not be strewn with rocks.

Eight years ago, Greg started publishing a newspaper. A PAPER newspaper. It's called The Downriver Review. And doggoned if he isn't making money.

Not lots of money.

But enough to support himself.

The Downriver Review is a one-man operation. Well, not quite. He gets a lot of help from his pal, Brad Swoveland. Brad designed Greg's Web site and helps him with accounting. Otherwise, the Review is Greg's baby. And the Web site is not exactly up-to-date. Paper is Greg's medium of choice.

He shoots the photos, recruits local writers and photographers, sells the ads, lays out the paper and picks it up from the printer. He trucks it from his home in Sturgis to Downriver communities like...

Wait a minute. Did I just type "Sturgis"?

Where the bing bong is Sturgis? WHAT is Sturgis?

Sturgis, friends, is a place — a town of about 11,000 people so close to the Michigan state line that a loud belch can be heard in Indiana.

Why, in Sturgis, when the wind blows hard from Hoosierland, the trees don't murmur, they drawl.

In Sturgis, they're so close to Tierra Hoosierra the cops once arrested a carload of drunken Notre Dame fans for violating the Interstate Anti-Riot Act.

If you fart in Sturgis — okay, you get the idea. It ain't exactly Downriver, that nebulous region south of Detroit. In fact, it's so far from Downriver, metro Detroit, that Greg has to drive his twice-monthly press run of 3,000 Downriver Reviews 150 miles from the Sturgis Journal printing plant to the nearest outpost that could reasonably be termed Downriver.

But back to my main point — he's running a PRINT newspaper! What kind of chuckleheaded thing is that to do?

Didn't he get the memo?

The one that said newspapers, the PAPER papers, are headed the way of the dodo, the mammoth, the saber-toothed tiger, Cro-Magnon man and every other extinct breed of livestock you can think of.

Wait a minute, though. Who wrote that memo?

Hmmm. Let's see, I get most of my news about newspapers from, golly gosh, from newspapers.

If you're betting on horses, which tout do you believe?

In the case of newspapers and their supposedly imminent demise, the tout is the industry, which echoes the same glum news day after day.

I won't belabor the numbers here, but refer new readers to my Chapter 27 on whether newspapers have a future. You know, I don't believe the early numbers for papers sold, so I have to doubt the decline has been as dramatic as the papers claim.

There's a saying in the newspaper business, so Greg tells me: "Newspaper people lie about their circulation and brag about their drinking."

Greg doesn't need to lie about his circulation. He prints 3,000 papers, carts them to Wayne County and sets them up — freebies — in bars, restaurants, stores, anywhere the owners will let him give away his Downriver Review. From Rockwood to Allen Park and points between. His "salary" comes from selling ads.

Why am I dwelling on this mite of a paper, 3,000 freebies, an upstart? Because I haven't read anything like this in the mainline papers. They're all moping about how the Internet is killing them. Baloney. They're doing it to themselves. And here's this guy with virtually no capital, just working away to make a living and incidentally showing us that there is a future for newspapers.

PAPER newspapers.

Greg is 55. He grew up with newspapers. His dad, August Rokicak, the real "Rocky" in the family, owned a weekly called Pulse when Greg was growing up. Pulse covered Gibraltar, a town several miles south of Detroit.

Greg's first love is music. He plays guitar and keyboard and has warmed up audiences for Ted Nugent. Now he plays for the Kalamazoo Civic Theatre and other venues. When he was young, it was all about music. That was to be his career. He slid into newspaper work because he knew the business. For years, he worked for a Sturgis shopper doing art and ads. The shopper was sold a couple of times and one day, his boss invited him to go for a walk. When Greg came back, his coworkers watched him clean out his desk.

It had been a good life. He'd had a $50,000-a-year salary and still had a 27-foot sailboat he docked in St. Joseph. The salary was gone. There was never a pension. After he started The Downriver Review, Greg motored Jam 3, his sailboat, around the Lower Peninsula. It's sitting on a rack in a Gibraltar marina.

In the years before I retired, I thought about starting a newspaper. But I'm quite different from Greg. I am a Journalist, a writer, and I'm jealous of my time. The idea of hauling newspapers around town, cold-calling businesses to try to sell ads, the layout and all the production — hey, that's not my cup of chamomile. When I considered the idea at all, I thought strictly in terms of a Web publication.

I wondered why Greg thought of putting out a PAPER paper in the first place.

"Common wisdom says print newspapers are dying," I told him. "What do you think?"

"People sit there in coffee shops with their laptops and computers, but let's face it, a newspaper article I want to read later, I just rip it out of the paper and set it up where I'm going to read it. I don't run my paper with experts. Every week I choose what news should go in. What is there to do with a newspaper? You put articles in it, you try to make it look nice, you try to make sure you've got as much profit to support your product."

"Is The Downriver Review making money?"

"I've been supporting myself for a number of years. Yes, we are, or I'd be out of business."

"How can you make money when the dailies supposedly are having trouble?" (Note that they still make money, just not as much as their owners want.)

"The corporations are fine. It's all about cutting the payroll. The corporations are making plenty of money. It's always said their profit margins are more than many other companies. They're greedy. [This just in: In March, 2010, Gannett revealed that it paid its CEO, Craig Dubow, $4.7 million, including a $1.5 million bonus, for the year 2009 when he fired 6,000 workers and ordered 'furloughs' for thousands of others. I'd agree with Greg when he says these companies are greedy — JT] They figure they can melt the papers down. They don't care about circulation rates going down, because half the time they lie about it. Newspapers lie about their circulation and brag about their drinking. They're gonna be okay. What will happen is when the corporations melt them down to nothing, someone will buy them."

"Will there always be a place for paper newspapers?" I asked.

"There will always be a place for newspapers because it's an easy-to-move-around vehicle. People that like to read books, you drive yourself crazy trying to read a book on the computer. A book is just a friendly vehicle. As Forrest Gump said, 'That's all I got to say about that.' "

Okay, here's what I've got to say about it. The idea of cold-calling people to buy ads, peddling papers to all kinds of businesses, why, if I had to do that, I'd never have time to write. For me, newspapers are all about writing. Thank God there are people like Greg who like selling ads and printing papers. They need people like me and I need them.

Publish a print newspaper? Ghastly thought! I'm a writer.

Give me stringing any day.

chapter 44

a thimbleful

An editor was sent at company expense to that august, preeminent and Journalistically anointed citadel of reportorial wisdom, the Poynter Institute. All the way down in Florida. He was paid, along with his salary, travel and lodging expenses, to attend a seminar on a topic that excites Journalists no end. It's called "Ethics in Journalism." When the editor returned to the newsroom, someone remarked approvingly on the reason for his absence, Journalistic ethics being a sacrosanct concept requiring instant obeisance at many newspapers.

"Ethics in Journalism — that's a thimbleful," wisecracked the editor.

Anyone contemplating a working life with at least one foot pointed over the transom of a newsroom needs to be aware how ethics — or the PERCEPTION of ethics — can dominate and distort the thought processes of otherwise intelligent human beings. Worse, wrong or stupid thinking about "ethics" can intrude on people's private lives, it can interfere with their right to take part in politics and it can ruin — through perceptions alone — otherwise fine friendships.

I thought of that piece of newsroom badinage — ethics, a thimbleful — when I read Clark Hoyt's January 20, 2008, dissertation in the Times on the private life of Times Supreme Court reporter Linda Greenhouse. Greenhouse is married to a lawyer who sometimes argues cases before the Supremes, and, Good God! Can you believe it? She failed to ask her editors' permission before she accepted this man's hand in marriage.

I'm not going to delve into how this discussion was prompted by some right-wing loony who wanted to make trouble for Greenhouse because he thinks the reporter and the paper are too "liberal." Nor will I discuss at this point the kind of latter-day McCarthyism and Big Brotherism that are the natural results of proscriptive, so-called ethics policies at newspapers. Later.

What I find fascinating is Hoyt's use of the old newspaper gambit of appearing to bolster his conclusions, or indeed making it appear that he came to his conclusions, through the quoting of self-proclaimed experts. In his essay, Hoyt quotes a professor of Journalism whom he allows to expound on conflict-of-interest as an ethical issue. This is nothing unusual. The normal course for Journalists promulgating rules of reportorial behavior is to dial up a J school prof.

As Dean of the Shoestring J School, I'd like to interject right here that this whole business of hunting for talking heads to proclaim conclusions that the reporter already has arrived at is one of the phonier though more ubiquitous tactics you'll find in news stories. At the Shoestring J School, we try to find the facts FIRST; we bolster our articles with facts, not with the ruminations of carefully selected "experts."

But Hoyt trundled out the usual expert, a J school prof, wouldn't you know.

Wait! Since when is ethics a branch of Journalism? I thought ethics was a subsidiary of philosophy. If you're so dead set on showcasing an expert, why not call a philosophy prof who's an expert in the broad field of ethics, not just "ethics" as applied in newspaper work?

I can think of a couple of reasons: Just didn't think of it. Too lazy to find out who the philosopher experts are.

Or, just maybe, asking somebody outside the thought-conditioned realm of Journalism might elicit the wrong answer.

Hmmm. Wouldn't it be neat to shrug off the J school pontifications and head for the P department?

Why not find out what prominent philosophers have to say about newspaper ethics policies? I'd like to start by having a panel of real ethicists analyze what some call the "gold standard" of newspaper ethics policies — that 54-page epic published by the Times. They call it "Ethical Journalism: A Handbook of Values and Practices for the News and Editorial Departments." It even has an index! Wow. This must be the real thing.

Maybe not. What I want to know is whether newspaper ethics policies are really meant to encourage honest, fair reporting, or are they, as I believe, simply tools for controlling the behavior, on and off the clock, of newsroom employees?

chapter 45

a TRUE ethics policy

"Ride hard, shoot straight and speak the shining truth."

Why would I write a one-line, nine-word chestnut that is open to a wide range of interpretation and claim it as my professional ethics policy?

Because it contains three elements missing in the long-winded, self-serving, so-called policies put out by many major and minor American newspapers to impose "ethical" standards on their editorial employees.

First, my policy is short. Second, it is actually possible to parse sense from it. And third, it contains a word missing from its supposedly more sophisticated brethren. More about that word later.

But now, time for a warning: I have an interest in this discussion that is more than academic. Six months before I retired, I was disciplined for behavior that managers decided, long after it happened, was "unethical." They agreed that what I did was not unethical at the time I did it, but after they found out about the horrible act I had committed three years previously, they tinkered with the language of their "ethics" policy to make it, ex post facto, a breach of their re-jiggered policy. In other words, don't do it again. If that seems convoluted, don't blame me. Having amended the meaning of "ethics," managers then asked me if I would ever again do what I had done three years before, which, by the way, was ethically okay according to Free Press policy three years earlier when I did what they thought was abhorrent. What they failed to tell me was that they had already decided that if I answered "Yes," they planned to punish me, possibly even fire me.

Sweet bunch of guys.

Anyone who thinks this episode towards the end of my 30-year career in Journalism didn't play a significant part in my decision to retire should read a book about the business practices of Gannett, the corporation that owns the Free Press. It's called *The Chain Gang*, by Richard McCord.

My supposed sin? As a citizen of the United States of America, I participated in the political process in fall 2004 by contributing $500 to the Michigan Democratic party.

But back to my ethics policy, which, following industry standard, is subject to change at my whim. I really think my ethics policy du jour has it all over those fatuous policies put out by the big-name newspapers.

Take a look at that supposed gold standard, which is to say the ethics policy of our nation's leading newspaper, the Times, where they're so proud of their 54-page tome on newsroom social control that they saw fit to attach an index.

An index! This thing must be really important. Hmmm. Gosh, I don't see any index entries for "Newspaper Guild," or "union," or "collective bargaining agreement" or "contract." Guess this hyped-up, overweight document isn't part of the Times contract with the New York local of The Newspaper Guild. Wonder how meaningful it really is...

I haven't seen another American newspaper ethics policy that reached quite the Times' height of self-importance and pomposity, but they all have these elements in common: florid, grandiose but murky verbiage in combo with goals or standards impossible to meet. The result is blatant hypocrisy.

Okay, I'll stop kicking the Times around. For a minute or two. Here's one of my favorite examples of a double standard, found in the Dec. 13, 1984, edition of the Free Press' "Ethics Guidelines." It says: "No staff member should write about, report on, photograph or make a news judgment about any individual related to him or her by blood or marriage or with whom the staff member has a close personal relationship."

That prohibition existed for years in the Ethical Guidelines, then disappeared without explanation. Here's what I think happened: Someone in management with the power to reassemble these relatively elastic ethics policies belatedly figured out that the ban on writing about family members was being violated with impunity every day of the week by then columnists Jim Fitzgerald, Susan Watson, Bob Talbert and others. Of course, lowly reporters like me had to abide by it or face recrimination from editors. But the columnists were and are the paper's superstars, paid far better than other writers to ruminate on anything that bestirred them, which often was a spouse, a kid or a grandchild. In direct violation of the paper's behavioral edicts.

That's the problem with so-called "ethical guidelines" or "ethical policies" — their lofty, pompous proscriptions too often collide with workplace reality. Everyone in the newsroom knew that those columnists were highly prized for their ability to spin homey yarns about pals or hubbies into highly readable essays that persuaded people to trade their spare change for the newspaper. Why, people would even trade good money to buy books that collected these family-oriented columns. Meanwhile, a rule that insiders know is being broken, if they think about it, is unknown to readers. How often do you see a newspaper's ethics policy in print where its readers can easily find it and compare what they're reading with the paper's ethical cant du jour? The hypocrisy goes unrecognized by the public and therefore it has no importance to newsroom managers who write the regs.

Here's another "ethic" I find entertaining, because it has survived and lives on in current iterations of many newsroom ethics policies. I quote from the 1984 document: "A staff member may not enter into a business relationship with a news source."

There was a time at the Free Press when a certain columnist had a book deal as coauthor with a certain famous but now-dead football coach whom he continued — despite the book partnership with Bo — to use as a news source. It was okay by management, despite the seemingly emphatic prohibition, that Mitch had this deal with the coach.

Really, the language is pretty vague. What does it mean to say "business relationship"? If I buy a book from a bookstore, then write a story about the store manager, was that deal a "business relationship" that violated the policy? If I pay for lunch at a restaurant, then write a review of that eatery, am I in trouble?

Don't ask me. I don't write the rules.

We know who writes them. Newspaper owners, or their managers.

I'm told the Times' ethics book is the "gold standard" of ethics policies. Wow. That is really impressive. It stands to reason. They are the classiest newspaper in the country. They must have the smartest writers, deepest thinkers, so it's natural to turn to them as the wisest of the wise.

On page 19 of their hefty book, I find rules for staffers regarding "Voting, Campaigns and Public Issues."

I'm interested in the opening line: "Journalists have no place on the playing fields of politics."

What a mouthful that is.

At risk of being branded a smart-ass, I'd like to know — can somebody explain to me? — what the phrase "playing fields of politics" means?

I picture an immense soccer field with goalposts all along the sides. Have I got the picture? No? Well, what the hell DOES it mean?

It is my understanding — correct me if I'm wrong — that reporters travel with political candidates and government officials either on campaigns or as part of the officials' governmental duties. It is my understanding that reporters attend press conferences called by officials and candidates for political office. Am I wrong to believe that reporters sometimes hold private conversations with politicians and government officials, that they sometimes shoot the bull about politics in off-the-record contacts and may even discuss the ins and outs of political maneuvering with people who have a political leaning of one kind or another? And that these unpublicized conversations between Journalists and politicos from time to time affect the course of political history? Hmmm: Could these scenes be construed as occurring on "the playing fields of politics"?

I'm sitting in the dining room of my home writing this, having perused the front page of today's (Jan. 20, 2008) Times. Oh, my; here's a headline, "VOTE OF WOMEN PROPELS CLINTON IN NEVADA CAUCUS; followed by a deck, "OBAMA IS STRONG 2ND" and a sub-deck, "G.O.P.'s Primary Goes Down to the Wire in South Carolina." The article was cowritten, we are told through a byline, by Jeff Zeleny and Jennifer Steinhauer.

Where did Mr. Zeleny and Ms. Steinhauer learn about these elections if it was not on the "playing fields of politics"?

Gosh. I wonder if these two reporters will be cited for ethical lapses if it turns out that they in fact conducted some or all of their reporting on "the playing fields of politics"?

Don't ask me. I don't make the rules.

Isn't it just possible that these very articles might have some impact on the behavior of the very politicians they cover? Might not politicians choose to do one thing and not another, based on conversations with reporters or based on their reading of the reporters' articles? How about the articles about National Security Agency wiretapping? Didn't those articles affect government behavior? It seems that the very publication of articles takes place on those "playing fields," doesn't it?

I'm not even going to get into the question of why the Times' ethics gurus chose that term, "playing fields of politics." Were they perhaps sportswriters or sports editors? It's a pretty lame metaphor, made more so by its choice of athletic lingo. But I'm tired of picking on it.

I'd just like to know this: Why do newspapers write these hyperbolic policies if they can be construed and re-construed to the point where they're meaningless?

The people who run newspapers see these rules as clubs they can use to beat on reporters when no other weapon is handy and whenever it suits them. Control. Keep those flunkies in hand. But that's not what the managers say, of course. I recently heard a top newspaper editor explain what these policies are meant to do: preserve the paper's credibility. You see, in this manager's view, readers lose confidence in the paper as a believable source of news if they find out their favorite writers have conflicts of interest.

Problem: All those exceptions. The sportswriter with the book deal, columnists writing about family members. Another problem: Those "conflicts" were known to readers, who likely never considered that they were "ethics" conflicts because they were never told about the policy. If they had known, would they have cared? Who knows? Who cares? Columnists provide entertainment. The whole paper can't be murder and mayhem or politics and courtroom folderol. Managers know it. They give those writers great latitude, freedom to break the rules because it sells papers.

Did readers give a rip, really?

According to the editor, though, if the public realizes there's a conflict, they will stop buying the paper. That would hurt the paper's bottom line.

Did it hurt the paper's bottom line to let writers wax on about their families or write about sources they had deals with? Not if readers didn't know. They continued to buy papers, maybe bought even more papers, thanks to the wit and homeyness of the columns.

But we then hear it's not even reality that matters. It is perception. If people PERCEIVE a conflict, they may stop buying. That would be bad. But all those years when columnists wrote about family members and didn't get caught, that was okay. There was no PERCEPTION of a conflict. So people kept buying papers and there was no economic harm to the publishers.

So what ethics is really about is not credibility at all. What "ethics" is about is selling newspapers. Ethics equals money.

Why is this important to me? I love newspapers. I see them dying. No, I see them killing themselves. I see them doing dumb things they got away with when they were the only show in town. But now, with competition from the Internet, they are like deer in a blaze of headlights. Either they're paralyzed with fear or simply lack the basic intelligence they need to survive. This is about the future of newspapers.

It's worth looking again at those highly paid columnists who write to a different standard from other staffers. Managers assume that readers buy more papers because they want to read those columnists. If what they write, even though it may violate ethical standards, sells papers, then everything is okay. No credibility problem as long as the cash flows in. And as long as nobody blows the whistle.

I keep reading these ethics policies, and there's one word that I don't find in any of them. "Credibility" runs rampant. But that word which readers REALLY prize more than credibility, well, I can't find that word in the index to the Times' "Ethical Journalism" manual.

I don't find it in the Free Press policies, of which there have been so many iterations that it's difficult to catalog them.

Okay, I made fun of the Times' pompous index, but maybe it can help us out here. Oops. No sign of the word that comes between "trustees" and "University of Missouri awards for consumer journalism."

My little policy is not 54 pages long. It has no index. It is only nine words long.

But yes, my policy has that most important of words. Here it is:
Ride hard, shoot straight and speak the shining TRUTH.

chapter 46

no free lunch

We've read about Journalists who were zapped by colleagues and a so-called "public editor" for such things as getting married or writing about family members. Who in the world would want to count himself in the midst of a self-styled "profession" where members denounce each other for simply getting married?

Assuming that you haven't tossed this book down in disgust and signed up for a course in selling real estate, how does the newbie stringer weave his or her way through the increasingly complex thicket of ethical conundrums? How does the seasoned veteran do it? Make no mistake, you are bound to encounter these issues.

I mentioned the case of a radio news reporter who was voicing ads for his station. This was thought to be leaping over the wall that supposedly separates editorial from advertising staffers. In fact, this was not an ethical issue. It was rather an issue of job description. The radio reporter's duties included whatever needed doing at the station, which had a small staff and couldn't afford to have anyone beg off doing work because of a supposed conflict between reporting and advertising. Put differently, do the work or get fired. It was a matter of survival for a small radio station that work be done regardless of some holy mission dreamed up by a frat-house-minded Journalism organization.

A bit over the top? Considering that SPJ once used Greek letters, it's not too much of a stretch to think that social conformity and policing behavior are still not far from the frat-house minds of SPJers, given that the group has a fairly restrictive "ethics" code.

It's interesting also that the organization appropriates the term "professional" in its name. Society of *Professional* Journalists. What makes them professional? They get paid, I guess. Otherwise, they ply a craft like tool and die makers, a good analogy since both require skills but neither requires a license.

Okay, so how does the nascent stringer deal with these arbitrary rules? Simple: Make up your own.

We are striving for independence. We want to think independently and write independently. We avoid anything that might compromise our independence.

We are trying to be honest with ourselves and with our readers. We want them to believe us, trust us, rely on us. Looked at that way, we should know without having to be told that writing stories about a business partner might impair our independence. Might. Depends. If the story is a survey of car repair shops and we happen to be partners in one of the shops we're writing about, our judgment should be questioned.

What if I'm writing a humorous story about something that happened involving my business partner, my wife, my son or someone else close to me? The aim in the auto shop survey was to present a fair and balanced account of services offered, and that fairness and balance might justifiably be questioned if the author is involved financially with one of the shops. But telling a family story in a newspaper column? As long as the account is accurate, fairness and balance are not criteria. It's a STORY, maybe containing a lesson or a laugh line.

What about those free lunches?

If you're doing straight Journalism, trying to be independent, then the rule should be that you pay your own way. That is very hard to do. People who are subjects of stories often want to pay for lunch or give you something of token or real value. It is very difficult sometimes to keep subjects from paying for lunch, especially if "no" is not in their vocabulary.

Will eating a free lunch, paid for by the story's subject or one of the subjects, bias you? Probably not. But you are still beholden to that person. You have to say, "Thanks for lunch, Charlie." It's in his head and it's in your head. Charlie may or may not think he's roped you into his corner by buying your meal. Question is, what do YOU think?

Couple of solutions. One is simply to always pay for the meal yourself. This is easy if you're a staff writer on a publication that allows you an expense account. But if you're an impoverished stringer, you may not be able to afford it.

Well, then at the very beginning, or better yet, when you're making the lunch or breakfast or dinner appointment, make it clear that you will each pay your own bill.

Now here's a radical idea: Don't interview people over lunch.

Really — ever notice how hard it is to take notes while you're trying not to slop a Reuben's juices onto your shirt? Eating while interviewing just doesn't work well. A social setting, in a restaurant, is not a good place to ask hardball questions. What if the subject gets angry, starts to yell?

Really, I never accept food or coffee during an interview — I need my hands to take notes. And I'm always afraid of spills.

Gifts that might help you write the story are, well, another story. For instance, a friend wrote an article about an ice cream maker. The ice cream people insisted on giving him some $40 worth of ice cream to take home because, they argued, how could he write about their ice cream without trying it? Now in his case, he had a choice: He could have insisted on paying for the ice cream and the paper would have reimbursed him. Instead, he took the ice cream home and tried it.

Was the ice cream a covert bribe? Well, if it was great ice cream, that's what he would write anyway. If it was bad ice cream, things are not so clear. Again, it boils down to what's in the head of the writer. Does he or she feel grateful for the free ice cream? As an ice cream gourmand, I am very aware of the price of ice cream. I shop for sales, twofer deals. If someone gave me forty bucks' worth of ice cream, I'd be calculating how long I could go without forking out money for my favorite dessert. There would be a certain amount of gratitude towards my benefactors — oops! I mean, my story subjects.

See what I mean? You don't want to put yourself in a position of servitude, of being beholden to someone you're writing about. No way around it, that ice cream is a gift, and independent writers don't take gifts from sources. Period.

My friend's decision to accept the ice cream was ad hoc, a judgment made on the spot under social pressure. Many gift situations are like that. Reporting about an apple cider mill, the writer and photographer in parting might be handed a small jug of cider. Samples. At the Free Press, we were allowed to accept "token" gifts of little or no value, though staffers argued endlessly about what was meant by "little or no value." That is the problem — the area is all gray.

Unless you simply don't accept gifts.

A stringer doesn't have colleagues to argue with, nor does a stringer have an expense account to cushion purchases spurred by the ethics conscience. The stringer also has no cushion against allegations that he or she accepted bribes. Read the public editor's column in the Times and you'll see that all too often stringers are caught violating the Times' verbose ethics guidelines. It has turned out that an op-ed writer was under contract with a company likely to get good publicity from the writer's essay. You'd think common sense would dictate to the writer that there was an obvious conflict of interest, but these cases keep on happening. The glory of having one's byline in the Times may blur the ethical issue for some writers. Don't let it happen to you. Your good name is the only cushion you have.

Years ago, many of us Free Press staffers joined together in pillorying Mitch Albom, the celebrated sports columnist who has transcended sports to become humorist, moralist and, by the way, a household name. Mitch had a business deal with the late Bo Schembechler, then the football coach at the University of Michigan. The deal was that they would coauthor a book about Bo. It seemed to some of us that Mitch had overstepped by interviewing Bo and writing Free Press columns about him while the deal was in force. Didn't our ethics policy ban business relationships with sources?

Yes, in fact, the ethics policy did. However, I never recognized the policy. It was imposed on us arbitrarily by the company. Our Newspaper Guild collective bargaining agreement said we would not do anything that would "compromise the integrity of the newspaper."

Did it compromise the newspaper's integrity to have Mitch and Bo selling a book, after which Mitch continued writing about Bo? I don't think so. Readers were aware of the book arrangement. What would we do, penalize Mitch for cultivating such an important source by telling him he can't cover him because he wrote a book about him? Well, not just about him. With him. Profiting jointly. But still, the cards were on the table. You knew what the deal was.

On the other hand, newspaper managers often kill stories they think might hurt the paper. An infamous example occurred during the 1980s when the Free Press spiked editorial cartoons by staff cartoonist Bill Day for fear they would displease Ed Meese, the U.S. attorney general who had a say in approving the then pending merger of the Free Press with the News. Those cards were not on the table, but they were exposed and I would say the censorship — prompted by business considerations — compromised the paper's integrity.

Just keep in mind: The key to the new Journalism is INDEPENDENCE.

Guard your independence, and you can't go wrong.

chapter 47

second opinions

Don't you run some legal risk being a stringer? Aren't you a sitting duck for plaintiffs' lawyers out to make a quick buck on a libel lawsuit filed by some disgruntled person you wrote about?

Well, sadly, yes, we stringers are vulnerable, just as doctors, lawyers, dentists, carpenters, plumbers and anyone else who plies a trade is, theoretically, a target of lawyers.

And it's not just theory, as I can tell you from sad experience. I have been sued. But I — or rather, my newspaper, on my behalf — have also sued others.

Once, I became — on orders of a lawyer — a fugitive wanted as a witness in a criminal trial. That was the most uncomfortable legal situation I was ever placed in by my paper. I was caught between the desires, prejudices and whims of my newspaper and a driving county prosecutor intent on having me testify in a criminal trial. I made a critical mistake in that case: My error was in listening to the newspaper's lawyer and not finding an attorney who represented MY interests.

The lesson of this chapter is that whether you are an independent contractor, i.e., a stringer, or a staff writer, you should always, ALWAYS have your own attorney separate from the lawyer whose fee is paid by your publisher.

Bert Lindenfeld taught me this important lesson: I was editor of the Berrien Springs weekly and I called Bert, managing editor of the Benton Harbor paper, for his advice about using the county prosecutor as the attorney for the cash-starved weekly newspaper I was running. I was dealing with violations of the Open Meetings Act by public officials. The Michigan sunshine law says that violations are misdemeanors that may be investigated by county prosecutors. Our impoverished paper couldn't afford to hire its own attorney, and I wondered what Bert thought about "retaining" the county prosecutor.

Not much.

"If you're not paying your lawyer, you can't control what he finds," Bert told me.

Simple, direct advice: As a stringer or a staff writer, you should make sure that any lawyer who speaks for you is representing YOUR interests and nobody else's.

In the next chapters, I'll unfold a couple of experiences I had with the legal system, and I'll outline mistakes I made that in one case were pretty devastating. This is so important, I'll repeat it: My errors boiled down to one fundamental and colossal oversight — not seeking my own counsel. Many staff writers have been screwed by their papers and their papers' attorneys and probably don't even know it. Always keep in mind Bert Lindenfeld's advice: Whoever pays the lawyer controls the outcome.

chapter 48

burial detail

Sometimes, it seems as if cops just don't have any sense of humor.

Or is it the undertakers who don't laugh?

In the case of Johnny Caver and his libel lawsuit against me and the Free Press, we got a dose of stone-face from a Detroit cop and mortician in one person.

This guy, who was both a police officer and a funeral director, just couldn't take a joke. And I just had to play for a laugh.

Caver's lawsuit came in 1993, after I wrote an article about another lawsuit — one that was filed against him by his partners in a funeral parlor.

My story was based almost entirely on court records and the few lines that were not from the file came from a lawyer whose comments were identical to the complaint he'd filed in court.

What is the best defense against a libel complaint?

Did I hear someone say, "The truth"? Aha! Well, truth can be a darned good defense if you can establish what the truth is. But lacking the certainty of verity, the best defense is in something called "privilege." Court records are absolutely privileged, meaning you or I or anyone may quote from them to our hearts' content without fear of being sued for libel. Yes, even if we print not the truth, but a slew of bald-faced lies, if those lies were part of a court pleading, or part of court testimony, they can't be attacked, be they ever so false and defamatory. There is even limited privilege for elected officials who make cockeyed remarks on the floor of some legislative assembly.

In those days, I was working in the paper's City-County Bureau in the Coleman A. Young Municipal Building in Detroit. Part of my job was to head down to the office of the circuit court clerk around 4:00 p.m. each day and speed-read my way through a tall stack of lawsuits that had been filed that day. I was looking for any suit involving someone famous or notorious. Failing to find bigwigs, I'd settle for anything that might give me a chance to make readers chuckle.

Johnell Caver Sr. was neither famous nor notorious as far as I knew, but the complaint his partners filed against him was the kind of gem a reporter is always hoping for. So goofy that it's hilarious almost without any help from a writer. Here's how I wrote about the complaint against this Detroit cop and undertaker:

Johnell Caver Sr.'s partners in Detroit's J.L. Caver Funeral Home say the man who gave his name to their mortuary is trying to bury their business.

Caver is being sued by fellow shareholders in J.L. Caver, who claim their erstwhile undertaker snatched one of their corpses, stole the keys from their hearse, changed their phone numbers and forwarded their mail to a new, unlicensed funeral parlor he calls Caver Memorial Funeral Home.

"They're fighting over dead bodies," said the partners' attorney, Michael Morse of Southfield.

In fact, my story added, one of the partners' complaints was that Caver had indeed made off with a body he moved from their funeral home to his new one. According to court records, he literally snatched the corpse, along with the funeral billing that went with it.

I had no way of knowing if any of those allegations were true, but it didn't matter: They were part of the court record and therefore enjoyed what is known as "absolute privilege." A remark made in court can be totally false, but because it is privileged, it can't be used in a libel suit.

But that didn't stop Johnell Caver Sr. from finding a lawyer to sue the Free Press. The lawyer waited to file suit, though, because according to libel law he needed to give the paper a chance to retract the story. Caver's lawyer mailed his demand for a retraction to "John Thurtell." Now, my name is not, nor has it ever been, "John Thurtell." There is accordingly no "John Thurtell" at the Free Press. But that didn't matter, because Caver's lawyer mailed his letter to the Detroit Newspaper Agency, not the Free Press, thus doubly ensuring it would not be received. There was no "John Thurtell" there, either.

Receiving no response, having sent his demand for a retraction to the wrong person at the wrong entity, the lawyer sued me and the Free Press for allegedly libeling Caver.

Had the Free Press attorney seen the letter, he might have persuaded Caver's attorney to drop the lawsuit. But the mail was not delivered. Wrong person, wrong company. Eventually, an attorney for the paper persuaded a judge to dismiss the case. Why? First, my story was accurate. But it was also based on court records that are privileged.

My bosses elected not to ask the judge to force Caver to pay the paper's legal expenses, and the lawsuit was dismissed. The paper paid roughly $12,000 in lawyers' fees and court costs for a lawsuit that should never have been filed.

chapter 49

struck out

Did I mention, always, ALWAYS get your own lawyer's opinion in legal cases involving you and newspapers? It's kind of like having a union to represent you, except that we stringers don't have the luxury of a union.

Next best thing: find a good lawyer. I know, I know — it costs money to hire an attorney. But consider the alternative.

Consider what happened to me a few years ago because I trusted an attorney hired by my paper, and went for a second opinion only when it was too late.

Too late to do me any good, but not too late for you.

Here's my story. Tell me if you think I did right by myself in trusting the company mouthpiece. Believe me, with police surrounding my house and threatening to break down the door, being hauled from Plymouth to Oakland County Circuit Court by two prosecutors' investigators and referred to as "the prisoner" while the company lawyer belatedly and futilely argued with the prosecutor and judge was an experience that upset me and left me depressed for a long time.

As with the undertaker story, you might say I buried myself with a clever lead. It started on a Sunday. I came into work and an editor told me to chase a story in the Saturday edition of another paper about a baseball coach who was busted for dealing dope. I called the coach at home and was rather surprised that he talked to me. But he did, and I wrote a lead that indirectly quoted him:

Pontiac Northern High School's baseball coach, David Chism, said it's true that he helped sell heroin to an undercover police officer.

Towards the end of the story, I wrote:

Chism, who is free on bond, insisted Sunday that although he knew he was handling illegal drugs and that last week's deal was morally wrong, he was only giving his friend, Cleveland Brown, a ride.

"It doesn't look too good," Chism said. "I did pass the drugs.

"The morally right thing for me to have done was to have said, 'No, man, I'm not going to pass this for you,' but I didn't do that, and I can't change that," Chism said.

Before I sent the story to my editor, I called the prosecutor's office. I repeated to one of the chief prosecutors what the coach had told me. The prosecutor said he'd want me to testify. He told me, correctly, I believe, that Chism had confessed to me.

What did that make me?

A witness for the prosecution.

The prosecutor made good on that promise. Prosecutors faxed a subpoena to a newspaper office in downtown Detroit. The paper's lawyer said that a fax subpoena was no good. Until a subpoena was handed to me, I had not been served, he contended. I successfully dodged testifying in the preliminary examination where a district judge decides whether there is evidence to support the charge. The judge ruled there was reason to believe Chism sold the heroin, and bound him over for trial in Oakland County Circuit Court.

When the trial got under way, the prosecutors were faxing subpoenas again, and again, the attorney said that wasn't good enough. It is also worth noting that there was a long feud going on between the Free Press and the Oakland County prosecutor. At one point, the paper's lawyer boasted that he warned the prosecutor not to do battle with an institution that buys ink by the tanker-load.

The paper's lawyer repeated that I didn't have to testify because I had not been properly served with a subpoena. He ordered me to stay out of the Oakland news office where a process server was most likely to find me. I worked from home, from my car, from a library — anywhere but from my assigned desk. This went on for days.

The judge didn't agree with the newspaper's attorney, though. Apparently, he didn't care how I was served. The prosecutor wanted my testimony and that was enough for His Honor. The Oakland prosecutor meanwhile enlisted help from Plymouth Township police in my Wayne County community. Two Oakland investigators with help from local cops staked out my house.

The attorney for my side was packing suitcases for a trip to Florida when I finished my morning run. I have a three-mile course through adjoining subdivisions, and as I rounded a corner by my house, heading for home, I noticed a township police cruiser parked oddly not far from my house. I thought maybe he was part of a speed trap.

My car was in our driveway. I'd left it unlocked on purpose, as I always did on mornings when I ran. I loped up to my car, opened the door, pushed the remote garage door opener button and watched my garage door wind up. I trotted inside and pushed the button to close the garage door. Just as the door was closing behind me, I heard somebody pounding on it. In our driveway there was a white car with stubby antennas. Now I understood that police cruiser I'd seen. There was a second cruiser toward the end of our street.

I called my editor. Her daughter answered. Mom was in the shower. A few minutes later, my editor called and I told her I was besieged. At some point, I took a shower. I also recall some time going by, because I went to my basement amateur radio station and listened to a shortwave radio, once in a while glancing out the basement window. I could see a police cruiser parked on our street a couple of good stone's throws away.

My editor, meanwhile, called the attorney, who called me and urged me to try to escape through my backyard, since, in his view, I had still not been properly served the subpoena. I looked out back and saw another cruiser covering my backyard. No, I thought, escape seemed to be ruled out.

A police lieutenant phoned to tell me they'd knock my door down if I didn't come out. I decided enough was enough. I said okay, give me five minutes to iron a shirt.

I put on a tie and a sport coat and rode to court with the investigators. There, the lawyer argued that I should not have to testify. During a recess, with the judge and jury out of earshot, the prosecutor and the Free Press lawyer loudly argued. "My interest is in seeing justice served!" the prosecutor proclaimed. "I have a higher interest," the Free Press lawyer intoned: "It's called the First Amendment."

The lawyer's First Amendment argument didn't work. The judge ruled that I would have to testify.

What did the prosecutor want from me? Not names of confidential sources. Not my notes. All he wanted me to do was to confirm what I'd written in the story — that the coach had confessed to me, and that I'd written his statement into my article.

Why were we trying to avoid having me say what the paper had already published? In retrospect, I realize that we had no case. I believe that I had a duty to testify as fully as the court required, just as any other citizen would have to do if called as a witness.

Beth Hand, the assistant prosecutor, told Judge Fred Mester that my testimony was critical to admitting the Chism quotes, which otherwise would be inadmissible as hearsay evidence.

"In essence, judge, this reporter took a confession. He made himself a witness," she said.

The judge ruled that my quotation of Coach Chism was "relevant, material and goes to the heart of the case."

But he strictly limited the scope of the testimony to include only information about Chism's quotes as they appeared in the story. "One of the most fundamental rights is the right to a free and aggressive press. This ruling will not limit this right," the judge said.

After all this happened, I called Lou Mleczko, administrative officer of the Detroit local of The Newspaper Guild. A Guild attorney researched the situation and let me know that there was no legal basis for ordering me to refuse to give testimony.

Dodging a subpoena is a poor approach to responding to a court, attorney John Adam wrote. Best to comply, or protest formally.

What have I learned?

Next time I'm subpoenaed, I will get a second legal opinion.

Next time I am a witness in a legal case, I will testify as any citizen would.

chapter 50

building the bullshit meter

Before long, if you start stringing, you'll be needing a sensitive, well-calibrated bullshit detector. For years, I kept an excellent feco-meter on my desk at the Detroit Free Press. It came in handy not only when talking to news sources, but often when I needed to filter out the excess, the hyperbole, the bile and bias from my fellow reporters and editors. This little passive electronic device was a godsend.

But my early bullshit-o-meter had some drawbacks. It was of the low-impedance design, meaning it was very sensitive to the slightest whiff of bullshit. As a consequence of this design defect — my own fault, really — it was impossible to measure the dynamic range — the highs and lows — of bullshit emanations. I couldn't tell the difference between low-level, third-rate crap from public relations mouthpieces

and the more sophisticated lies floating out of government offices. That is a real defect.

Moreover, because my detector's tolerance for bullshit was extremely low, it simply could not differentiate between several simultaneous caca-phonous emissions. In short, while it could detect the presence of bullshit, it could not tell me whence the offending material came, nor could it read the level. Calibration of my boweliar propaganda gauge was virtually impossible.

Obviously, a higher-impedance design was as mandatory as it was suppository. What was needed was the sensitivity to merde-ish palaver contained in the original largely resistive-capacitance-coupled unit, along with an automatic insertion of impedance, i.e., the product of inductance times resistance divided by the trans-conductance of feces measured in micro-Colons.

Here might be as good a place as any to mention that the Colon was recently adopted by the International Consortium for Standards in Bullshitometry as a universal test of veribullimitude. The Colon itself is computed by multiplying the actual measurement of fecal material in Tauri (defined elsewhere, or not) times credibility level measured in Dutos, itself an archaic derivative of the Anglo-Hispanic root word for "doubt," by now long out of fashion. All measurements in this paper will be given in micro-Colons except when they're written in pico-Colons, unless stated in nanobulls.

Now, a word on fecal transducers. My design calls for two of these mechanico-electrical devices, one at input and one at the post-fecal exit port. But please don't be misled. There's no need to purchase a high-end fecal transducer. As most know, the word "transducer" is a Latinate word made up of "trans" for "across" and "ducere," which means "to lead." Therefore, to "lead across," in our case, means the transition from fecal presence in the material sense converted to electrons for measurement. In short, it's a microphone. And any cheapy mike will do. When it comes to BS technology, always aim low.

My bullshit-o-meter is housed in a wooden box. In truth, it is a very old and venerable instrument, and has a wooden handle useful for holding the detector in the face of a subject who is making questionable remarks. The user plugs headphones into a jack on the indicator box and listens for the telltale squeals and squawks of bullshit harmonics being truly detected. Once the fecal gauge has been hoisted into service, the operator merely turns the dial to determine if untruths, exaggerations, fudgings of fact or theory, stretchings of the bounds of veracity and the

Chapter 50

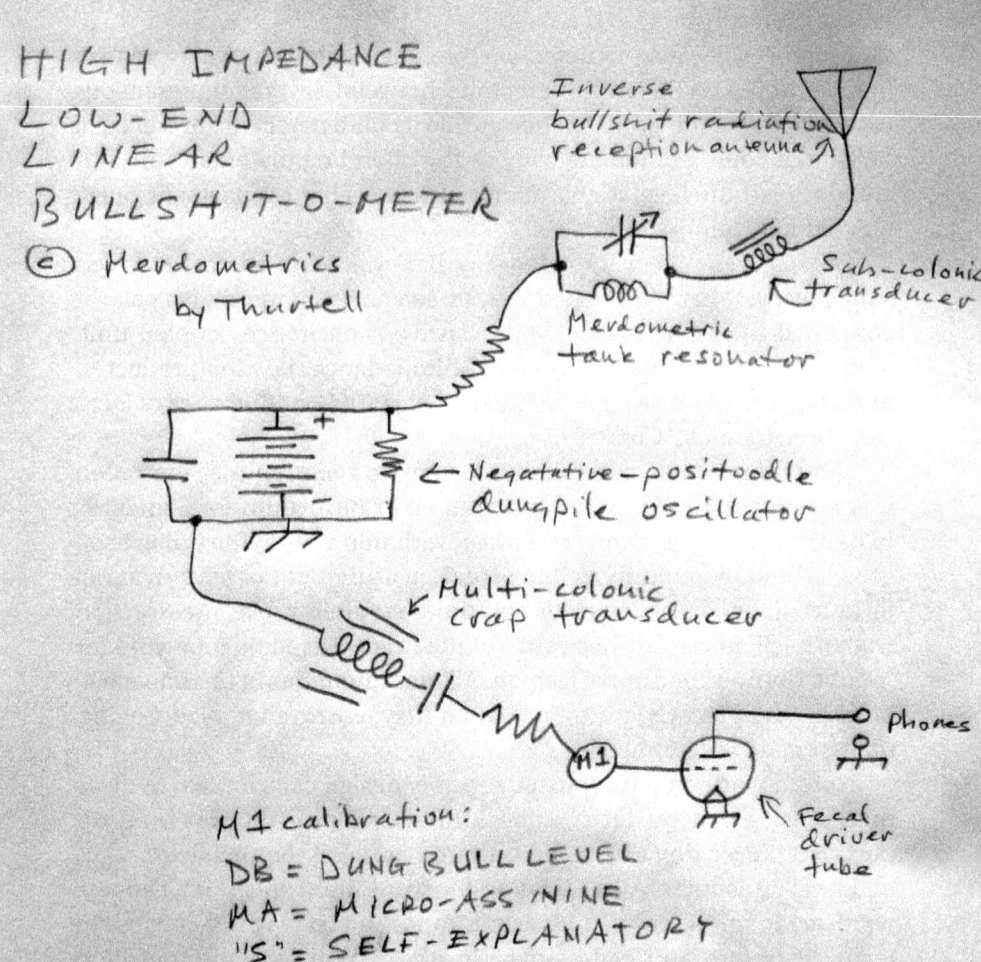

like are being emitted. The dial is necessary because bullshit is emitted on various frequencies.

You will need these materials:

Wooden box approximately 3 x 4 x 8 inches

Wooden handle — a stick will do

A ¼-inch phono jack

Variable capacitor — any value or range that will fit in the box

Inductor or coil — small enough for box

Wire for inverse bullshit radiation reception antenna — four inches is the max because bullshit radiation can be quite potent and might otherwise swamp the device.

Instructions for building a bullshit-o-meter:

Don't do it!

Hey, this whole chapter has been utter, sheer, unmitigated, unadulterated, unexpurgated and premeditated crap, poppycock and nonsense. In fact, it was a test: If you believed in my crap-o-scope, you need serious remediation if you are ever to become an effective stringer.

But don't worry — this book was designed to make cynics of the most naïve.

Read on.

Oh, yes, also for relaxation, please pick up at your local bookstore or at my Web site a copy of *Stringer* and *Cross Purposes* — novels intended to help develop bullshit sensitivity in the most idealistic of readers.

And don't forget *Shoestring J School*.

Now, do you detect any BS?

I learned about bullshit at an early age. I had my Uncle Charlie as a role model. I used to argue with him, but I learned that he made up his "facts" and would cite fictitious "sources." Often they were nonexistent articles that he claimed were from Reader's Digest, which in my small western Michigan hometown carried the power of Holy Writ. In short, Uncle Charlie was the biggest bullshitter I've ever known.

Why do I consider him a great role model? Because he trained me, unintentionally, to disbelieve, to test everything he told me. Don't believe Uncle Charlie, and by extension, don't believe anyone, not even — sorry, Mom — your mother, because she may have bad information. In fact, don't even believe yourself. Test your own ideas and preconceptions.

That's how you build a bullshit meter — by listening hard, and distrusting what you hear.

chapter 51

prosecuting the messenger

It was my second visit to the newsroom of The (Benton Harbor) Herald-Palladium. This time, I wasn't looking for stringer work. I had that, with the South Bend paper and other news outlets and magazines. I was by then editor of The Journal Era in Berrien Springs. This time, I was on a mission — to interview the managing editor of The Herald-Palladium, Bert Lindenfeld.

This was the man who had rejected my Jesse James story proposal two years earlier, but seemingly eons ago. In that bygone era, I thought a stringer was part of the architecture of a house. By now, I knew it as a way of life. It was fall 1980. My first son, Adam, had been born in April. I'd been editor of The Journal Era about a year. Our paid circulation was approaching 2,000 — not bad, given it was 700 when I took over as editor.

I wanted to interview Lindenfeld for an article about the Benton Harbor Citizen, a muckraking weekly newspaper published across the St. Joseph River in the worn-out city of Benton Harbor. Depopulated, with white flight an almost accomplished fact, with factories shuttered or closing and the government virtually bankrupt, the city of Benton Harbor was mostly black and considered by all-white neighboring communities as a lost cause. There was lots of crime, and that was fodder for the Herald-Palladium.

The Citizen, with editor Terry Kelly, thought otherwise. She was out to expose corruption in city, state and federal agencies, and it seemed that every week, this former Roman Catholic nun would unearth and publish some new bombshell. Over in St. Joseph, the staid H-P ignored the Citizen's revelations and continued publishing its steady stream of crime reports, many of them stemming from Benton Harbor. There were many social problems in Benton Harbor, and it seemed to me that the Palladium, standoffish, self-righteous, was all too gleeful about publishing the mugs of black felons while willing to ignore corruption on its own side of the river.

By this time, there was more history between Lindenfeld and me than a failed story proposal about an outlaw. I'd found him helpful when I needed advice about prying public information out of resistant government agencies. But the biggest lift Bert Lindenfeld gave me came through the lead editorial he wrote for the Herald-Palladium of April 22, 1980, defending me and The Journal Era against a threatened investigation by the Berrien County prosecutor, John Smietanka.

We didn't subscribe to the Herald-Palladium, so I was not aware of the editorial that evening, 20 days after the birth of our first son, Adam, when I walked into the meeting of the Berrien Springs school board. All eyes were on me as I found a chair and set my steno pad on my knee. Somebody wisecracked about the "celebrity" and when I looked puzzled, somebody muttered about "today's News Pollution" and a copy of the Palladium was shoved my way. There on page two, under the masthead, was a big headline, "Journal Era's Editor Rates Medal, Not Probe."

I'll be writing in more detail about my experience with the Berrien County legal system in *Shoestring J School*. This story began in fall 1979, about when John and Pat Gillette bought The Journal Era and hired me to be their 20-hour-a-week editor. People — in Journalese we call them "sources" — told me that Michael Johnson, a high school student from Stevensville, had been arrested for rape and, because he was under 17 years old, was lodged in the county juvenile home's locked ward under the supervision of the Berrien County Probate Court Juvenile Division.

At the juvenile home, staffers evaluated the 16-year-old Johnson and recommended he be held rather than released. Despite that commonsense advice from professionals, Berrien County Probate Judge Ronald Lange ordered Johnson released to live at his parents' home, though he had a separate apartment with his own entrance and use of a car.

I wanted to write about the case. Problem was, my sources, who knew the details of the case, refused to tell me which police agency had arrested him. They wouldn't tell me the kid's name. Because he was a juvenile, his court records were confidential. Anyone who revealed information about him could be prosecuted for a misdemeanor. Nobody would give me the specifics I needed to start asking questions.

Several months later, all that reluctance vanished when news broke that a 16-year-old Stevensville classmate of Michael Johnson had been found raped and strangled. Johnson was convicted of second-degree murder. The conclusion was obvious to those in the know: Had Judge Lange heeded the pros' advice, Johnson would be behind bars and Sue Ellen Machemer would be alive.

Suddenly, people were willing to risk giving me information. One of the concerns I heard was that Michael Johnson's father, a prominent lo-

The Herald-Palladium

EDITORIAL PAGE

Editor And Publisher, W. J. Banyon
Managing Editor, Bert Lindenfeld

Were it left to me to decide whether we should have government without newspapers or newspapers without government, I should not hesitate to prefer the latter. — Thomas Jefferson.

Journal-Era's Editor Rates Medal, Not Probe

John Smietanka, Berrien county prosecutor, has been asked to investigate the Berrien Springs Journal-Era for possible violation of juvenile court confidentiality laws. It would be far more appropriate for the Berrien County Board of Commissioners to strike a medal acknowledging the public service performed by the weekly newspaper's editor, Joel Thurtell.

Thurtell's article about the purported inner workings of juvenile court, published last week in connection with the death of a Lakeshore girl and the arrest of a young suspect, lifted the curtain on the Berrien court at a time when the public really needs to know what's going on.

Quoting un-named sources from within juvenile court, Thurtell reported that Berrien Probate-Juvenile Judge Ronald H. Lange released Michael J. Johnson on probation even though professionals at the center had recommended incarceration.

Johnson, now 17 and legally an adult, is charged with the April 3 murder of Sue Ellen Machemer, 16, a classmate at Lakeshore High School. He was sentenced to probation from juvenile court on Jan. 30 in a case in which he had originally been charged with raping a woman. Because he was 16 at the time, Johnson's case was handled in juvenile court, and details of the case and its disposition were not released.

Judge Lange denied he had ever seen a recommendation for incarceration, according to the Journal-Era. The Herald-Palladium published salient features of the Journal-Era story after futilely trying to get confirmation or denial from the court. Judge Lange was reported on vacation and unavailable. Charles Kehoe, director of juvenile court services, said he'd like to tell the "complete picture," but his hands were tied by secrecy laws.

Kehoe said he had asked the prosecutor's office to investigate the possibility that state and federal statues may have been violated in connection with the Journal-Era story. Kehoe stressed he is not a lawyer but believes there are laws protecting privacy in cases like the Johnson matter.

He may be right insofar as agents of the court are constrained by law from discussing the court's confidential business. But, fortunately for the Berrien county public, the Journal-Era and its editor have something better than law to back them up: namely, the United States Constitution.

The First Amendment to the Bill of Rights says "Congress shall make no law . . . abridging the freedom of speech, or of the press; — " Editor Thurtell will have a lot of help from his colleagues in the publishing field if anyone tries to take that right away from the little weekly.

Moreover, attempting to identify and prosecute Thurtell's sources is preposterous. They had the courage to speak out in public to expose what they thought was a grave miscarriage of justice. Are they now to be tried for exercising their right of free speech in answer to conscience? It will be far better if the prosecutor concentrates on unraveling the full story of why juvenile Michael Johnson was freed to become an accused adult killer.

Reprinted courtesy of The (Benton Harbor) Herald-Palladium

cal businessman, had influenced Judge Lange to release his son. I was not able to confirm this. But it seemed evident from the judge's behavior — rejecting sound advice from court staffers — that the judge must have had some reason for flouting guidance from experts in the system.

My story in The Journal Era, "Staff said no, but judge freed boy," challenged the credibility of a court system that had — till then — operated with the seeming approval and complicity of the daily newspaper. Court officials were furious about the story, and focused on my anonymous sources and the fact that information about juveniles is confidential and protected by law. Charles Kehoe, director of the juvenile court, asked prosecutor Smietanka to investigate The Journal Era's Journalism.

This was scary. The Journal Era was small, a real shoestring newspaper. There was barely money to pay an editor, let alone retain attorneys to defend us against an attack from a government attorney. But I was lucky. Tipped that juvenile court officials routinely released "confidential" information about juvenile offenders to military recruiters,

Reprinted courtesy of The (Berrien Springs) Journal Era

I called the Army, called the Navy, called the Marines and called the Air Force. The recruiters told me they were able to get any information they needed about supposedly protected juveniles. They told me that court officials were quite willing to break the law for them. Cute, isn't it? The court gets to break the same law they want my sources to obey. They want us prosecuted, while they get to skate away. This information helped me develop a counterattack. In a follow-up story, I gave prosecutor Smietanka a new target for his probe: the Berrien County Court itself. Why, his witness list was right there in my story. I'd done his job for him!

'Course, the prosecutor wasn't about to go after other county officials. But I think it's safe to say that this little Recruitergate quenched whatever enthusiasm the prosecutor might have had for making me and my sources talk.

Bert Lindenfeld's editorial was a big boost. The Herald-Palladium was the beacon for polite and respectable Berrien County society. By supporting me as a worthy colleague and defending our little newspaper, Bert encouraged people to sympathize with us and reject the court's bullying.

"The First Amendment to the Bill of Rights (sic) says 'Congress shall make no law...abridging the freedom of speech, or of the press; —' Editor Thurtell will have a lot of help from his colleagues in the publishing field if anyone tries to take that right away from the little weekly.

"Moreover, attempting to identify and prosecute Thurtell's sources is preposterous. They had the courage to speak out in public to expose what they thought was a grave miscarriage of justice. Are they now to be tried for exercising their right to free speech in answer to conscience? It will be far better if the prosecutor concentrates on unraveling the full story of why juvenile Michael Johnson was freed to become an accused adult killer."

If you become a stringer, you'll learn that stories seldom disappear for good. So it was with the Johnson story. In summer 2009, I learned that Michael Johnson's family had petitioned the Michigan Department of Corrections to release their son, the man who murdered Sue Ellen Machemer. I asked my old friend Scott Aiken, still a reporter with the Herald-Palladium, if the H-P had ever written about a possible contact between Michael Johnson's family and Judge Lange. No, Scott replied. Nothing in the clips.

I still wonder why the judge made that awful decision to overrule the court staff and send Michael Johnson home, enabling him to commit the gruesome crime juvenile court staffers foresaw. It seems that the full story of why Michael Johnson was allowed to rape again and add murder to his crimes is still to be revealed.

That was the history of my relationship with Bert Lindenfeld from Jesse James to Ronald Lange. I asked him my questions about the Benton Harbor weekly. He answered them. Eventually, I wrote a two-part series for his paper's rival in South Bend. As we chitchatted that day, he abruptly changed the subject. He asked if I'd like to be a reporter on the Herald-Palladium at the then impressive salary of $17,000 a year.

Wow! Steady work, steady pay.

I thought about the offer. And I turned him down.

Why didn't I take that real job in Journalism? As a stringer, you're likely to face a similar dilemma. Well, I'd had two looks at the Palladium newsroom. All male, with the exception of two women allowed to write "society" columns. All white. But for me, they would all be military vets. Bert once had one of those vets, a reporter, stand at attention while he chewed him out for some reportorial infraction.

I didn't serve in the military. No, sir! I'm a veteran of the Peace Corps. I kind of suspected that in the Palladium newsroom, I'd have been a misfit.

At The Journal Era and as a stringer, though my pay was erratic, I had a huge advantage: I got to pick the stories I worked on. I got to write them the way I wanted.

Mostly.

At the time Bert made his offer, I was facing a serious problem with independence at The Journal Era. My stories about a local cable television company's efforts to get a franchise with the township were being censored by the publisher, who was intent on selling ads to the cable company. The problem was that I was sending my cable TV stories to the Tribune to be published a few days before they appeared in the weekly. That gave the cable people time to read them and put pressure on my publisher. It didn't matter when I argued that my stories were accurate.

"I've predicated the future of this newspaper on having those cable television ads," John Gillette told me.

Thus, at the time of Bert's offer, I needed to leave The Journal Era to preserve my independence. But the Palladium looked like more of the same, only worse. Had I taken the Palladium job, it would have been harder to leave a full-time job with benefits than to dump a part-time job without frills. Best not get started in that direction.

I told Bert no, and soon, because of the cable company's censorship, I cut loose from the weekly. I needed income, so I took a staff job at the South Bend paper, where I worked from home, picked many of my stories, wrote deeply researched articles while covering meetings, trials, fires and ostensibly doing my editors' bidding. I was headed down a slope, though, that led from more to less independence. I didn't have a book like *Shoestring Reporter* to warn me of the perils ahead. By 1984 I'd taken a job at a then-big Detroit daily, where the definition of anathema is independent thought.

chapter 52

why not sell insurance?

Why NOT be a salesman? You could sell insurance, I'm sure, and make more money than most reporters. With far less hassle.

Oh, yes, the hassles are myriad for newspeople. For good reporters, at least. And the bad ones sometimes take flak, too.

Good reporters, aggressive seekers after truth, will inevitably run into opposition from colleagues, if they're staff reporters. They may well have their work suppressed by editors, a practice I learned about firsthand in my 23 years at the Detroit Free Press.

As a stringer, you will not be immune to the innate human penchant for censorship. But if you're not tied to one news outlet, you can shop stories around until you find an editor friendly to your idea. In these times, unlike the old days, you can also post an independently reported story on your blog. You may not (most likely will not) be paid, but at least you can publish your particular approach to the truth.

You will not avoid angering people and hearing criticism of your work. Some may well be justified. That is the price of hanging your work out for everyone to see. The insurance salesperson would not have to endure such insults. So why choose a path that leads to angry denunciations rather than fat paychecks?

Here's a reason: The satisfaction of having exposed a wrong and, just maybe, the elation of realizing that your work led to a correction, a reform.

There is something else intangible but nonetheless significant: Power. Have you ever felt like events in the world were beyond your control? You look at the morning's headlines and think: These goings-on are simply beyond the reach of a minor person such as I. Or, you realize that you have somehow been shafted by a system that rewards those who screw their way to riches, people who find legal or less-than-legal ways of stealing, either directly through scams, or indirectly through, say, usurious fees and interest charges on credit cards, overcharges on cable television bills, puffed-up phone bills, bait-and-switch at car dealers and so on.

The normal person may have to resign him- or herself to being, once again, a victim. A Journalist can take action. A Journalist can do something about conditions that are unjust. In my forthcoming book, *Shoestring J School,* I'll be writing about cases where the lies and scams of politicians, businesspeople, even churches, schools and, yes, universities, were vulnerable to one singularly potent weapon: The published truth.

The quest for righting wrongs and finding and revealing truth should not involve satisfying personal grudges. And it is wrong to use Journalism to feather your own nest. This is no idle concern. A reporter who masters a beat, a topic, a subject of interest to the Journalist and the public, may become an object of interest to powerful people who would like to mute that voice, or at least put a muzzle on it. Reporters who move into public relations, especially when they go to work for people or institutions they covered, open themselves to the suspicion that they may have colored their previous reporting to please a potential new boss.

Whenever I feel like I'm being beaten up, by editors, by sources, by readers, and in a low moment nurture a fantasy of leaving Journalism, I ask myself: How would it feel to be selling insurance?

The answer comes back instantly from my heart: NOT VERY GOOD!!

But there is another temptation that can lure the best of reporters astray. It is the temptation of becoming — at higher pay and greater authority, supposedly — an editor.

Do you want to work long hours? By that, I mean REALLY long hours.

Do you want to be a target for everyone's ire, from reporters to editors higher up the food chain, readers, advertisers, anyone with a grievance against your paper?

Did I say long hours?

Do you want to get ingratitude from everyone, even other editors at your own level?

Knives constantly being sharpened, fall guys constantly being lined up, sacrificial lambs having their throats cut, beset by fools from every direction?

If you look forward to that kind of life, please have at it: Be an editor.

My forthcoming novel, *Cross Purposes, Or, If Newspapers Had Covered the Crucifixion,* lays out the nasty reality of a junior — or for that matter, ANY — editor's position at a major though made-up daily newspaper, the Detroit Filibuster:

Caesar O'Toole is an assistant city editor, or ACE. ACEs at the Filibuster are the lowest level of executive, roughly equivalent to, say, a sergeant in the Army. They are the crowbars used by higher-level editors to move the foot soldiers — reporters and photographers — into action. By definition, the ACE, therefore, is held in contempt by everyone above and below. This is so obvious, in fact, so fundamental a truth, that all who work in the newsroom know it.

Except the ACEs.

Caesar O'Toole is as blind on this issue as all of his compadre ACEs. He holds this thankless job solely because he believes — foolishly and falsely — that it's a step toward real executive power at the newspaper. For, as all but fools know, there is no such thing as executive power at a newspaper. Of course, a newspaper is not a lonely place for fools, and oh, how Caesar would not only love to have the status of a Chester Bontemps, the paper's executive editor, or even of Chutney Vipes, the city editor. But worse for O'Toole, he believes it is possible. Why, he would even settle for being in the chair of Don Strodum, the deputy city editor.

Want stress?

Want ingratitude?

Want indignity?

Be an editor.

Otherwise, strive for Journalistic independence.

Be a reporter.

Be an independent reporter, one who thinks for him- or herself, questions everything, and whets that wonderful reportorial curiosity by looking hard and deep at things other reporters miss.

Be a stringer.

stringer's oath

1) I will never work gratis.

2) Obey the first part of the Cub Scout Oath and to hell with the rest: Repeat after me: "I (your name), promise to do my best to do my duty in finding the truth and revealing it, to be square with my readers in honestly reporting what I have learned, and damn the pack.

3) I will be curious to the nth degree.

4) I will never take "no" for an answer.

5) I will never forget a good story idea no matter how often my editors turn me down.

6) I will strive to teach and spread my values of honest Journalism wherever I go.

7) I will take no compensation for a story other than what I am paid by the publication that hires me.

8) I will not be in thrall to government officials or business or religious leaders or other power brokers.

9) I will be the servant of my readers.

10) I will die writing.

END

index

A

absolute privilege, 194, 195
academic degrees, 8, 9–10, 11, 12, 32, 98–99, *129–30*, 154, 172
  See also self-training; traditional journalism and training
adventure reporting, 10–11, 39–40, 44, 89–93, 141
advertising
  coverage areas and redlining, 97–98
  newspapers, profits, 118, 119
  online sales, 123, 175
  radio, voice work, 125, 188
  self-publishing, 175, 177, 178
  story placement and, 146
Agee, Warren, 110, 111, 112
age issues, 39–41, 128, 130, 134
Aiken, Scott, 4, 21, 23, 31–32, 34, 35, 45, 49, 71, 155, 156, 208
airplane crashes, 151, 152
Albom, Mitch, 184, 191
Alexis, Mark, 149, *150,* 151, 152
Andrews University, 56
antitrust issues, newspapers, 131–32, 133–34
application processes, 21, 37–39, 41, 98–99, 128, 154, 155–58
  See also hiring, newspapers
art. *See* photography and photographers
arthritis, 105
Associated Press (AP)
  government contacts, 49
  history, 17
audiences. *See* readers
Ault, Phillip, 110, 111, 112
autobiographies, 158
automation, radio, 154

B

Banyon, W. J., *206*
Battle of Little Bighorn, 1876, 17
beat reporting. *See* crime reporting; local news coverage; police
Beck, Patricia, 39–40, 59, 160
"beer allowance" payments, 59, 64
Benton Harbor, Michigan, 204
The Benton Harbor Citizen (Benton Harbor, Michigan), 204, 209
The Benton Harbor Herald-Palladium. *See The Herald-Palladium* (Benton Harbor, Michigan)
The Berrien Springs Journal Era. *See The Journal Era* (Berrien Springs, Michigan)
bias
  interviews/information gathering, 169, 189, 203
  newsrooms, 148–49, 170
  political reporting, 74, 142
blogs
  joelontheroad.com, 4, 14, 40, 164
  as journalism, 15, 16, 175
  "printosphere" opinions and debate, 14, 15

board meetings. *See* meetings, coverage
books, by columnists, 184, 191
Bowling Green State University, 12
brain power, 103–4, 107, 148
bribery, 142, 189–90
briefs, 75
Brundrette, Tom, 21
budgets
    investigative journalism, 8
    kill fees and, 139
    staffers vs. stringers, 57, 139
"bullshit detection," *200,* 200–201, *202, 203*
Bush, George W., 133, 134, 142, 185
business vs. news, and conflicts of interest, 125, 184, 188, 191
bylines, 94, 138, 156, 162, 163, 164

C

caffeine, 116
cameras, 73, 160–61
campaigning, political, 133, 134, 185
Campbell, John, 71
cartoons, 191
Cass County, Michigan, news coverage, 57, 59, 64, 65, 66, 68, 70, 114, 115
Castine, John, 74, 152
cause and effect, 169–70, 174
Caver, Johnell, Sr., 194–95
censorship
    geographic "redlining," 97–98
    inter-paper competition, 21
    publishers/editors, 131–35, 142, 143–44, 151, 152, 191, 209, 211
    self-, 125, 126–27, 132–33, 142, 143
    staffer power struggles, 108, 109, 112
CEO salaries, 178
The Chain Gang (McCord), 182
Chicago Tribune
    employment applications, 37–38, 39
    stringer work, 138–39
Chism, David, 196–97, 198
chronological considerations, events, 168–70, 174
Cichan, Cecelia, 152
circulation, newspapers, 83, 119–22, 123, 166–67, 175, 177, 178
city council meetings. *See* meetings, coverage
city services. *See* fire departments, news coverage; fires, news coverage; police
clip files
    applications and personal portfolios, 21, 37, 56, 146, 158
    blog material, 175
    story ideas, 36, 164–65
coffee, 116
collective bargaining, journalists, 19, 183, 191
collective reporting, 109–10, 112, 148
college degrees. *See* academic degrees
college newspapers, 101–2
Columbia University, 39
columnists, 12, 156, 163, 183–84, 186, 191
commentary in modern culture, 15
compensation. *See* income examples
competition between newspapers
    circulation, 120–21, 122
    content correction opportunities, 121, 152, 153
    double-dipping, ethics, 27
    and exclusivity rules, 21, 30, 153
    monopolies vs., 131–32, 133–34
confessions, 196–97, 198–99
confidential information, 205, 207–8
conflicts of interest, 186, 188–91
    business vs. news, 125, 184, 188, 191
    local organizations, 142–43
    personal/family, 180, 183–84, 186
    political, 125–26, 131–35, 142, 143, 180
    press-police relationships, 74
    story examples, 49, 131–32
    See also ethics standards; objectivity
constitutionality, public records, 174
content exclusivity
    staff writer regulations, 27, 30,

153
  stringer limitation examples, 21, 23, 99
content limitation. *See* censorship
content shortages, 25-26, 28, 101, 128, 141, 142
Conyers, John, Jr., 133, 134
cops. *See* police
copyright ownership, 59, 64
  See also intellectual property
courage, 13, 120, 124
court records, 194, 195
courts, news coverage, 146, 194-95, 205, *206,* 207-9
See also criminal trials
craft vs. profession debate, 11, 15-16, 18, 125, 188
creative writing, 31, 32, 74, 94-95, 155, 163-64
credibility, 120, 124, 186-87
crime reporting, 35-36, 74, 75-78, 88
  age and, 39
  journalistic addiction, 94, 162
  juvenile cases, 146, 205, *206,* 207-9
  story placement, 146
  style issues, 106, 109-10
criminal trials, 192, 196-99
criticism, of published work, 211
Cross Purposes, or, If Newspapers Had Covered the Crucifixion (novel), 5, 13, 37, 41, 212-13
Cureton, John, 12
curiosity, 13
Custer, George Armstrong, 17

D

daily newspapers
  content needs, 25
  industry struggles, 1, 2-3, 121, 178
  stringers, 18-19
  See also competition between newspapers; newspaper industry
Day, Bill, 191
degrees, academic. *See* academic degrees

Department of Natural Resources, 79, 81, 83, 84
Detroit, Michigan, coverage areas, 97-98, 168, 176, 177
The Detroit Free Press
  circulation history, 120-21, 121-22, 167
  criminal trials and, 192, 196-99
  delivery schedule, 121, 122
  editorial direction, 145, 149, 151-52, 163, 191
  employment history and stories, 2, 6, *7,* 12, 19, 30, 41, 90-91, 92-93, 120-21, 122, 140-41, 151-53, 157-58, 162-63, 174, 182-83, 194-95, 196-97, 210, 211
  employment policy, 157
  ethics policy and conflicts of interest, 134-35, 182, 183-84, 187, 190, 191
  libel suits, 192, 194-95
  1995 strike, 19, 122
  stringer work, 19, 27, 102
  style and format, 68
  See also Joint Operating Agreement, Detroit daily newspapers
The Detroit Free Press Magazine
  stringer work, *22,* 23, 46, 49, *50-52,* 53, 57, 59, 102, 159
  submissions, 21
The Detroit News
  circulation history, 121-22, 167
  delivery schedule, 121, 122
  inaccuracies, 121, 152, 153
  layoffs, 101
  1995 strike, 19, 122
  stringer pay, 101
  stringer work, *24,* 27-28, *29,* 30, 32, 45-46, 71, *72,* 101, 149, *150*
  See also Joint Operating Agreement, Detroit daily newspapers
dictation, story filing, 23, 32, 68
discrimination, 39, 128, 130
documentation of sources, 173-74
donations, political, 133, 134-35, 182

"double-dipping," 27–30, 32, 45–46, 101, 156
The Downriver Review (Sturgis, Michigan), 176–78
Dubow, Greg, 178

E
economics of cities, and content decisions, 97–98, 204
editing of stories
    censorship, 108, 143–44
    stories changed via, 102, 108
editorials
    newspaper solidarity, 205, *206*, 208
    political influence, 135
editors, 212–13
    collecting as contacts, 46, 58, 98, 102, 137, 157–58
    content management: censorship, 142, 143–44, 151, 152, 191
    content management: story ideas, 76, 77, 89, 127, 145, 148–49, 170
    content management: story placement, 145–47
    content management: story rejection, 27, 77, 121, 138–39, 149, 151, 152
    fee agreements, 101, 136, 139
    querying and pitching, 20–21, 98–99, 149
    stringer and staff management, 18, 25–26, 28, 37, 98, 101, 140–41
    turnover, 46, 58, 101, 102, 136
education. *See* academic degrees; traditional journalism and training
egotism, 94, 162, 164
election coverage, 185
Emery, Edwin, 110, 111, 112
employment, newspapers. *See* hiring, newspapers
ethics standards
    bribery and censorship, 142, 191
    double-publishing, local markets, 27
    objectivity vs. conflicts of interest, 49, 125–26, 131, 134–35, 184, 186–87, 188–91
    papers' policies, 134, 180, 182, 183–86, 187, 190
    personal policies, 182, 183, 187, 214
    police scanner usage, 36
    as social control, 16, 131–33, 134–35, 180–81, 182–87
    validity and credibility of stories, 74, 142, 152–53, 186–87
    See also theft of ideas
European Union, study abroad fellowships, 39, 128
exclusivity, content. *See* content exclusivity
"expert" interviews, 162, 180–81

F
favoritism, 145–46, 147
feature stories and reporting
    adventure ideas and assignments, 10–11, 39–40, 44, 89–93
    magazines, 21, 46
    reassignment, from investigative reporting, 132, 134
    soft style usage, news content, 110, 111, 112
federal abuses of power, 133, 185
Federal Bureau of Investigation (FBI), 133
Federal Communications Commission (FCC), 132
fellowship programs, 39, 40, 41, 128, 130
fiction writing. *See* novel writing
financial records, 174
fire departments, news coverage, 71, 72, 74–75
fires, news coverage, 73, 74, 79, *80*, 81, 106
firings
    experiences described, 101–2, 141
    industry layoffs, 136–37, 178
    threats, and freedoms, 134, 135, 153, 182

First Amendment rights, 10, 132, 135, 198, 208
fishing rights, news coverage, 49, 56-57, 64, 65, 66, 102
Fitzgerald, Jim, 183
Florence, Italy, 28, 30
Fox, Noel, 49, 57, 66
freedom of information laws, 34, 101, 174, 192
freelance journalists. *See* stringers
free newspapers, 177
front-page story placement, 138, 145-47
full-time employment. *See* staff writers
future of journalism
    pessimism and predictions, 1, 118-19, 122-24, 186
    saving journalism, vs. saving newspapers, 1-2
    self-publishing options, 175-76, 176-79
    See also newspaper industry

G

Gannett Company, 121-22, 133-34, 135, 178, 182
gifts, 190
Gillette, John, 83, 85, 87, *137,* 146, 156, 205, 209
Gillette, Pat, 83, 85, 87, *137,* 146, 156, 205
Gjesdal, Janna, 21, 22, 159
Good, Dave, 149
Gorham, Wade, 79, 81
government industry control, 74, 131-35, 142, 143, 185, 191
The Grand Rapids Press, 65, *67,* 136
Greenhouse, Linda, 180
Griffin, Tony, 113, 154-55
Gross, Michael, 59
Grosse Ile, Michigan, 168
group reporting, 109-10, 112, 148
Gruber, Tom, 23, 45, 46, 49, 128, 156, 157

H

Haight, Debra, 4
Hand, Beth, 198

hard copy documents, 106, 107, 173-74
hard vs. soft news style, 110, 111, 112
head shots, 159-60
health insurance, news coverage, 127
The Herald-Palladium (Benton Harbor, Michigan), 21
    editorial direction, 204, 209
    editorials, 205, *206,* 208
    pitches, 20-21
    policies, 21, 23, 34, 156
    stringers, 4, 18, 21, 23, 35, 155-56
Henry VIII, 169-70
Hinga, Don, 113
hiring, newspapers
    freezes, 157-58
    interviews, 21, 23, 99, 128, 155-56
    preparation and research, 96-100
    resumes and applications, 21, 37-39, 41, 98-99, *129-30,* 156, 157-58
    word of mouth information, 6, 96-97, 154-58
    See also query letters
historical record, creation, 35, 168-69, 172-74
history degrees, 10, 31, 154, 172
home delivery changes, dailies, 121, 122
"hooks," 89, 93
Howe, Doug, 154-55
Hoyt, Clark, 180-81

I

ideals of journalism, 1, 5, 49, 124, 187
ideas, stories
    inspiration and creativity, 168, 170-71
    intellectual property/theft, 49, 56, 108, 149
    stringer experiences, 141
inaccuracies in reporting
    avoidance methods, 106-7
    daily newspapers, and competition, 121, 152, 153
    post-print revelations, 71
income examples
    "beer allowance," 59, 64

CEO salaries, 178
columnists, 186, 191
"double-dipping," 27–30, 32, 45–46, 101
fee quibbling, 136
kill fees, 138, 139
research, 97
staff writers, 19, 32, 57, 101, 138, 144
stringers, 19, 21, 23, 24, 28, 31–32, 57, 101, 136, 139
independent contractors. *See* stringers
Indianapolis Star, 61–63, 64
Indianapolis Star Sunday Magazine, 57, 59, 60
Indian rights. *See* Native Americans, news coverage
indirect quotations, 196–97
industry trends. *See* newspaper industry
inspiration, 168, 170–71
  See also ideas, stories
integrity. *See* credibility; ethics standards
intellectual property
  copyright ownership, stories, 59, 64
  personal story ideas, 49, 56, 108
  stringer rules, 21, 23
Internet
  journalism industry competition, 118, 123, 175–76, 177
  journalism industry embracement, 1
  local news Web sites, 4
  story ideas, 149
  See also blogs
internships, 39
  See also fellowship programs; mentoring relationships
interviews (job), 21, 23, 99, 128
interviews (sources)
  chronologies and attention to detail, 169, 170
  methods and skills, 34, 35, 36, 104–5, 189–90
  power and importance, 173
  subject matter experts, 162, 180–81
  tragedy stories, 140, 141, 152
  training, 34, 154–55
inverted pyramid format, 75–76, 106, 108–9, 110
investigative reporting
  budgets, 8
  documents, procurement and usage, 173–74
  story placement, 146
  techniques, 35
  unpopular truths, 132–33, 134, 152
  value to community, 74–75, 204, 208, 212
Iraq War (2003-), coverage, 74, 142

J

James, Jesse, 20–21
job hunting. *See* hiring, newspapers
job security, 136–37, 209–10
joelontheroad.com, 4, 14, 40, 164
Johnson, Michael, 146, 205, *206,* 207, 208–9
Johnson, Ruth, 86–87
Joint Operating Agreement, Detroit daily newspapers, 121–22, 133
Jonas, George, 15
The Journal Era (Berrien Springs, Michigan), *33, 82, 85, 87, 119, 137*
  circulation, 83, 119–20, 123, 166–67, 204
  controversial content, 146, 205, *207,* 207–9
  employment history, 18, 32, 56, 57–58, 119–20, 125, 156, 204–5, *206,* 207–10
  legal issues, 192, 205, *206,* 207–8
  stringer policy, 3–4
journalism, style and format. *See* news writing, style and format; quotations
journalism industry. *See* newspaper industry
journalistic ethics. *See* ethics standards
journalists
  defining, 15–16, 103

"official" documentation, 14
personal success traits, 6, 13, 174, 214
power, 211–12
social control, 16, 131–33, 134–35, 145–47, 180–81, 182–87, 209
workloads, 18, 19, 45, 68, 162–63, 212
worldviews, and objectivity, 126, 184–85
See also editors; staff writers; stringers; traditional journalism and training
J school. *See* academic degrees; self-training; traditional journalism and training
judges, news coverage, 146, 205, *206,* 207–9
juvenile crime cases, 146, 205, *206,* 207–9

K
Kalamazoo College *Index,* 101–2
The Kalamazoo Gazette stringer work, 21
Kehoe, Charles, *206,* 207
Kellogg, Mark, 17
Kelly, Terry, 204
Kesterke, Edgar, 79
kill fees, 138, 139
Kinkopf, Eric, 157–58
Kirk, Bob, 24, 30, 45–46, 71
Knight Ridder, 121–22, 133

L
labor. *See* strikes; unions
Lange, Ronald, 205, *206,* 207, 208–9
language, objections, 87, 141, 146
large newspapers. *See* daily newspapers
Lawrence, Dave, 120–21, 158
lawsuits. *See* libel suits
layoffs, 101, 136–37, 178
leaks, political stories, 142, 143
   See also scoops
LeBlanc, Big Abe, 49–52, 56, 102
Lee, Jimmy, 110
legal advice

probative power, 174
self-representation, 192–93, 196, 198–99
legislation, newspaper industry, 131–32, 133–34
libel suits
   J. Caver/*Detroit Free Press* case, 194–95
   risks and vulnerability, 170, 192
licensing and certification, 9–10, 15
Lindenfeld, Bert, 20–21, 192, 193, 204–5, *206,* 208, 209
lobbying, media corporations, 132, 135
localization of stories, 28, 30, 36, 149
local news coverage
   corruption, material, 74, 204–10
   crime and tragedies, 35–36, 73–78, 88, 109–10, 146, 204
   meetings and city business, 18, 21, 23, 32, 79, 81–88, 99, 106–7, 155
   national interest, 57, 65, 68, 114
   press-release-driven content, 142
local newspapers. *See* local news coverage; weekly newspapers; specific papers
Lowell, Michigan, 12, 28, *29,* 30
Lowell Ledger (Lowell, Michigan), 12
Luther, Martin, 169–70

M
Machemer, Sue Ellen, 146, 205, *206,* 208
magazine content, 21, 46
marketing. *See* advertising
marriage, 180, 188
Marsh, Jan, 34, 36, 156
mastheads, 137, *137, 206*
May, Jeanne, 130
McCord, Richard, 182
meals, 189–90
media consolidation, 132, 133–34
media owners
   antitrust issues, 132, 133–34
   ethics policies, 184
   political lobbying, 132, 135
   treatment, newspapers, 1, 2–3,

222 | Index

media owners (*continued*)
178
See also publishers
medical news coverage, 152
Meese, Edwin, 191
meetings, coverage, 18, 21, 23, 32, 79, 81, 86, 99, 106–7, 155
memory, 104, 107
mentoring relationships, 34, 35, 36, 45–46
Mester, Fred, 198–99
Michigan Democratic Party, 134
Michigan Farmer, 67
Mierau, Charlie, 85
military, and confidential information, 207–8
Miller, Judith, 142
mistakes. *See* inaccuracies in reporting
Mitchell, Bill, 158
Mleczko, Lou, 199
monopolies, 131–32, 133–34
Morris, Sue, 34, 35–36
Morris Volunteer Fire Department (Michigan), 71, 72
motivation, 42–43, 138
Mumford, Lou, 34, 36
Murdoch, Rupert, 132, 135
music, 116–17
myths
objectivity as, 126–27, 131, 135
sentimental stories, 152

N

names, style/format, 65, 68–69
national interest stories and topics, 57, 65, 68, 114
National Security Agency wiretapping, 133, 185
Native Americans, news coverage
culture reclamation story, 149, *150*, 151
fishing rights story, 49, 56–57, 64, 65, 66, 102
natural disasters and phenomena, news coverage, 73–74, 83, *84*, 85
networking
article querying, 56

employment leads, 6, 96–97, 154–58
journalistic skill development via, 34–36
organizations, 45
See also mentoring relationships
"news-hole," 25–26, 28, 101, 128, 141, 142
The Newspaper Guild, 19, 183, 191, 199
newspaper industry
Detroit, Michigan papers, 121–24
format evolution, 118–19
government control, 74, 131–35, 142, 143, 181, 185
profits, 3, 118, 178
self-harm and struggles, 1, 2–3, 121–22, 186
self-publishing, 175–76, 176–79
stringers within, 2
Newspaper Preservation Act (1970), 131–32, 133–34
newsroom biases, 148–49, 170
news writing, style and format
inverted pyramid, and format diversions, 75–76, 106, 108–9, 110
name styles, 65, 68–69
professional tips, 65, 69
quotations protocol, 36, 113–15
writing techniques, 42, 44, 105–6
The New York Times
article style and format, 65, 68–69, 114–15
ethics policy and document, 135, 180, 181, 183, 184–85, 187, 190–91
online readership model, 123
queries, 53, 56–57, 65
reporting, G. W. Bush administration, 74, 142
reprints policy, 59, 64, 69
stringer work, 57–58, 59, 64, 65, 157
2008 election reporting, 185
The New York Times Book Review, 169–70
Niemiec, Dennis, 74

Niles Daily Star, 66
non-fraternization policies, 34
"nontraditional" job applicants, 6–7, 37–39, 41
Northwest Flight 255 crash, 1987, 151, 152
note-taking, 105, 107, 189–90
    See also quotations
novel writing, 31, 32, 74, 94–95, 155, 164

O
Oakland County (Michigan) Circuit Court, 196, 197
oath, of stringers, 214
objectivity
    contested, business/political relationships, 125–26, 133–35, 184
    as myth, 126–27, 131, 135
    official-driven content, 74, 127, 142, 185
    story examples, 49
    See also conflicts of interest
official-driven content, 74, 127, 142, 185
official records, 173–74, 194, 195
    See also freedom of information laws
off-the-record comments and conversations, 86, 185
"1A" story placement, 138, 145–47
one-time use rights, 59, 64
Ongley, Betty, 23
open meetings laws, 34, 174, 192
organizations. *See* professional organizations; service club organizations
originality, as stringer technique, 76, 88, 89, 124, 127
owners. *See* media owners; publishers

P
page one story placement, 138, 145–47
Pastor, Susan, 56
pay rates. *See* income examples
percentages, 166–67
personal characteristics, 6, 13, 214

personal ethics standards, 182, 183, 187, 214
Peterson, Iver, 56
philosophy, and ethics, 181
photography and photographers
    credits, 79, 81, 87–88
    do-it-yourself processing, 27–28, 120, 160
    editors' handling, and relationships, 25, 159
    nonfiction books, 39–40
    photos as "proof," 168–69
    staff writer responsibilities, 163
    stringer work, 73, *80,* 81, *82, 82*–83, 87–88, 149, *150,* 159, 160–61
    style issues, 159–60
photography requests, as writing tool, 43
placement of stories, as leverage, 138, 145–47
plane crashes, 151, 152
police
    corruption, 74
    libel lawsuits, 194–95
    officers as sources/police beat stories, 34, 35, 39, 74, 75–78, 88, 106, 109–10, 131, 161
    scanner transmissions, 36
    subpoena deliveries, 196, 197–98
political affiliations and activity
    journalists, 125–26, 131, 134–35, 142, 180, 182, 184–86
    media corporations, 132
political cartoons, 191
political influence of journalism, 74, 142, 185
    See also government industry control
politics, in newsrooms, 145–47, 148–49, 170
politics and politicians, news coverage
    conflict of interest accusations, 125–26, 134–35, 180, 182
    example story copy, 76–77
    objectivity, validity, and conflicts of interest, 74, 142, 143, 170, 184–85

Ponte Vecchio (Florence, Italy), 28, 30
portability, newspapers, 178–79
Poynter Institute, 180
press release-inspired stories, 127, 142
price fixing, 131–32, 133
primary sources, 173–74
privileged records, 194, 195
procrastination, 42, 43, 116
professional organizations, 45, 125, 188
profession vs. craft debate, 11, 15–16, 18, 125, 188
professors of journalism, 6, 9, 12, 180–81
profit margins, newspapers, 3, 118, 178
The Progressive, 53, *53–55*, 64
Protestant Reformation, 169–70
public records, 173–74, 194, 195, 204–5
public relations
    news content, 127, 142
    positions, 212
publishers
    social control of journalists, 16, 131–33, 134–35, 145–47, 180, 181, 183, 184, 185–86
    and state of newspaper industry, 3, 121–22, 123–24, 176–77
    stringer and staff management, 25, 147, 209–10
    See also self-publishing (print)

Q

query letters, 20–21, 53, 56, 65
quotations
    confessions, and outcomes, 196–97, 198–99
    gathering methods, 104–5
    inaccuracies in stories, 152, 153
    journalistic protocol and techniques, 36, 113–15, 141, 173
    See also interviews (sources)

R

radio news
    advertising and, 125, 188
    employment examples, 12, 23, 99, 113–14, 154–55
rates of change, 166–67
readers
    ethics standards, knowledge/ignorance, 184, 186, 191
    journalism's broad reach, 173
    reporters' obligations, 143, 189, 214
readership. *See* circulation, newspapers
"real" journalists. *See* traditional journalism and training
"redlining," 97–98
Reformation, 169–70
Reitz, Cleon, 79, 81
rejection notices
    article re-submission, 27
    pitches, 20
reporters. *See* journalists; staff writers; stringers
Reporting and Writing the News (textbook), 110, 111, 112
reporting skills, 103–7
    See also interviews (sources); investigative reporting; writing skills; writing techniques
reprint fees, 59, 64, 69
repurposing, stringer stories, 27–30, 45–46, 53, 71, 156
    See also one-time use rights
résumés, 37, 38–39, 41, *129–30*, 156, 158
    See also application processes; clip files
retirement, 116, 117, 143, 164–65
retractions, 195
Rokicak, Greg, 176–79
Rouge River (Michigan), 39–40, 141

S

salaries. *See* income examples
schedules, writing, 68, 94
Schembechler, Bo, 184, 191
scoops
    conflicts of interest and, 142, 143
    group reporting avoidance, 109–10
    stringer story offers, 27, 36

self-censorship, 125, 126–27, 132–33, 142, 143
self-publishing (print), 175–79
   See also blogs
self-representation, legal, 192–93, 196, 198–99
self-training, 6, 10–11, 12–13, 34–36, 154–56
senses, as reporting tools, 79, 81, 103–4
service club organizations, 142–43
Shafer, Jan, 32
Sherefkin, Bob, 35, 45–46
Shine, Neal, 158
Shoestring J School (nonfiction), 4–5, 41, 101, 106, 205, 212
shootings, news coverage, 77–78
shorthand techniques, 105
skepticism, 203, 213
   See also "bullshit detection"
small newspapers. *See* weekly newspapers
Smietanka, John, 205, *206,* 207, 208
snakes, 10–11, 78, 89–93, *90*
Society of Professional Journalists, 45, 125, 188
soft vs. hard news style, 110, 111, 112
Sonneborn, Bill, 28, 30, 46, 71
sources. *See* interviews (sources); quotations
South Bend Tribune
   articles, textbook examples, *111*
   employment history, 18, 23, 34, 36, 74, 108, 112, 142–43, 146, 157, 210
   stringer use and experiences, 3, 23, 28, 32, 45, 46, *47–48,* 49, 53, 73, 79–81, *80, 84,* 99, 101, 149, 156, 209
   style and format, 68
   Sunday Michiana magazine, 28, 30, 46, 71, 157
staff writers
   compensation, 19, 32, 57, 101, 138, 144
   content production, 18, 25–26, 76, 95, 140–41, 162–63
   employment applications, 37–38

lack of copyright, 59, 64
legal guidance, 192–93
networking opportunities, 97
political limitations, 134–35, 180
publishing limitations, 27, 30, 133–34, 135, 143, 153, 209–10, 211
state secession, news coverage, 57, 59, 64, 65, 66, 68, 70, 114, 115
Steinhauer, Jennifer, 185
storytelling
   journalistic methods, 42, 43–44, 106, 110, 113, 171
   sentimental topics and myths, 152
strikes, 19, 122
Stringer (novel), 5, 28, 32, 95
stringers
   American history, 17–18
   compensation, 19, 21, 23, 24, 28, 31–32, 57, 101, 136, 139
   daily newspapers, 18–19
   defined, 8, 17, 31–32, 78, 103
   editors and content management, 25–26, 28, 37, 76, 77, 88, 98, 101, 102, 128, 141, 149
   employment conditions/rules, 21, 23, 99, 103, 135
   employment searches, 21, 23, 96–100, 154–58
   freedom and independence, 6, 27, 135, 140–41, 143–44, 147, 188–89, 213
   legal guidance, 192–93
   oath, 214
   weekly newspapers, 3–4, 18–19
   See also editors; journalists; local news coverage; photography and photographers; specific newspapers
Stuart, Reginald, 56–57, 57–58, 65, *66,* 68, 69
student reporters and reportage, 101–2
subject "experts," 162, 180–81
subpoenas, 196, 197, 198, 199

subscribers. *See* circulation, newspapers; readers
suicides, 77-78, 140-41
Sumerix, Lyle, 34, 36, 73, 74-75, 160-61
sunshine laws, 174, 192
swear words, 87, 141
Swoveland, Brad, 176
syndication, 27
    See also columnists

T

Talbert, Bob, 183
taxes, news coverage, 57, 65, 71
teachers, 140
    See also professors of journalism
television
    cable advertising, 209
    news, effects on print content, 148, 149
textbooks, 110, 112
theft of ideas, 49, 56, 108, 149
timeframes, story assignments, 68, 163
Time magazine, 157
time management habits, 94, 116
township financial records, 174
township meetings. *See* meetings, coverage
traditional journalism and training
    academics, 8, 9-10, 11, 12
    avoidance, 4-5, 6, 9-13, 32, 34-36, 38, 125, 128
    culture, 104, 131, 188
    professors, 6, 9, 12, 180-81
    résumé coverage, 38, 39
    status quo, industry attitudes, 2, 6-7, 157
    textbooks, 110, 111, 112
tragedies, news coverage
    on-scene reporting and investigation, 73-74, 88, 151-52
    photography, 73, 88, 160-61
    suicides, 77-78, 140-41
    See also crime reporting
truth, 187, 194, 211-12

U

unions
    authors', 59
    journalists', 19, 183, 191
    news coverage, 162
United Press (UP), 17
university degrees. *See* academic degrees
University of Michigan
    coaches, 184, 191
    fellowship programs, 40, 41, 130
    news coverage, 140, 141
Up the Rouge! Paddling Detroit's Hidden River (nonfiction), 39-40, 60, 163

V

VanderMolen, Francie, 3-4
village council meetings. *See* meetings, coverage
volunteer positions, 154-55
voting, 126, 184
    See also political affiliations and activity

W

Walden, Gene, 156-57
watchdog role of journalism, 1, 5
    See also investigative reporting
Watson, Susan, 183
Weakley, John, 86-87
weekly newspapers
    circulation statistics, 83, 119-20, 123, 166-67, 204
    content and coverage, 18, 21, 23, 32
    See also local news coverage; stringers
"who, what, where, when, how" information (inverted pyramid), 75-76, 106, 108-9, 110
wire services, 27
wiretapping, National Security Agency, 133, 185
witnesses, trials, 192, 196-99
WMUK-FM (Kalamazoo, Michigan), 23, 99, 113-14, 154-55

workloads, journalists, 18, 19, 45, 68, 162–63, 212
  See also content shortages
writer's block, 42–43, 116
writing skills, 42
  See also reporting skills
writing techniques
  atmosphere and stimulation, 94, 116–17, 170
  quotation-related, 113
  story development, 69, 170–71
  storytelling, 42, 43–44
  studying others' writing, 105–6
  time management, 94, 116
  See also news writing, style and format

Y

young readers, 123

Z

Zeleny, Jeff, 185

about the author

Joel Thurtell has been reporting news for more than 30 years. He never took a class in Journalism. He's a graduate of Kalamazoo College and earned a master's degree in history from the University of Michigan. As a Peace Corps volunteer, he supervised building schools and a well in northern Togo, West Africa.

He's won awards for his investigative and feature work at The (Berrien Springs) Journal Era, South Bend Tribune and Detroit Free Press. He writes a popular blog, **joelontheroad.com**, that was named "best independent blogger raising hell" by Metro Times.

He wrote *Up the Rouge! Paddling Detroit's Hidden River*, published by Wayne State University Press, with photographs by Patricia Beck. Other books by Thurtell are *Plug Nickel*, essays on restoring wooden sailboats, and *Seydou's Christmas Tree*, the story of a Muslim kid in West Africa who changed the author's concept of Christmas.

He and his wife, Karen Fonde, have two sons, Adam and Abe. Joel and Karen live with their lapdog, Patti, in Plymouth, Michigan.

www.ingramcontent.com/pod-product-compliance
Lightning Source LLC
Chambersburg PA
CBHW070641160426
43194CB00009B/1538